THE
AMERICAN
EAGLE

THE
AMERICAN
EAGLE

The Ascent of Bob Crandall and American Airlines

DAN REED

St. Martin's Press New York

Design by Judy Christensen

Library of Congress Catologing-in-Publication Data

Reed, Dan.
    The American eagle : the ascent of Bob Crandall and American Airlines / Dan Reed.
        p.   cm.
      "A Thomas Dunne book."

    1. American Airlines, inc.—History.   2. Airlines—United States—History.   3. Crandall, Bob.   4. Airlines—United States—Biography.   I. Title.
    HE9803.A95R43   1993
    387.7'06'573—dc20   92-44216
                                                                    CIP

To Janet, Joshua, Christopher, and Timothy.

In the four of you I find more joy and happiness than any man has a right to experience.

CONTENTS

PREFACE

I HAD barely gotten out my "Hello" when the voice on the other end of the phone came at me with an intriguing question.

"Quickly! What individual had the biggest impact on the airline industry in 1992?"

My questioner was Scott Hamilton, editor of the small but influential airline finance trade journal *Commercial Aviation Report*. He was surveying several dozen airline and financial industry executives, as well as reporters who, like me, cover the airline industry. His survey was to provide the meat for a more light-hearted piece in the year-end edition of his publication. His question was one of those classically great debate starters like "Who was the better basketball player, Larry Bird or Magic Johnson?" Regardless of the field being discussed, such questions provide aficionados an opportunity to match their analytical skills and wits and to engage in a heated but still friendly debate.

After much debate—both with Hamilton and with myself—I finally cast my vote for Bob Crandall, chairman of American Airlines. I was hesitant to do so, partly because he is the central character of this book, which at the time of his call was in the final stages of being edited. Also, I hesitated to name Crandall partly because Sir Colin Marshall, deputy chairman of British Airways, deserved strong consideration for his role in trying to forge a partnership between his own airline and a major U.S. carrier, USAir. If that deal had been approved (President George Bush turned it down on December 22) it would have had a huge impact on the future of the global aviation industry. And even though the president rejected it, Marshall's and British Airways' efforts to gain greater access to the huge domestic U.S. airline market, along with the policy issues raised as objections by other U.S. carriers, have helped illuminate the need for Congress and the new administration of President Bill Clinton to review and revise the national policy concerning the globalization of the airline industry.

I picked Crandall largely for his bold gamble in introducing American's Value Plan fare-pricing system. The Value Plan, which was an attempt to radically alter the way airlines sell their services, ultimately failed when competitors refused to adhere to its simple but rigid principles. Accordingly, Crandall finished second to Marshall in Hamilton's poll. And most of the respondents' comments regarding Crandall were quite negative. Most blamed him personally for the huge losses suffered in the otherwise almost always profitable summer travel season.

But in the course of my phone conversation with Hamilton we agreed that had the question been phrased a little differently to ask who has had the biggest impact on the airline industry in the last decade or two, Crandall would have won hands down.

While others played big roles in the development of the U.S. airline industry following passage of the Airline Deregulation Act of 1978, no one seriously disputes Crandall's preeminent role. He has cast an enormous shadow over the entire industry. Indeed, it is difficult to think of any industry in which one man or woman has had a greater impact than Crandall has had on the U.S. airline industry. Perhaps there are others who do not come to my mind, but the only one I can think of who comes close to Crandall in that regard is Sam Walton. The late founder of the incredibly successful Wal-Mart chain of discount department stores had a huge impact on retailing in the last twenty years. Like Crandall, Walton challenged long-held assumptions about the way his industry operates and about his customers' tastes and preferences. And, like Crandall, Walton recognized both the value of computers as inventory management tools and the substantial economies of scale that could be achieved if the company could retain its low unit of production costs even as it grew rapidly. But even Walton didn't have as big an impact on some of his competitors—Sears, J.C. Penneys, and Dillards, for example— as Crandall has had on all of his rivals. All of American's competitors—United, Delta, Northwest, Continental, USAir, America West and, to a small extent, even the industry's highly successful oddball, Southwest Airlines—now consider many innovations pioneered by American under Crandall to be standard operating procedures.

That, I suppose, is why I wanted to write this book. Love him or hate him—and there are plenty in both camps—Bob Crandall is a living legend. And people like to read about and talk about living legends. Fortunately for me, I happen to have covered this particular living legend longer than anyone else. I guess that makes me an expert on the man, though I must add that no one outside his small circle of family members and close personal friends can ever be a true expert on Crandall.

Invariably, upon learning that I was writing this book, colleagues, friends, and business associates asked me whether I like Crandall. The answer to that question is yes, I do like him. And in many ways I admire him. He is one of the most fascinating people I've ever known and I have learned much from my close observation of him over the past nine years.

But that is not to say that Crandall is faultless. Indeed, his faults— his world-renowned temper, his inability to see things as his opponents see them, his intellectual arrogance—are every bit as remarkable as his abilities, which include his personal loyalty to those whom he loves and with whom he works, his love for open and honest philosophical debate, and his intellectual honesty. In fact, that might be what makes him such a compelling and controversial character.

One thing that most definitely is *not* fascinating about Bob Crandall (and a host of other people quoted in this book) is his language. As one who played and then covered sports, I've heard in locker rooms every profane and vulgar thing one person can say to another, so I'm not shocked by such language. But as an evangelical Christian I am offended by it. And I don't understand why such highly educated people can't find better, more accurate, more specific, and even more colorful ways to express themselves. Their cursing doesn't mean that they're morally deficient people. But it reflects, sadly, I think, a deterioration in American culture that such language has become an acceptable part of everyday life.

As a journalist and as a serious Christian, I faced an ethical dilemma as to whether I should repeat the profane and vulgar language of people quoted in this book. My decision—with which I'm still not completely comfortable—was to remove such language from direct quotations where it was unnecessary to the meaning of what was said and provided no insight into the mindset of the speaker. However, in a few instances I have left profane and vulgar language in direct quotations because that language had an important impact on what was being said.

I WOULD like to acknowledge the work of Robert Serling, author of the corporate history of American Airlines, *Eagle*, and of John Nance, author of *Splash of Colors* about the demise of the old Braniff International Airways in 1982. Both books provided valuable details and insight into those parts of American's history that are touched on in this book but which occurred before I arrived on the scene. I also would like to thank retired American executives Dave Frailey, Otto Becker, and Gene Overbeck and retired American Board member Hooks Burr for their time and assistance in helping me piece together events that took place long before my time.

I also would like to thank everyone in American's corporate communications department for their assistance in helping me track down obscure bits of information and sometimes hard to nail down interview subjects. In particular I'd like to thank Al Becker, John Hotard, Tim Smith, Tim Doke, Marty Heires, Cara Acker, Kathy Fryske, Carolyn Hutchison and Ginger Hummel.

Additionally, I want to thank Mike Blackman, vice president and executive editor of the *Fort Worth Star-Telegram*, who granted my request for leave and who offered me encouragement. Mary Jo Meisner, the *Star-Telegram*'s managing editor, and business editor Mike Norman, my boss, had to cope with my many absences from the office because of my work on this book. Yet they never complained about having to find people to do my work while I was out. For that I am deeply appreciative.

To my colleagues and friends on the business news staff at the *Star-Telegram*—Phyllis Stone, Steve Zuckerman, Jim Fuquay, Jack Z. Smith, Dan Piller, Steven VonderHaar, Michael D. Towle, Scott Nishimura, Worth Wren, Jr., Mark S. Leach, Todd Mason, Sandra Baker, June White, Meg Hart and Sharon Dunn—and to my former colleagues on the business news staff there—Jim Smead, J. Lynn Lunsford, Julie Truck, Barbara Rose and Kristen Moulton—I want to say thank you for covering for me so many times. I also want to say thanks for being such classy professionals and wonderful supporters of me in this work. I am proud to have been your teammate.

My attorney, Mike Lax, gave me valuable advice and twenty-five years of invaluable friendship.

To my agent, Jane Dystel of Acton & Dystel; thanks for taking on a rookie and doing a great job for me.

To Tom Dunne and Pete Wolverton at St. Martin's Press, thank you for your understanding and your encouragement. As a rookie, I needed a lot of both and you provided it freely.

I've also enjoyed the support and encouragement of many relatives, friends, colleagues, and business associates around the nation who are far too numerous to mention. It's corny to say, but you'll never know how much your words of affirmation and encouragement have meant to me over the past couple of years.

Finally, saying "thank you" to my family somehow seems so inadequate in light of the price they paid in relation to my work on this book. My sons—Joshua, Christopher, and Timothy—are too young to understand that all the time I spent shut up in my room writing, or working at my office late into the night, was necessary to complete this book. All they know is that they didn't get to spend as much time with me as they would have liked. For that I am sorry.

Of course, though my sons got to spend less time with me while I was writing this book, they got to spend even more time with their mother. That's good, because my wife, Janet, is a marvelous mother. She, however, also got to spend even more time with them. And that's not so good. Our boys currently are six, four, and two years old, and they are more than any one adult can handle alone. Yet Janet did it for prolonged periods of time, and kept her sanity doing it—well, most of the time, anyway.

Her support, her willingness to be my sounding board, her advice, her prayers, and, most importantly, her love for me sustained me through some very long and trying days when I wasn't always able to be the kind of husband that I wanted to be. I told her when I married her that I considered her to be a special gift from God and that I would always cherish her as such.

I still do.

—Dan Reed
December 1992

THE
AMERICAN
EAGLE

1

Wednesday, October 4, 1989

MOST EVERYWHERE else around the nation it was fall. But it was still warm in the Metroplex. That's the techno-babble name someone dreamed up a decade ago for the sprawling, nearly one-hundred-square-mile region between and around the twin princes of the North Texas prairie, trendy Big D, Dallas, and down-home Fort Worth, Cowtown. The mercury had reached 92 degrees the day before and would top out that day at 88 degrees.

It was the kind of pleasantly warm, late summer day in Texas that made the one thousand or so American Airlines employees who'd relocated to the Metroplex ten years earlier not miss New York City, from whence they had come. Sure, the sultry, sometimes suffocating triple-digit heat of late July and August in North Texas was unlike anything they had ever experienced in New York. But the fact that there were so many days each year in North Texas just like this wonderful day is what made it such a great place to live and work. A comfortable breeze was blowing, softening the effects of the moderate heat. The sky was a brilliant blue, broken only by high, wind-swept puffs of cloud.

It was, in short, a day to kill for.

Not much could ruin a day like that for American executives Don Carty and Ann McNamara, two refugees from colder climes. But late that afternoon, sometime between five and five-thirty, one of those things that could ruin it did.

Carty, an expatriate Canadian, was the airline's top financial executive and chief strategist. That morning the local newspapers had carried short stories noting that he'd been promoted to the newly created position of executive vice president for finance and planning at American and its parent company, AMR Corp. That, in effect, made him the co-number-two executive at the world's largest and most profitable airline—if you don't count the Soviet Union's Aeroflot. A tall, gregarious man with prematurely gray hair and a booming voice, Carty was one-third of the triumvirate that reigned over all of American's far-flung and rapidly expanding empire.

McNamara, a down-to-earth daughter of an Associated Press news photographer who had grown up in the Northeast, had risen in just fifteen years at American from staff lawyer to senior vice president for administration and general counsel. Not counting board members, she was the highest-ranking woman in the U.S. airline industry. As one of five senior vice presidents, McNamara ranked a notch below Carty and Bob Baker, American's executive VP for operations. But she clearly was among the eight to ten people at American generally considered to be part of Chairman Bob Crandall's trusted inner circle.

Of the airline's two dozen senior officers, Carty and McNamara were the only two who actually had their offices in the boss's executive suite. And on that day the boss was in Tulsa, Oklahoma, speaking at a training session for managers in American's data-processing division. So it was to Carty that Ellen Howell, one of Crandall's three secretaries, brought a short letter that had just come in on Crandall's fax machine.

The big Canadian took one look at it and immediately called to McNamara, whose office was connected to his via a shared private executive washroom. McNamara stepped through the washroom and into Carty's office, where he shoved the fax at her.

At the top of the page was the distinctive three-dimensional block of interlocking Ds and Ts. At the bottom were the words "The Trump Organization."

The letter—really a note—was from Donald Trump, New York real estate developer, Atlantic City hotel and casino impresario, big-league investor, owner of a small but highly visible airline, and internationally known bon vivant.

McNamara didn't need to read the letter to know what it was about. She, like Carty, had been waiting for it for months.

*   *   *

BY THE early fall of 1989, Donald Trump was reaching his zenith. He had ridden a self-generated wave of publicity to a level rarely achieved by a mere financier—a level usually reserved for glamorous movie and rock stars. He was, in fact, becoming a more frequent subject in such publications as *People* magazine and the *National Enquirer* than in the more sober business periodicals such as *Fortune*, *Forbes*, or *Business Week*.

Despite his wealth and apparent success in the eat-or-be-eaten world of high finance, there had always been a certain hard-to-explain tawdriness associated with Trump and the ego that apparently compelled him to stamp his name on his many conspicuous possessions and to trumpet his own successes. Though he obviously wanted to be perceived as someone with Park Avenue class, more often than not he came across like a Brooklyn hustler. He was gaudy instead of graceful, slightly sleazy instead of sophisticated.

That he had worked hard—at least in the way wheeler-dealers work hard—was undeniable. Back in the late 1970s, when he was still a relative unknown, Trump had taken a huge risk by using tax breaks to help finance his acquisition and extensive remodeling of the decaying old Commodore Hotel, built over New York's Grand Central Station. The glitzy Grand Hyatt Hotel opened in September 1980 and triggered the revitalization of a whole section of Manhattan. And it became Trump's springboard to even bigger and more ostentatious undertakings.

In April 1983 he opened the Trump Tower on Fifth Avenue in New York. With its huge marble atrium and cascading waterfall, the Trump Tower quickly became a must-see on many tourists' itineraries, ranking right up there with the Empire State Building and the Statue of Liberty.

At about the same time, Trump, unable to buy a high-profile National Football League franchise, instead bought the New Jersey Generals in the ill-fated United States Football League.

By 1984 Trump the business risk-taker had become Trump the real-life gambler. He opened Harrah's Hotel and Casino at Trump Plaza in Atlantic City, New Jersey. The Harrah's name was dropped and the establishment became known simply at the Trump Plaza. A year later Trump's vision of turning dirty, gamey old Atlantic City into the East Coast's version of Las Vegas came into sharper focus with the opening of his second upscale hotel-and-casino operation named, ever so modestly, Trump Castle. The price tag: an estimated $90 million.

The deals kept rolling in for Trump in the late 1980s. He bought Adnan Khashoggi's 282-foot yacht, one of the world's biggest, for $28 million, changed its name to the *Trump Princess*, and made it the ultimate symbol of his extravagant life-style. He bested crooner-turned-TV-talk-show-host-turned-TV-gameshow producer Merv Griffin in a highly publicized takeover battle for the Resorts International Hotel chain. In that deal, he took possession of the Taj Mahal, an enormous, garish Atlantic City hotel and casino that, at the time, was still under construction.

In his book *Trump: The Art of the Deal*, he crowned himself king of the deal makers. In the text he condescended to give the rest of us, whom he naturally assumed wanted to follow in his successful steps, instruction in how to become great deal makers too.

In 1988 Trump acquired New York's famed Plaza Hotel from a partnership led by Robert M. Bass, the third and wealthiest of the four incredibly wealthy Bass brothers of Fort Worth, for about $400 million. A year later he stepped in after former Major League Baseball commissioner Peter Ueberroth and his team of investors failed in their attempt to buy bankrupt Eastern Airline's Washington–New York–Boston shuttle division, plunked down $365 million for it, and changed its name to the Trump Shuttle.

Despite Trump's boasts about his grand deals, experienced executives in both the hotel and airline industries had howled at both the Plaza Hotel and Eastern Shuttle deals; they believed Trump had paid way too much.

They were right. By the late 1980s, Trump's ego had grown so large that he knowingly and purposely overpaid for his acquisitions. He rationalized that because he was THE Donald, people expected him to pay top dollar for whatever he bought. And besides, in order to maintain his image, the reasoning went, he was obligated to pay the highest prices.

In any case, Trump always felt he could rest easy in the knowledge that he wasn't really putting much, if any, cash in his acquisitions. Trump was the king of cash flow, the lord of leverage. Nearly everything he bought was financed to the hilt.

The Plaza was a classic example. Trump took out a $425 million loan for the Plaza deal. That covered the hotel at $400 million and an apartment building adjacent to the Plaza at $7.5 million. Then he had the loan overwritten by $17.5 million, primarily to finance improvements he wanted to make in the hotel. His bankers asked Trump personally to guarantee $125 million of the $425 million loan. But he didn't invest one dime of his own money in the deal. All it took for Donald Trump to become the owner of the world's most famous hotel was the title to the grand old building itself and his promissory note covering $125 million—or 29.4 percent of the loan amount.

The Plaza deal also was a classic example of how Trump's ego got in the way of what once had been good business judgment. The $400 million he paid for it was a stiff price, especially since Bass had paid only $250 million for a 71 percent stake in it a year earlier. Indeed, once he had taken possession of the grand old French Renaissance palace, Bass had become so fond of it he determined that he didn't want to sell it, at least not quickly. But Trump was so willing to be fleeced, Bass couldn't justify not doing the deal.

Actually, Trump had bargained Bass down from $450 million. But Bass, dealing through one of his lieutenants, Tom Barrack, had bargained Trump up from $350 million. Bass and his partners walked away from the Plaza, which they had owned for only six months with a paper profit of $107 million. Bass's own profit from the deal totaled more than $75 million, less the small amount of interest he had to pay on a $300 million loan he'd taken out on the building when he bought it.

As with several of his other late-1980s deals, Trump knew he was overpaying. The prestige and publicity that came with owning the world's most famous hotel apparently made the deal worth the price.

"I WAS almost indifferent to it," Don Carty said, recalling his emotional response to Trump's faxed letter to Crandall offering to negotiate the sale of American Airlines.

In the days leading up to October 4, 1989, American's senior management had heard indirectly that Trump would be making a bid for AMR. The information may have been leaked by Trump; nevertheless, the source was reliable enough for McNamara and other senior managers to consider it seriously.

In any case, just *who* was making the offer didn't really matter anyway. "With all that was going on in the industry, and all the talk, you'd have to have been on Mars not to have been expecting something like that from someone. I mean, it seemed fairly obvious to me that somebody would take a run at us," said Lowell Duncan, American's vice president for corporate communications at the time.

Sure enough. Northwest Airlines already had gone in a leveraged buyout engineered by Los Angeles financier Al Checchi. And United Airlines was the subject of a $300-a-share takeover bid made by its pilots' and flight attendants' unions. Most everyone on Wall Street agreed that the takeover wave seemed destined to run through the airline industry the way it had, for example, the processed food and the grocery store businesses. Obviously, American and Delta Air Lines were the next likely targets.

And many investors were betting American would be the next to fall victim to a takeover bid. One share of AMR common stock rose from a closing price of $71.50 on August 7, 1989, to $91.50 a share on August 29. The stock price runup had begun the day former oilman and movie studio owner Marvin Davis offered $240-a-share in an unsolicited takeover bid for UAL Corp., United Airlines' parent company. He later boosted his bid to $275 a share. Ironically, it had been Davis who had started the airline takeover game with an unsuccessful $2.7 billion bid for Northwest.

During the three weeks following Davis's first offer to buy United, American's stock was a fixture on the New York Stock Exchange's most active list. On Monday, August 28, nearly 1.4 million shares of AMR's stock were traded. The next day a whopping 3.86 million shares were traded. Previously, AMR stock had been trading at an average of only about 680,000 shares a day.

When no bid materialized, the price fell from a peak of $96 a share down to $81 a share. Then *USA Today* financial columnist Dan Dorfman reported on September 11 that Trump had acquired a substantial amount of AMR stock and that the boyish-looking billionaire might seek federal permission under the Hart-Scott-Rodino Act to acquire up to $15 million worth of the company's stock. That antitrust law required that Trump seek a federal waiver to go over the 5-percent level in his ownership of AMR since he already owned one airline, the Trump Shuttle. AMR's per-share price jumped again, but this time by only $2.25 a share. Dorfman also reported in the same column that Kevin Murphy, an airline analyst at Morgan Stanley & Co., had estimated that AMR could go in a takeover for a price between $120 and $140 a share.

Actually all the speculation in AMR's stock had helped the company in some ways. If nothing else, it turned up the fire under the company's efforts to get ready to defend itself, efforts that had been under way to one degree or another for months.

In fact, by the time Trump's fax arrived in Carty's office, Mike Durham, at the time American's VP and treasurer, had been exploring for more than two years the question of what to do if someone tried to take over AMR. He and a team of senior people from his finance department and from the legal department also had been working on ways to beef up the company's takeover defenses. And after it became clear early in the summer of 1989 that American was a likely target, Durham, his internal team, and more than a dozen legal, financial, and public relations crisis management specialists brought in from the outside spent thousands of man-hours putting together the final pieces of American's defense strategy.

In truth, the project had gotten started in 1986, when Durham sat down for a what-if discussion with John C. "Jack" Pope, American's chief financial officer—who left in 1988 to become executive VP at rival United—and Doug Hacker, Americans corporate services VP.

One of the smart things American had done back in 1986 was to retain the services of Marty Lipton, a partner in the New York law firm of Wachtel & Lipton and the man credited with inventing the so-called poison pill takeover defense tactic, in which stockholders are given certain rights that can be exercised only upon certain events related to an unsolicited takeover attempt being launched and which have the effect of making the company much more expensive to acquire. Shortly after retaining Lipton, American put its first poison pill into its bylaws at the 1987 annual meeting.

Then less than two months before Trump submitted his bid, and at Lipton's suggestion, the company's board had voted in a teleconference call to put bigger teeth into its poison pill.

Actually, the mere fact that the company had hired Lipton—the best in the business—indicated how management would respond in the face of an attempted takeover. Lipton advised companies on takeover defense moves not only because it made him a lot of money, but because he fervently believed that most takeovers harmed the target companies, their shareholders, their employees, their customers, and the nation.

WHEN McNAMARA called with word of Trump's offer, Durham's initial reaction was "a combination of trepidation and eagerness."

"The initial emotional response is that there's trepidation as you look at the future, which twenty-four hours before seemed reasonably clear and now there's a lot more grayness. You don't know what the next couple of months will hold for you and the company.

"On the other hand," he said, "you spend most of your career preparing for something just like this and there's a sense of challenge. Everything you've ever done has prepared you for this moment and now it's time to put all your training, all your ability, all your knowledge and all your instincts on the line. It's definitely a challenge. And I like a challenge."

The challenge, as Durham saw it, was whether American could remain both independent and financially strong. Losing a takeover battle was not the only danger involved. Another, perhaps more unpleasant result of a takeover battle would be to prevail but only at the price of self-mutilation. Would portions of the company have to be sold to pay off nervous shareholders? Would the company's future have to be mortgaged by selling assets, then leasing them back at higher costs, so that shareholders could be paid off and pacified? Would new investors friendly to management—perhaps even employee groups—have to be invited to become significant stockholders in return for special considerations such as wage or benefits concessions and promised loyalty to management in a takeover battle?

None of those scenarios was particularly appealing to the people who ran American Airlines. To say that they were proud of what they had created at American would be a gross understatement. Indeed, American's executives were—and still are—flat-out arrogant in expressing their confidence in their own managerial superiority. It is an arrogance born of success, of the knowledge that together they had created the best-run airline in the industry's history.

Like the Green Berets, American's top managers viewed themselves as an elite corps, endowed with greater abilities and better trained to use those abilities than their contemporaries. Anything short of total victory over a would-be corporate raider would be a huge disappointment.

Of course, in this case total victory meant running off anyone trying to buy the company and doing so without adding debt to the airline's balance sheet or mutilating the company.

That's why American had to be prepared long before it received a takeover bid. Typically, when a company becomes the target of an unwanted takeover proposal, time is at a premium. Lots of very tough decisions that can have a huge impact on the outcome of a takeover battle have to be made very quickly. Lots of very difficult analyses that normally would take months have to be performed in a matter of hours. Hard-to-find answers to tough questions must be found quickly.

Typically, most companies that receive takeover offers are not as well prepared as they should be. So their first response usually is a faltering statement of defiance, a kind of corporate stammer that management thinks will be perceived as toughness but that usually is regarded as nothing more than foolish bluster.

But in American's case, Durham knew what the company's first response would be long before Trump's letter dripped out of the fax machine in Crandall's office. American's plan was to try to delay the action in order to buy time. Durham and his teammates believed they needed that time to analyze properly the specific offer vis-à-vis the different financial models they already had loaded into their computers; time to check out the market's response to the bid; time to determine which, if any of the possible legal maneuvers they'd prepared might be used; time to make the best-informed decisions possible.

"One of our primary goals early on was to be able to make decisions under less pressure and with better information, and to do it more quickly. We felt we might be able to put the ball back in Trump's or whoever's court faster than they expected and that way buy ourselves some more time," Durham said.

ONE OF the least enjoyable tasks of Carty's job was that either he or colleague Bob Baker were usually the ones to break bad news to the boss. They both knew Crandall well enough to know that his famous outbursts of anger usually were directed at the problem, not at the messenger. Still, Carty was less than thrilled at the prospect of calling Crandall, who was still in Tulsa, to tell him that Donald Trump wanted American for his trophy case.

Since this matter of a takeover offer clearly fell on the financial side of the company and not Baker's operations side, "I called Bob," Carty said. McNamara also was on the line.

"He didn't sound very surprised," Carty recalled. "Of course none of us were. Still, I could tell from his voice that even though we were ready for this, it kind of made him a bit mad."

Crandall, who caught the next flight back to D/FW, admits that he was less than shocked. "I knew we were ready, so what was there to say? What I thought emotionally was 'Dammit! We don't need this now.'

"Demand was starting to fall off domestically and fuel prices were jumping up on us, and we were starting to look at a little downturn that we hadn't been expecting and that we thought might run awhile. We'd slowed down our budgeting process in order to get a better idea of what was going to happen to the economics of this business. That was something that needed our attention. But we were going to have to put that down and deal with this thing with Trump. It was all so unnecessary. What a waste!"

After they hung up with Crandall, Carty and McNamara began phoning everyone who needed to know: all of the senior officers, including Baker and Mike Gunn, senior VP for marketing.

McNamara called Durham, who in turn called several of his financial staff members to tell them to tie up a few loose ends on the defensive plans before morning. Durham also alerted the mergers and acquisitions specialists from both Goldman Sachs & Co. and Salomon Brothers, Inc., that American had put on retainer several months before. They were the company's principal outside financial advisors.

Then McNamara called Chuck MarLett, American's corporate secretary, and a few other key people in her legal department. Marty Lipton and his associates at Wachtel & Lipton were called in. Those who weren't already in town were asked to catch that night's late flight from New York.

McNamara then called Debevoise & Plimpton in New York, American's longtime primary outside counsel. While not specialists in mergers and acquisitions, the Debevoise & Plimpton lawyers knew American like no other outsiders. Their understanding of the company made them essential members of the defense team.

One problem was that George Adams, Debevoise & Plimpton's senior partner in charge of corporate law and the firm's primary contact with American, was vacationing in France. Adams had done his first work for American back in 1958, when he handled the contract that allowed the airline to open a ticket office in New York's Grand Central Station. He'd worked closely with American's legendary founder and longtime chairman C. R. Smith and with every chief executive since. His presence on the defense team was felt to be critical.

"I got the call around eleven-thirty that night in my hotel room in Brittany. I'll never forget it. My wife and I had just had the most wonderful dinner," said Adams, who wasn't exactly surprised by the call. He'd left his phone numbers and itinerary with McNamara.

"The next day my wife and I rented a car and raced across France. But we just missed the last flight to New York out of Paris. So we ran over and caught a flight to Amsterdam, where we were able to get a later flight into New York. I will never forget that day as long as I live, doing probably eighty-five mph. across France, missing the plane and having to go to Amsterdam to catch another flight," said Adams, who also lost about two weeks of vacation in the process.

"We got back into New York late on Thursday, October 5, the day the offer from Trump was announced publicly. By that time we had some of our people down at American's office in Texas, so it was determined that I could do more by staying in my office in New York and working from there on Friday and over the weekend rather than waste half the day on an airplane. Then I would come on down and be there by Monday morning."

Next McNamara called Duncan. His job was to call Hill & Knowlton, the big New York public relations firm, which had assigned to American a team that included top specialists in the areas of crisis management and mergers and acquisitions. That done, Duncan then called his top three lieutenants in corporate communications, Al Becker, John Hotard, and Lee Elsesser, to brief them. Those three alerted their staff members at home and told them to be in the office and ready to handle a barrage of media phone calls by 7 A.M.

WHEN CRANDALL arrived back at American's headquarters in the early evening, he, Carty, and McNamara called members of AMR's board of directors. Crandall especially wanted to talk to one board member, Al Casey, the company's former chairman and Crandall's mentor. Two men couldn't be more dissimilar in personality than Crandall and Casey. Indeed, some of their frequent and sometimes quite sharp disagreements gave many the impression that they did not like each other. But somehow they had made a good team when they ran American together. And Crandall valued Casey's advice like no other board member's.

A brief board meeting was held via conference call, with the board quickly authorizing management to release word that Trump had made an offer. Getting that authorization wasn't hard. Management had kept the board well informed on what it was doing to prepare for a possible buyout bid and on its likely defensive steps. The statement the board authorized for release had, for the most part, been written weeks earlier. All that was needed were the particulars of Trump's offer and final reviews by the legal team, senior management, and the board's members.

Then Crandall sent word to all forty board-elected officers of American and its subsidiaries, ordering them to attend a staff meeting at seven the next morning. Those who couldn't be there in person were told they would be hooked in to the meeting via conference call.

Ted Tedesco, the vice president for corporate affairs, arrived early the next morning, eager to hear what Crandall had to say. Though Tedesco had been with American only about two years, he knew Crandall probably as well as anyone. They had been fraternity brothers in the 1950s at the University of Rhode Island. In those days, they often went on double dates, each with the woman they eventually married. Tedesco recalled thinking in college that Crandall was different from "the rest of us screwups." While he could cut up and have a good time like other college kids, Crandall had an intensity that Tedesco said made everyone believe he was destined to reach much higher and farther.

In 1987 Crandall brought his old college friend in to be American's chief lobbyist with state and local governments. He didn't hire Tedesco just because he was a friend who needed a soft place to land after bailing out as the original executive director of the controversy-plagued Dallas Area Rapid Transit system, better known as DART. Crandall recognized that he and American needed someone with Tedesco's feel for local governments. American needed to soften its image as something of a bully when it came to dealing with local authorities. Crandall, who is noted for assembling a talented and deep staff of top officers, also liked the idea of adding someone who long ago had won his trust and respect, someone off whom he could bounce ideas and expect to receive an honest answer, even if that answer wasn't the one he wanted to hear.

"This was serious stuff," Tedesco said of the tense atmosphere in the room as nearly all of American's corporate and senior VPs gathered. "He doesn't call us all together that often."

"So Bob just wades into the room and says, 'Last night I received this formal letter about what we've been thinking about, about somebody being out there. It's Trump.' Then he read Trump's letter to us. Then he read what he was going to say and what he was going to tell the employees.

"He said the board was going to meet in two weeks and what our posture was going to be and that we were going to get the word out that morning before the market opened. Really, he was very calming. He asked if we had any questions. A few guys did. He answered them. Then he said, 'Okay, back to work. We'll let you know if we need you, but the best thing you can do right now is make sure you and your people do everything you can to make this the best airline it can be.' Thirty minutes. That's all. It was over.

"On the way out I looked at him as I walked by him and said, 'Christ!' and he said, 'Ah, shit!' He wasn't concerned so much that we might lose but that this was going to make him take his eye off the ball. This kind of thing was just going to disrupt the health of the company. Even if we won—and you never know how you might get whipsawed around in something like this—it was probably going to screw up the company, and that made him mad. This was his company, his life, and somebody was messing with it."

Indeed, Trump was messing with Crandall's life, even his personal life, more than his old friend Tedesco knew.

It just so happened that Trump faxed his offer to Crandall's office a couple of days before the American CEO and his wife, Jan—his high school sweetheart back in Barrington, Rhode Island—were to go to Morocco to attend billionaire Malcolm Forbes's seventieth birthday party, a legendary affair that turned out to be perhaps the most lavish, expensive, and star-studded blowout in the history of birthday parties.

On Thursday, the day after Trump's offer came in, Crandall briefed his management team, monitored developments with AMR's stock on the New York Stock Exchange, met with lawyers, investment bankers, board members, and his top lieutenants to make sure the takeover defense was coming together as planned.

Then, on Friday morning, he left, somewhat reluctantly, for Morocco.

Even though Forbes's party wasn't scheduled to begin until Saturday, a who's who list of movie stars, musicians, politicians and top corporate executives from around the world already was assembling in Morocco by the time the Crandalls arrived on Friday evening, just in time for dinner. The American CEO, who despite his well-deserved reputation as a no-nonsense businessman, knows how to let his hair down and have a good time. But he could not relax and enjoy the party atmosphere. He spent most of Friday night trying to get through on the phone to his takeover defense team back in Texas.

Finally, anxiety won out over the urge to party. At five A.M., Morocco time, on Saturday, hours before the party officially got under way, "The Capitalist Tool," Forbes's private Boeing 727, began its takeoff roll. With an assist from the flashy Forbes, Bob Crandall was returning to the battlefield.

ABOUT THE time the meeting was breaking up at American's headquarters, the bells began ringing on Dow Jones News Service wire machines in newspaper offices around the country. American had issued the statement announcing that Donald Trump had offered to meet with the AMR board and senior management to discuss the sale of the company for $120 a share. That came to a total of about $7.5 billion, far more than the $6.4 billion United's unions were offering for its parent company, UAL Corp.

Although American officials and their advisors debated whether Trump's carefully worded letter actually fit the formal definition of a takeover offer, they decided to treat it as if it did.

"Actually, all Trump had done was to suggest we discuss the possible sale of the company for $7.5 billion. He had invited us to tea at Trump Tower," Durham said.

American's statement said it had received a "unilateral, unsolicited letter from Donald J. Trump proposing an acquisition of the common stock of AMR in a cash merger price of $120 per share." The statement also noted that while Trump said he believed that the financing could be obtained, he had provided no particulars in his letter to Crandall.

Then, after saying the AMR board would consider the proposal "in due course," the statement included the company's view of these developments. American's corporate mind-set had remained unchanged. Management held fast to the notion that AMR's shareholders would be best served by the company remaining independent and that "excessive levels of debt in the airline industry are not in the public interest."

AMR's stock, which had closed the day before at $83 a share, did not open for trading on time that morning because of a huge order imbalance. Predictably, arbitrageurs, the Wall Street buzzards who circle over a company they sense is in trouble, were placing so many orders to buy AMR stock that not enough sellers could be found quickly. When trading did begin, AMR's stock price jumped immediately to $106.50, up $23.50 from the previous day's close.

Then it gradually settled back down to end the day at $100 a share. While that price was $17 above where it had been only twenty-four hours earlier, it was $20 less than what Trump had offered. In effect, the market had voiced its skepticism about Trump's price and his intentions. At the same time, major investors also had sent a message to American.

But it was left to Crandall and company to decipher the message. Did the market want American to issue a one-time dividend to buy its loyalty? Did the market expect American's management, perhaps with labor's help, to take the company private in its own leveraged buyout? Was the market saying that it anticipated someone else, perhaps with greater credibility and more financial strength, to enter the picture and create a true bidding war?

From a historical perspective, American found itself in an odd position in early October 1989. Only sixteen years earlier airline industry watchers had wondered whether good old American would be around much longer.

In those days it had a gas-guzzling fleet of Boeing 707s and Boeing 747 jumbo jets that, on good days, it half filled with paying passengers. Indeed, American had invented the flying piano lounge in the early 1970s not out of any desire to offer passengers a special service, but because it was looking for some way to make the planes seem less empty. The piano lounges had taken the place of several dozen seats on American's 747s that otherwise would have flown empty.

George Spater—the man who had moved into the corporate captain's seat in 1967 after American's founder, C.R. Smith, retired to become Lyndon Johnson's secretary of commerce—resigned in disgrace in 1973 after admitting that he authorized an illegal contribution of corporate funds to the infamous Committee to Re-Elect the President (CREEP) during the 1972 presidential campaign.

One senior executive was convicted on embezzlement charges. Another wanted in connection with the embezzlement case was a fugitive, living somewhere in Europe.

But Spater's ritualistic corporate suicide and the well-publicized embezzlement case were only the most notable of a whole series of demoralizing incidents and events that rattled American in the late 1960s and early 1970s. The leadership vacuum that developed was so severe that Smith, who in 1973 was seventy-two years old, had to be summoned out of retirement to run things until a new chief executive officer could be brought in from outside the company.

Then, when in 1974 Smith introduced his surprise choice to run American permanently—a Boston Irishman named Al Casey—no one at American was particularly enthused. Casey had run a newspaper and broadcasting company, Times Mirror Co., parent of the *Los Angeles Times*, for a decade and was known primarily as a "finance guy." He had no airline experience at all. Most employees figured Casey would have to hire a good "airline guy" to help him figure out the difference between a DC-10 and a Form 10 K.

What Casey had discovered quickly upon entering American's old headquarters in New York was that morale was at the lowest point in the carrier's history. Attitudes weren't much better out at the airports, in the maintenance hangars, in the cockpits, or in the passenger cabins for that matter.

Casey also had found that there was a lot of suspicion at headquarters, and elsewhere, of the new guy running the finance department. Bob Crandall had come from Bloomingdale's, of all places, where he'd spent six months licking his wounds after being passed over for the chief financial officer's job at TWA. He was pushy and had a temper that was enormous, even by the airline industry's rather indulgent standards. Crandall was poking his nose into all sorts of places where American's corporate culture said someone from finance—even the senior VP—should not be poking his nose. And he was upsetting people with alarming regularity.

Of course, most of the old heads around American's corporate offices figured Crandall wasn't an American kind of guy and probably wouldn't hang around long. He didn't fit in.

They were partly right. Bob Crandall didn't fit in well at the old American. But, in fact, he would hang around long enough to surpass even C.R. Smith in terms of his impact on the company. Casey first shifted Crandall from finance to marketing, where he promptly gave birth to SABRE, the world's first computer reservations system used by travel agencies. Then he made Crandall president and eventually picked him as the heir to the chairman's throne.

As he gained more and more power, Crandall changed American's devil-may-care corporate personality to reflect his own. Like him, American became a company driven to win. And like him, American—always one of the more analytical companies in the industry—became absolutely obsessed with numbers and studies. No other company would do a cost-benefits analysis to determine how much fuel could be saved by removing one olive from the lunch salads served onboard its flights. But American not only performed such a study, Crandall ordered the olives removed to save about $40,000 annually.

American also became, like Crandall, supremely confident. As outsiders began to notice his influence within the company, American as a corporation—and its managers individually—began acquiring a reputation for managerial excellence and arrogance. That perceived arrogance stems from their profound sense of "rightness." They have a rock-solid faith that their disciplined study of the facts and their methodical number-crunching always leads them to make the correct decisions. That attitude—which permeates every office cubicle, airport ticket counter, and cockpit at American—is pure Crandall.

That was the American Airlines that Donald Trump offered to buy, not the lackadaisical, demoralized airline that had existed sixteen years earlier or the money-loser that had abandoned its expensive New York headquarters in 1979 in favor of less expensive digs in Texas.

No one can say whether Trump fully understood what it was he was bidding for. In hindsight, his analysis of American as a possible takeover target seems to have been quite poorly done. Still, in a left-handed sort of way, Trump was paying Crandall the ultimate compliment. The man who claimed to be interested in buying only the very best of anything offered to buy American for $7.5 billion. That was more than $1 billion more than anyone was willing to pay for United, the airline that had ruled the world back in 1973.

The takeover offer served as a blinking neon sign declaring that American had indeed arrived, right on time, at the top of the heap, where Crandall always had wanted it to be.

Trump's bid was confirmation that by the clarity of his vision and the sheer force of his remarkable will, Bob Crandall's relentless sixteen-year drive—really more like a holy quest—to make American the world's preeminent airline had succeeded. Now Trump threatened to take away the airline into which Crandall had poured his very being in order to exploit it for what Crandall regarded as ego-driven personal gain.

Crandall's public stance on the possibility of a takeover always had been "If anybody can come into this company and do a better job than we can running it, and can give the shareholders a better return on their investment than we can, then let 'em." But he carefully guarded what he really believed. He never said it, but he was certain that there wasn't anyone alive who could run American better than he and his team of senior managers were running it in 1989. His sense of rightness told him so.

He also never said it, but those close to him believe that Crandall determined that if it became impossible to retain control of his airline on his own terms, then he would not allow it to be lost to a pompous, smooth-talking, image-conscious huckster like Trump.

If Donald Trump wanted to take over American Airlines, he was going to have to take on—and beat—Bob Crandall, the toughest executive in corporate America.

2

The Wrong Man

C. R. SMITH, who for all practical purposes created American Airlines out of a bizarre financial amalgam of dozens of small, poorly financed airlines in the 1930s, was more than just American's chairman for nearly forty years. He was the carrier's heart and soul. In addition, Smith was the undisputed leader of the entire U.S. airline industry for his entire career.

Largely because of Smith's unmatched managerial abilities and natural ability to find and groom talented young managers, American was known as the industry's best executive breeding ground. Over the years the senior executive ranks at many other airlines have been populated by many former American executives.

So it is both ironic and incredible that when it came time for Mr. C.R.—as he was universally known—to replace himself, he picked a man whose education, experience, and personality clearly made him the wrong man for the job.

In the early 1960s it looked as if a former schoolteacher who'd become a hotshot salesman for the airline would replace Smith. Marion Sadler literally wrote the book on how to sell airline tickets for American Airlines. Sadler's sales manual, written on his own initiative in the early 1950s when he was American's district sales manager in Buffalo, was adopted by the company as its standard training curriculum for its sales representatives. It earned him the company's highest honor, the Distinguished Service Award for Merit, and a promotion in 1955 to an important staff job, director of passenger sales at American's Manhattan headquarters. In 1957 Sadler was named VP of customer services. Two years later he was named VP and general manager of the airline.

Along the way he impressed nearly everyone, including C.R., with his understanding of the business side of the airline business. At some point in the early 1960s, C.R. began grooming Sadler to be his successor. And in January 1964 American's board named him president.

Sadler had a charmed tenure as American's president. Not only was he a capable manager and popular leader, the mid-1960s were very good years for most U.S. businesses. The national economy was exceptionally strong. And the country had not yet gone through the traumatic period of social change brought about by the dissatisfaction with the war in Vietnam and a decline in the national economy. In 1964, Sadler's first year in the job, American's profits rose 70 percent, to $33.4 million. The next year the company earned $39.6 million. In 1966 the company earned $52.1 million and placed its order for ten Boeing 747s at a then-astounding cost of $16 million each. Profits dropped slightly, to $48 million, in 1967. Still, Sadler presided over four of the most successful years in American's history.

But in the summer of 1967, Smith shocked American's employees and the entire airline industry by naming George Spater, American's general counsel, to the new position of vice chairman. The move was widely—and correctly—perceived to mean that the academic Spater, not the popular Sadler, would be C.R.'s successor.

A few days later Sadler underwent surgery for colon cancer.

A talented lawyer with strong political ties in Washington dating from his days as TWA's chief Washington lobbyist, Spater was the antithesis of a good airline manager. While C.R. himself was some-times perceived as being aloof, the bespectacled, quiet, even shy Spater widely was perceived as being an intellectual snob. Com-municating with the troops was a virtual impossibility for him.

As a corporate lawyer, it had been Spater's job to present all the possible options to his boss, who then would make the final decision. But he never learned to make the tough decisions himself. So, as chief executive Spater was notoriously indecisive. His problems were compounded by the fact that his understanding of the airline business was gained solely through the legal department. He had no expe-rience in operations, sales, or finance.

While Sadler's surgery in mid-1967 went well and the prognosis was good, his corporate fate was sealed. Late that same year, at American's annual officers' marketing meeting, C.R. stood up, and in his typically blunt way said simply that he and Sadler would be retiring.

Sadler officially left American in January 1968, but he returned at Spater's request in 1969 to serve as vice chairman. Though it was primarily an honorary and advisory post in which he acted as senior management's mouthpiece in dealing with employees, Sadler stayed active in the company until 1972, when circulatory problems forced the amputation of one of his legs. He learned to walk with an artificial leg and remained as a director of the company until 1981, a year after his other leg was removed because of continuing, painful circulatory problems.

In 1983 the man who probably should have run American Airlines for at least eight years died, having never achieved what twenty years earlier had seemed would be his destiny. One can only imagine how American and the U.S. airline industry would be different today had Sadler been at American's helm during the tough years between 1968 and 1975, the year he turned sixty-five and probably would have retired.

GEORGE SPATER's surprise ascension coincided with a serious reversal of American's and other airlines' fortunes. The year 1968 has been well chronicled as a watershed in U.S. history. For better or for worse, American politics, culture, and society all were changed dramatically and irrevocably that year. Hippies. Tet. Chicago's Democratic National Convention. Nixon. Draft-card burning. LSD. The assassintions of Martin Luther King, Jr. and Bobby Kennedy. It was a tumultuous, violent year of change. The positive feelings generated by the vibrant economy of the early and mid-1960s and the blossoming youth culture that spoke of love and peace gave way that year to worry about inflation and disillusionment with the way the government was conducting an increasingly unpopular war in Vietnam.

No matter whom C.R. chose as his successor, he would have faced some tough challenges between 1968 and 1973, the years Spater served as American's president and/or chairman. Despite steady revenue gains throughout those six years, the airline's profits were lackluster in 1968 and 1969 and virtually nonexistent in 1971 and 1972, when the company made $3 million and $5.6 million respectively. In 1970 the company lost $26.4 million. American lost another $48 million in 1973, one of its worst years ever.

American wasn't the only carrier suffering during those years. In 1968 the industry began a slow downward trend. And by 1970, when the industry's traffic growth rate dropped like a rock to just 0.3 percent, virtually every carrier hit the skids.

But by 1973 some carriers were making a modest comeback. American, however, was not one of them. That year American, Eastern, and Pan American were the only carriers to lose money. Eastern had been a chronic money loser for more than a decade, and Pan Am, primarily an international carrier, was hurt by the dollar's weakness abroad. But that American, historically one of the most consistently profitable airlines, was included in such company had more than a few heads shaking.

"American never made as much money as it should have after 1966," said Gene Overbeck, who in 1967 became senior VP-administration and general counsel. "The early '70s were especially bad. It was one of the really bad times in the industry's history. You had the deliveries of the first 747s, and that coincided with a tremendous downturn that affected the whole economy. The whole industry was doing poorly. And American was probably doing more poorly than most.

"But no one then was able to put their finger on why. It's not fair to say that American was poorly managed then. Maybe it wasn't as well managed as it should have been, but compared to other airlines at the time, it was no worse than most and better than some. But the money losses at American, relative to the rest of the industry, were a little worse. Even when American made money, it didn't make as much as it should have compared to what the rest of the industry did," Overbeck said.

Overbeck, who was close personally to Spater, agrees with the general assessment that inasmuch as the chairman did nothing to effect a turnaround, he was a big part of American's problems.

American's problems stemmed from the industry's addition of too many widebody jets just as passenger demand reached an unexpected plateau. The industry's financial condition also was hurt by the nation's first really serious energy crisis, which pushed up fuel prices.

Yet there is no doubting now that Spater was ill-prepared to face the challenges he encountered. He provided neither the visionary leadership nor the managerial force one might have expected from the CEO of a company going through such difficult times. Because he delayed making decisions—or made no decisions at all—on most of the important issues taken up by American's senior management, he created a leadership vacuum in the company. Eventually that vacuum would become so apparent that a newspaper headline would ask "Who's Running American Airlines?"

Otto Becker spent forty years at American Airlines before retiring in 1980 as senior VP-field sales and services. He joined the airline in the sales department at New York's LaGuardia Airport station and over the years came to be widely respected as an intelligent, hardworking, rock-solid executive who knew how properly to balance the corporate need to make money and the importance of treating his employees with respect. In many ways, Becker was the paradigm of the C.R. Smith–trained American Airlines executive. Convinced of the paramount importance of sticking to the fundementals of airline sales and operations, Becker also was intensely focused on running a smooth, high-quality airline. Yet even Becker, who to this day speaks reverently of his mentor, calls naming Spater to run the company "C.R.'s big mistake."

"Spater was a very bright guy and, I imagine, a very capable lawyer. He just was not an executive. He was not a manager. We would sit in his staff meetings and he always had an agenda, very well organized. But I don't think we ever, ever finished a topic. We never came to a real conclusion to a lot of the subjects we discussed. He just plain did not know how to delegate and hold responsible people who were working for him. He was, however, a fine gentleman, just a super man. A very nice man," Becker said. "He was misunderstood. Or maybe it was more that he was misplaced."

Becker recalls a picture that ran in the *Scientific American* magazine of Spater sitting in front of "a solid wall of books. He was sitting there in a rocking chair, with a sweater on. I thought to myself, 'That's Spater.' He should have been a college professor."

Fittingly, after Spater left American he spent most of his time in England, where he wrote two critically acclaimed books, one a coauthored study of authors Leonard and Virginia Wolff, the other an individually written two-volume biography of eighteenth century English journalist William Cobbett. Spater's death in 1984 cut short his writing plans.

Overbeck, who'd been hired by Spater in 1959 as American's first in-house lawyer ever (other than the general counsel) and who succeeded him as American's general counsel, agrees that Spater was out of place at American's helm. "George was sort of professorial. He had these wire rims he always wore. He didn't drink. He didn't smoke. He didn't tell jokes. He wasn't a raconteur.

"C.R. had that wonderful intangible called charisma. Spater didn't have any charisma. Not one drop. There's all sorts of old stories about some of the things C.R. would do. For example, C.R. used to carry flight attendants' bags for them. The girls—that's what we used to call 'em back in those days when they were stewardesses and all female—just loved it. They would carry on with him and make a big joke out of the chairman carrying their bags. But if Spater had tried that, the girls probably would have said 'Let go of that!'

"There's three things I think a CEO should have. One, he's gotta be smart, bright, intelligent. Two, he's gotta have a tremendous energy level. You can't be a good CEO if you don't have a lot of energy. And three, you gotta have charisma. C.R. had all three. Spater had the first two, but he didn't have any of the third one," Overbeck said.

In fairness, not every negative thing that happened during Spater's four-year reign at American was all his fault. By rights, American's unhappy experience with the Boeing 747, for example, should be hung on C.R. Smith and Marion Sadler. They made the decision to acquire 747s against the strong advice of some of American's route planners and the less forceful—but still expressed—misgivings of other executives, including Spater.

Pan Am, then the United States' unofficial "flag" carrier serving dozens of foreign capitals and nearly every major city in Europe, Asia, and South America, placed the first order for 747s in 1965. TWA, Pan Am's primary competitor in the transatlantic markets, followed suit. So did United, which thanks to its merger with Capitol Airlines in 1961 had passed American to become the nation's largest carrier even though it had no international routes. American followed the crowd in 1967. It placed an order for ten of the big, bump-nosed beasts and took out options to buy six more.

If nothing else, that decision shows that even good managers like Smith and Sadler can make bad decisions. While the 747 was ideal for the kinds of routes that Pan Am operated in those days—long-haul international flights on routes where it was protected by law from competition with other U.S. airlines—it was too big for the kind of routes American flew. As a result, the 747 became a huge albatross around American's corporate neck. To make matters worse, the first

747 to join American's fleet arrived in 1970, at precisely the worst moment of a particularly severe downturn in demand for air travel.

Still, Spater must get a big portion of the blame for the problems while he was CEO—both for what he did do and, perhaps more important, for what he didn't do. In some ways Spater was his own worst enemy. His own sense of integrity and honesty ultimately betrayed him by making it obvious just how little control he had over the goings-on inside his own company.

Juan Homs, a flashy young Spaniard who had been an up-and-coming executive in Pan Am's promotion department, was hired in 1966 by then-President Marion Sadler to design, edit, and publish an in-flight magazine similar to the one Pan Am had begun in 1947 and the one United had launched in 1957. His creation, *American Way*, was an instant hit. Today it continues to enjoy a reputation as the best in-flight magazine available and one of the better magazines of any type in the nation. Not only did Homs's magazine impress senior management, so did his tireless work habits and his managerial success. Every project in which he was involved came in at or under budget.

Unfortunately there was a dark secret behind Homs's success at American. When he negotiated any deal with an American supplier, he had three nonnegotiable demands. First the supplier had to agree to provide maximum quality and perfect on-time performance. Second, Homs demanded the right to cancel the contract if the supplier failed to deliver as promised. Last, and most important, the supplier had to pay Homs a kickback—typically 5 percent of the total value of the American contract. Most of the kickbacks went into two dummy corporations Homs had set up.

Sometime in early 1972, Spater found out about Homs's scheme from a supplier who blew the whistle. The subsequent internal investigation not only confirmed what Homs had been up to, it also uncovered a simpler case in which Melvin Fante, American's staff VP for corporate design, had diverted for his own personal use such things as chairs and carpeting he'd orderd for the airline's Admirals Clubs. Fante, it was learned, also had finagled himself a discount on business suits made by Hart Schaffner & Marx, suppliers of American's flight attendants' uniforms. Fante paid restitution to the company and resigned. Homs refused to do the same and was fired.

Had Spater left it at that, the matter would have gone down as just another ugly but relatively minor incident of white-collar crime. But at about the same time the Homs matter was coming to light, Spater read a column in the *New York Times* in which U.S. Attorney Whitney N. Seymour, Jr., had criticized the habit of most businesses of sweeping their white-collar crimes under the rug and being satisfied with firings and resignations. Businesses, Seymour argued, had a moral and ethical obligation to turn their white-collar crime cases over to the appropriate law enforcement agencies. Something in Seymour's opinion touched Spater's own high sense of moral and ethical propriety. The airline chairman may have already been leaning that way to begin with, but when Homs refused to make restitution, Spater responded by turning his case over to the Federal Bureau of Investigation and a U.S. Attorney for investigation. After being questioned by the attorney and a grand jury, Homs fled to his native Spain to avoid prosecution.

Unfortunately for Spater, the Juan Homs affair did not end when Homs skipped the country. In his quest to root out corruption in the company, Spater asked all senior officers to reveal in writing what gifts or money, if any, worth $100 or more they had received from Homs over the years. Walter Rauscher, American's senior VP-marketing, responded honestly and admitted to having borrowed $14,000 from Homs. Rauscher also reported that Homs, without Rauscher's prior knowledge, had paid the hotel bill run up by Rauscher and his family during a Hawaiian vacation, and that Homs had arranged it with a New Jersey Volkswagen dealer he knew so that Rauscher's wife could have a loaner car while her VW was being repaired after a wreck.

Rauscher had no college education, but that had not prevented him from rising all the way to American's senior vice presidential level. In 1959 he'd won American's Award for Merit for coming up with the industry's first successful overbooking plan. In 1972 he was Homs's boss. But his rank did not render him immune to the kind of personal financial pressures faced by millions of other members of the upper middle class in the inflation-ridden 70s. He had a $40,000 home mortgage, $6,000 in the bank, and three sons in college. On top of that, Rauscher had dabbled in the stock market, apparently not successfully. At one point, in need of a loan, he had turned to Homs, who, for reasons that became known only after the scandal broke, always seemed to have money to lend co-workers and with which to shower them with extravagant gifts.

Rauscher freely admitted to Spater the full extent of his financial involvement with Homs. But he really thought nothing of what he believed were his innocent dealings with the slick Spaniard, at least not until he arrived home that night to word that an agitated Spater had just called and wanted an immediate call back. He returned Spater's call and was told that the paper he'd signed earlier that day had been turned over to the U.S. Attorney's office.

Ultimately, with the government's lawyers arguing that his $14,000 loan from Homs actually was a kickback, Rauscher was indicted and stood trial. Rauscher then took the advice of his attorney, who despite the lack of hard evidence feared the country's attitude about official misconduct following the Watergate scandal. So largely because his attorney worried that in such a politicized and cynical environment the government could, and would string the process out well beyond his ability to pay for legal help, Rauscher entered a guilty plea. He was sentenced to thirty days in prison and served fifteen before being released. Later he received a letter from Homs, who was in Spain and contemplating a return to the United States to face trial. Homs's letter made it clear that the $14,000 indeed was a loan and not a kickback, and that Rauscher had had no knowledge of Homs's scheme. Based on that evidence, shortly after he took office in 1976 President Jimmy Carter pardoned Rauscher.

The whole affair was played out pretty much in public, giving American a black eye. And it got worse.

Spater was informed that Jack Mullins, American's longtime senior VP-marketing who had been bumped up and out to vice chairman in 1971 to make room for Rauscher, also had taken kickbacks. Instead of confronting Mullins, who by then was in semiretirement, Spater enlisted American board member Manly Fleischmann, an attorney who also had directed the company's investigation of Rauscher, to find out what happened. Fleischmann found no evidence of any kickbacks going to Mullins through Homs or anyone else. But the Wall Street Journal found out about the internal investigation and published a story saying Mullins was suspected of having bought a car and carpet for his house with company money. None of it was true, and at Spater's insistence the Journal ran his strong denial of those accusations against Mullins. Still, there was a growing perception that "everyone in management at American Airlines had their hands in the cookie jar."

IN 1972 Richard Nixon won the presidential election by a record landslide over Senator George McGovern. In retrospect, he probably could have won the election even if he'd taken a year-long vacation.

But, as we know only too well now, Nixon and his campaign officials were very busy boys during the 1972 campaign. The infamous break-in at the Democratic National Committee offices in Washington's posh Watergate complex eventually led to Nixon's becoming the only U.S. president to resign from office.

The Watergate break-in, and the much broader political scandal to which it was tied, also led to Spater's early resignation.

Dave Frailey, head of American's public relations department in 1973, said that during the '72 election campaign, "the arm was put on corporations to ante up." Behind the strongarm tactics was the now-infamous Committee to Re-Elect the President, or CREEP, as reporters who covered the unfolding of the Watergate scandal reveled in calling it.

"Spater was approached by a guy with CREEP named Herbert Kalmbach. He knew that Kalmbach, in addition to working for CREEP, was a lawyer who did work for United [Airlines]. Spater was just in a dither. Knowing George, I imagine that he couldn't eat or sleep. Whatever the case, he was finally told that $100,000 would satisfy everyone," Frailey said.

Spater's dilemma was clear. The thought of making what he knew would be an illegal contribution to the Nixon campaign went against everything he'd ever stood for. Doing so also would put his company at risk should the contribution ever come to light. However, the airline industry in the early 1970s was a very politically sensitive one. As a fully regulated business, airlines needed government approval to add new service on any route, obtain new domestic and international routes, change fare prices, or discuss with another carrier almost anything more important than the weather or the time of day. Therefore, American could not afford to make enemies in the administration. And refusing to make the solicited contribution almost certainly would have made enemies. That was even more true if American's chief rival, United, was on CREEP's hook too, as Kalmbach's role in putting the pinch on American suggested.

Without the knowledge of his board of directors, Spater knuckled under to the Nixon campaign's extortion and came up with $75,000, $55,000 of it from American's accounts.

"I'm convinced that the guy was doing it conscientiously to protect his company even though he knew full well as a lawyer that it was illegal," said Frailey, who was shocked not so much by the fact that American had made an illegal political contribution but more that the ethically minded Spater had been the one to do it.

Of course, had the CREEP burglars not been caught red-handed at the Watergate, Spater's illegal contribution likely never would have been detected. But once the Washington news media finally realized just who those unlikely burglars were and what they were doing in the offices of the Democratic National Committee, the race was on to see which news organization could get the newest, hottest scoop in one of the deepest tales of official wrongdoing in the nation's history. CREEP's operations provided the media with dozens of scandalous stories, all of which pointed to Nixon's moral and ethical unfitness for office.

Unfortunately for American Airlines, one of the stories uncovered during the media feeding frenzy surrounding the Watergate scandal was CREEP's coercion of illegal campaign contributions from a long list of major U.S. corporations.

Frailey recalls visiting American's office in Washington in the spring of 1973 and receiving a call from a reporter at the *Washington Star* whom he'd known for years. "He called me and said, 'Hey, Dave, do you know some of the things that are going to happen soon? The announcement is going to be made soon.' I said I didn't know what he was talking about and he said, 'I can't tell you what it is, but I've got a word of advice for you. I suggest you get the first plane back to your office this evening and first thing in the morning you get to George Spater and tell him things are getting ready to happen. He'll know what you're talking about.' Frailey tried to get more information, but all he could come away with was that "it had something to do either with Nixon or with CREEP."

Ralph Nader's Concerned Citizen organization was attempting to get Nixon's campaign records on corporate contributions made public. And Frailey's reporter friend knew that Concerned Citizen was about to get what it wanted; the names of some companies on the list of those that made illegal contributions.

Frailey did return to New York that night. At eight-twenty the next morning he was standing in front of the bank of elevators on the seventh floor of American's headquarters at 633 Third Avenue in New York. When Spater got off the elevator, Frailey requested an urgent meeting. Spater invited him into his office.

"As he was taking off his hat and hanging up his coat, I said 'I don't know what this is about, but I was in Washington yesterday and I got a call and the reporter said things are going to happen soon, something about the election,' Frailey said.

"And Spater said, 'Dave, I should have brought you up to date about this a long time ago. I'm sorry I haven't. Sit down and I'll tell you all about it.' That's when he told me what he'd done and who had asked for it.''

Frailey quickly recognized that Spater, who had set very high ethical standards for the company's senior executives, was about to be fingered publicly for participating in the illegal political contributions scheme. Spater decided to meet the bad news head-on in hopes of blunting its impact and the damage it might do to American. He had Frailey set up a couple of news conferences, one in Washington and one in New York, where he planned to display his own dirty laundry.

But if Spater had been expecting a kind and forgiving reaction because he had voluntarily confessed, he must have been quite disappointed. The public's reaction was both swift and negative. He and American were heavily chastized, both by the political hounds in Washington who were nipping at Nixon's heels and by the average American who was fed up with corruption in high places and with the manipulation of the electoral process that had been going on.

"You know, Spater took a lot of heat for that, but he was far from the only head of a major corporation who made such a contribution.'' Frailey said. "A few weeks later the whole list came out and there were a lot of major companies on that list . . . By then . . . it was becoming obvious that Nixon's people had coerced all these companies into making their contributions. The funny thing is, had George kept his mouth shut and just let the news come out later, American would have come off as being just one of the many companies involved. As it was, American was the first company to come forward and, therefore, the one everyone remembered,'' Frailey said.

Spater hung on at American for a couple more months, then resigned as chairman in September 1973, five months before his sixty-fifth birthday and his scheduled retirement date.

FRANCIS H. "Hooks" Burr remembers how Manly Fleischmann kept getting more and more exasperated. Fleischmann, from Buffalo, and Burr, a Bostonian, were both lawyers and members of American Airlines' board of directors in the early 1970s. They were among Spater's closest friends on the board. Yet they and Dallas businessman James Aston led the lynching party that was behind Spater's forced retirement.

"We kept looking at the financial results of the company getting worse and worse. We would lose a lot of money one year, make a little the next year, and then lose even more the following year," Burr said. "Manly, who was a wonderful guy, would look at that and want to know what was going wrong. And nobody in management could ever give him an answer that would satisfy him. And I kept wondering when George was going to come up with some sort of plan to solve all of American's problems. But he never did come up with anything that addressed the real problems. There was always this unavoidable cost item here, or that revenue problem there. No one was making the tough decisions to change the way things were done in an effort to make money."

Burr, who served on American's board for nearly thirty years, recalls how difficult a decision replacing Spater was for him, Fleischmann, and other board members. "We would have dinner with George from time to time, and he was a very nice, wonderful guy. And it killed us because we all were fond of him. But we had to do it. He was the guy on the bridge and had to be held responsible," Burr said.

The real shock, however, wasn't Spater's de facto firing. Most everyone who'd been paying attention in those days had figured such a move was inevitable. The real surprise was who the board chose as Spater's replacement: C.R. Smith.

"We couldn't find anyone else we were satisfied with on quick notice, and we figured it was going to take us quite a while to find the right man. So we contacted C.R. to see if he'd be interested in coming back to run the airline for a year or so while we conducted a search for a permanent chairman," Burr said. "C.R. really didn't want to do it. He was tired and I think he believed he was slipping a bit. But we expressed our extreme need to him and he accepted our offer with only two provisos. One, he made it clear he didn't want to hang around very long, no more than a year. And two, he didn't want to be paid anything more than his expenses."

C.R.'s return was like a dose of insulin to a diabetic. His mere presence helped revive the sagging morale of American's workers.

"When C.R. came back as caretaker chairman, he was there mainly as a symbol for the employees because morale was so bad, and for those outside, many of whom had questioned whether anyone was running American Airlines," Overbeck said.

But that's not to say that C.R. didn't do anything important during his interim chairmanship. Most significant, C.R. fired American president George Warde, who had run American's aircraft maintenance base at Tulsa, Oklahoma, before being promoted by Spater to executive VP and general manager in 1971 and then to president a year later. The popular and gregarious Warde got high marks for his work at Tulsa and his handling of employees. But he was out of his league as president.

Overbeck recalls that initially upon his return to American, "C.R. virtually ignored Warde, treated him as if he didn't exist."

That changed when Warde, fulfilling one of his most important responsibilities as president, developed the company's 1974 operating budget and took it to C.R. The old man was aghast. Warde's budget projected a loss! While in the past C.R. may have put up with American's underperforming ways, going into a year with a budget that projected a loss was something he was not prepared to do. He rejected Warde's budget and ordered him to make any cuts necessary to produce a projected profit. Warde did as he was told. But if he had any hopes of being allowed to stay on under whoever replaced C.R., Warde's initial willingness to accept a budget projecting a loss took care of that.

"C.R. went ahead and fired Warde, who really was a nice guy, so that whoever came in after him wouldn't have to do it," Overbeck said.

"C.R. also made the decision to sell the South Pacific routes we'd gotten from the government. And he fired John Andersen," who had replaced Walt Rauscher as senior VP-marketing, over Andersen's plan to cut loose American's longtime advertising agency, Doyle Dane Bernbach.

"But other than those few things, C.R. pretty much was a caretaker."

3

New Blood

BY 1973 Albert Vincent Casey had been president of the Times Mirror Corp., parent company of the *Los Angeles Times* newspaper, for seven years. Before that, he'd served as Times Mirror's executive VP for two years, and prior to that he'd been the company's senior VP of finance for a year. After nearly ten years of tap-dancing his way through one board room battle after another between warring factions of Times Mirror's dominant Chandler family, Casey was fed up. A gregarious Bostonian with nearly perfect comedic timing, Casey had used his considerable financial acumen to convert Times Mirror from a simple holding company whose flagship property was the *L.A. Times* into one of the fastest-growing and most highly regarded media conglomerates in the nation. Yet by 1973 he and everyone associated with Times Mirror knew he was approaching the end of the line there.

For eleven years he had played one side of the fractious Chandler family off against the other in order to do what he thought was best for the publicly owned company. Still, the Chandlers, or at least some of them, continued to view Times Mirror as their family's private concern. At one time or another Casey had managed both to oblige and to anger nearly all of the Chandler family members on the board. But no one, not even someone with Casey's charm, wit, and intelligence, can walk that tightrope forever. Ultimately he lost the support of too many board members, Chandlers and nonfamily members alike. Several quietly began working to oust him, going so far as to suggest that his drinking habits were starting to affect his job performance. To those who knew Casey well in those days, such a suggestion was preposterous. While he was no stranger to hard drink, Casey was not, his friends insist, anything close to being a drunk, as some of the Chandlers had implied. Nevertheless, while no one can say whether his opponents on the Times Mirror board could muster enough votes to oust him, Casey knew his days of effective leadership in Los Angeles were over, and he was looking for someplace to go.

A lifelong Republican, Casey thought he'd found a way out of his predicament in 1973. President Richard Nixon nominated him to head up Conrail, the government-subsidized passenger rail service in the Northeast. The only problem was that Casey, who was ready to give up his $300,000-a-year job at Times Mirror to take the $60,000-a-year job at Conrail because of his long-standing interest in politics and government, had to be approved by the U.S. Senate. And in 1973 no presidential appointment, not even one as far out on the edge of the political universe as the head of Conrail, was going to be approved by a Senate in which half the members were bent on drumming Nixon out of office.

JAMES ASTON, chairman of Republic National Bank in Dallas and one of the stronger voices on American Airline's board since the mid-1950s, is credited with coming up with the idea of bringing C. R. Smith out of retirement to serve as interim chairman. In the early summer of 1973 American's directors named Aston, Hooks Burr, Manly Fleischmann, and Detroit banker Charles T. Fisher III to a committee to deal with "the Spater problem." After several meetings they realized they had two problems. The first was that they had to replace Spater as quickly as possible. The airline's condition was deteriorating quickly and, by staying on, Spater was hurting more than he was helping. The committee's second problem was that it didn't have enough time to do a good job of finding a new CEO. So Aston, who as an officer in the Air Transport Command during World War II had reported to Brigadier General C. R. Smith, hit upon the notion of recalling the man he still addressed as "General" to active duty.

Aston, who also was a Times Mirror director, played a similarly critical role in bringing Spater's permanent replacement to American.

The executive search firm of Ward Howell Associates provided American's board with detailed information on more than thirty executives at other companies. Al Casey's name was on that list. But that doesn't mean that American's board was attracted to him instantly, or that Casey actively sought the job. Indeed, even though committee members at first were impressed by Casey's credentials, especially his strong background in finance, they delayed in contacting him. Aston, a Casey supporter on the Times Mirror board, didn't even realize Casey wanted to leave the media company. In fact, Aston initially scratched through Casey's first name on his copy of the list of candidates and penciled in "John," assuming that Ward Howell Associates had gotten Al mixed up with his older brother, a senior VP at Dallas-based Braniff International Airlines.

Meanwhile, C.R., who met regularly with the committee, favored someone with direct airline experience. In particular, he supported the candidacy of Pan Am chairman and former American senior VP Bill Seawell, a West Pointer whom C.R. had met and come to respect during World War II service together in the Air Transport Command. So, while Casey's name remained on the list, he was not contacted for several months.

There was also strong sentiment among some board members in favor of Arthur Lewis, a longtime airline industry executive who then was chairman of F.S. Smithers & Co., a Wall Street investment banking firm that years later was swallowed up in a merger with what is now The PaineWebber Group. Lewis had begun his airline career with American in Austin, Texas, in 1939. By 1954 he was C.R.'s head of planning. But he left in 1955 to become president of the fledgling Hawaiian Airlines. Lewis left Hawaiian in 1963 to become Eastern's president and general manager. In 1969 he quit Eastern, where management infighting was legendary, and went to Wall Street. That background gave him a combination of experience in both airline operations and finance that was appealing to American's board members. Still, Casey's ebullient personality was hard to beat.

When the committee finally began to consider Casey seriously, it soon realized that he had what they believed American Airlines needed. During his years at Times Mirror, Casey was an active West Coast fundraiser, recruiter, and supporter of the Harvard Business School, of which he was a graduate. Burr, who had never met Casey, also was active on behalf of Harvard on the East Coast. He turned to the network of Harvard Business School grads to do his personal background check on Casey, and liked what he heard.

"At Harvard they said Al was a real wiseguy, a great after-dinner speaker and sometimes a bit of a loose cannon. But nobody said anything bad about his character. And they had very high praise for his honesty and frankness," Burr said.

Jim Aston didn't have to do a personal background check on Casey. He was perhaps Casey's biggest fan on the Times Mirror board. The banker in Aston deeply appreciated Casey's keen understanding of finance. At the same time, as a former military man Aston marveled at the way Casey mixed hard-nosed decision making with genuinely warm-hearted humor in order to both drive and lead the people who worked for him to do their best work. Aston knew that Casey was a tough, demanding boss who drove his people hard, who did not suffer fools gladly, and who was not afraid to fire people who couldn't keep up with the furious pace he set. Yet Aston also noted that those who could keep up and perform up to Casey's standards would run through walls for him. In fact, Aston had only one problem with American going after Casey: He could not in good conscience be party to an effort to induce Times Mirror's leader to leave. So when Burr, Fleischmann, and Fisher asked him to approach Casey on American's behalf, Aston declined for ethical reasons. But he did agree to talk about the opportunity at American if Casey called him first.

A couple of weeks later, Aston's phone rang. Casey was on the other end. The two arranged to meet in Dallas to discuss the American opportunity the following week, when Casey was scheduled to pay a Christmas visit to his brother. They met, and Aston dispassionately explained both the positives and negatives that Casey could expect to find at American. Before their meeting was over, Casey made it clear that, since he was planning to leave Times Mirror in any case, he was interested in the American job. Casey said he wanted to meet with the other members of the committee and to hear more about American's situation.

At their first meeting, Burr found Casey to be everything his friends in the Harvard network had said he would be, and then some. Fisher and Fleischmann also felt that Casey could bring to American the C.R.-like charisma and leadership it so badly needed. In addition, they believed Al Casey could bring two things to the party that even American's legendary old chairman could not offer. Whereas C.R., an accountant by education and early career experience, knew enough about corporate finance to understand what his chief financial officer and investment bankers told him, Casey was a bonafide expert in modern high finance. And, while C.R. possessed the marvelous, innate ability to manage American Airlines through what essentially were its entrepreneurial years, Casey was a proven master at both managing and leading a large, complicated, technically sophisticated, and somewhat bureaucratic organization.

The rest of American's directors would go along with the committee's choice. The only person left to convince was C.R. Smith, who as interim chairman lacked real authority to block the committee's nomination. But because of the huge shadow he had cast over American for forty years, and because of the personal loyalty and respect he'd earned from every board member, C.R. did have the very real power to block Casey's selection, if he chose to do so. And initially C.R. was opposed to Casey.

"He'd say, 'What the hell does he [Casey] know about running an airline? He's a newspaperman,' " Burr said. "But we convinced him that American's problem was not operational but financial, and that we needed a financial man in here. We had plenty of good operational people already on board."

Once C.R. was on their side, the committee took Casey's name to the full board at its February 1974 meeting. It made its decision just in time. MGM Studios, unaware that American was interested in Casey, had determined to steal away Times Mirror's president for itself. American's board named Casey president, while C.R. retained the title of chairman. Three months later, just as Casey had demanded as a condition to his coming to American, C.R. officially retired again. But for all practical purposes, C.R.'s last official act at American was to nominate Casey as his own replacement.

"That was my idea," Casey once said. "If I was going to be the boss I didn't want C.R. looking over my shoulder, and he agreed with me. The board wanted C.R. to stay on for a while as chairman just to help make the transition look orderly to the employees and the public. So we settled on having C.R. stay around through that spring. But I ran the company."

After his initial opposition to Casey was reversed, C.R. took a quick liking to him. But he worked hard to stay out of Casey's way. They visited several times prior to Casey's election by the board, with Casey asking the expected questions and C.R. providing the expected briefings. But they rarely saw each other after Casey moved into headquarters. That's because C.R. never came around, preferring to offer what little advice he had through several of his famous terse, often humorous, self-typed memos.

*   *   *

WHEN HE read the news that Al Casey had been named American's new president, Otto Becker also thought there had been a typo and that *John* Casey was meant.

That was a common reaction around the insular airline industry, where everyone knew and respected John Casey but most had never heard of either the Times Mirror Corp. or Al Casey. But it didn't take little brother Al long to make his own mark in his big brother's industry. What he found when he arrived at American was worse than what he had expected—and he had expected it to be pretty bad. Casey quickly determined that American's situation called for radical action and sweeping change, if for no other reason than to send a message to American's demoralized employees that management finally was willing to make the tough decisions that it should have been making through the previous decade.

Within days of his ascension to chairman in May 1974, Casey appointed himself interior decorator at American's corporate headquarters in Manhattan. His principal tool was the sledgehammer.

For most of its history, American had had both a chairman and a president. C.R. had filled both roles simultaneously at various times, but usually someone acted as president while he retained the title and authority of chairman. C.R. apparently preferred to have a trusted hand serving as sort of the chief manager of bureaucracy, running the day-to-day aspects of the airline. That freed him to do the three things he liked most: traveling around the system, visiting with American's employees, and focusing on the bigger corporate and industry issues.

Casey preferred to operate the same way. As a finance man and as a big-picture guy, Casey would much rather leave things like day-to-day operations, marketing, and personnel matters to someone else. But early on at American, he faced two problems that more or less forced him to retain the title and responsibilities of president even after he became chairman. As an outsider, Casey had no one in the company—or, for that matter, within the entire industry—he felt he could trust completely. Also, as a newcomer to the industry, Casey recognized that he had a lot to learn, and that to learn it he had to roll up his sleeves and get his hands dirty in the daily operation of the airline.

"I didn't know a soul when I came here. I didn't know anything about the airline business. And I needed time to evaluate the people

I inherited, to find out which ones were worth a damn and which ones weren't. I didn't know who I could trust. Besides, when I got here, everyone in the company, or at headquarters in New York, anyway, was wondering who I was going to name as president, figuring that whoever I named would really run the airline," Casey said.

"So I fooled 'em. I named myself president and knocked down the wall between the chairman's office and the president's office in the old headquarters. I wanted to send the clear message that I was the one who was going to run the airline, no one else."

In addition to the sledgehammer, another one of Casey's favorite tools was the ax. In his first eighteen months at American Casey got rid of a dozen vice presidents, firing some, demoting several more, and reassigning a few others. More radically, at least for a high-rolling airline in those days, Casey put the formerly spendthrift American on a spending diet. And, largely because of his conglomerate building experience at Times Mirror, where deep pockets made growth and profitability possible, Casey decided American needed to start hoarding cash.

Indeed, it was American's lack of cash that most appalled Casey upon his initial inspection of the company's finances. American ended 1973 with $74.6 million in cash and short-term investments. In those preinflation days, that amount was not generally considered cause for alarm. Still, by Casey's standards it was a paltry sum, especially when compared with the company's $587.4 million in long-term debt, its limited credit resources, and the growing sense of urgency regarding the need to replace its many aging, inefficient jets.

"When I got here I started looking for the money, and I couldn't find any. There was no money. The balance sheet said there was a little, but I couldn't find it. Not real cash, anyway. We didn't have any money to do any of the things that I thought we should be doing."

In those days, just as is the case today, an airline with only a small amount of cash on hand is playing a high-stakes game of Russian roulette. When the economy is good, when passenger demand and fares are high, and when fuel prices are relatively low, an airline can be an incredibly productive cash cow. But because its fixed costs are so high and virtually impossible to pare down without major negative ramifications, an airline beset by a recession, slack demand, insane price competition, high labor costs, and fuel prices or international terrorism can be bled dry very quickly. All it really takes to kill a cash-poor airline is one relatively strong or long recession, one particularly frightening act of international terrorism, one major maintenance-related accident, or one major fare war. The actual death may be years in coming, depending on how skillfully the carrier can manage the bankruptcy process and/or its many creditors. But any one of those circumstances can determine its fate.

For American, the lack of cash was made worse by the carrier's inability to significantly improve its cash position by "leveraging" its fleet. When an airline leverages its fleet, it sells its aircraft to financial institutions—banks, insurance companies, specialty leasing companies, and the like—in order to convert them to cash. Then it turns around and leases those same airplanes back. The resulting lease payments cause the airline's monthly operating costs to rise. But the carrier can invest part of the proceeds from the aircraft sales in stocks, bonds, or interest-earning accounts partially to offset the higher monthly costs. The airline then can use the rest of the proceeds to acquire new equipment, new routes, or other assets, all of which are designed to build the company's total asset value, its market strength, and, it is hoped, its profitability, over time. Or the carrier can use the money to pay big dividends to stockholders.

But Casey quickly discovered that American had only minimal ability to leverage its fleet of 237 airplanes because most of them were aging gas guzzlers. Thanks to the first Arab oil embargo in 1973 and 1974, airlines—like the rest of the western world—were getting a very vivid illustration of how dangerous it was to be totally reliant on low fuel prices for growth and prosperity. Also, a whole new generaton of decidedly more fuel-efficient commercial aircraft was then moving from the drawing board to the production line. Together, the anticipated availability of those new jets and the inefficiency and age of American's old jets were conspiring to push the value of its first-generation jets like the Boeing 707 through the floor. Even those aircraft that did have some value in terms of sale-leaseback deals, such as American's sixteen Boeing 747s, already were under lease, often at terms better than the airline could get in a refinancing.

Nevertheless, by the end of 1974, Casey had built American's cash and short-term investment pile up to nearly $115 million, a 54 percent improvement over the previous year, while simultaneously cutting the company's long-term debt 19.3 percent, to $474.3 million. The company also posted a $20.4 million net profit in 1974—a $68.5 million positive swing from 1973's $48.1 million loss—despite soaring fuel costs and fuel shortages that led to a sharp schedule reduction in the first half of the year. Those achievements, and the airline's decision to order twenty-one of Boeing's new, very popular and versatile trijets, the 727, gave Casey plenty to be happy about as his first year at American came to a close. But the company was not yet out of the woods, and there were growing indications of more trouble ahead. Casey referred to those concerns in his message to shareholders in American's 1974 annual report. Passenger traffic was projected to decline in 1975, he wrote. Meanwhile, fuel prices remained very unstable and various proposals floating around Washington had the potential of raising fuel prices so much that the net profits of the entire airline industry would have been erased.

Casey also referred to one other troubling item in his 1974 report to shareholders. "I view with considerable misgivings suggestions advanced in the Congress that the regulatory framework under which airlines now operate be dismantled." Although Casey admitted that there was room for improvement in the regulatory process, he wrote: "I have found that on balance the existing scheme of regulation has served the public well. . . . Proposals designed to eliminate regulation must be carefully evaluated lest they jeopardize the integrated air transportation system that our country has come to enjoy—certainly the finest in the world."

AL CASEY may have studied at the Harvard Business School, but the professors there are still scratching their heads, trying to figure out just where he came up with his unique theory of management. But while Casey's management theory wasn't born at Harvard, you could argue that the principles Casey learned there are resident in his theory. The refreshingly direct Casey—who is widely regarded for his ability to explain broad, complicated issues in the simplest of terms—just cut out all the high-sounding rhetoric. What he arrived at was a management theory so simple and self-evident that others before him must have overlooked it, perhaps because of the common but mistaken assumption that any theory good for managing complicated business organizations must itself be complicated.

"There's only four jobs in any company, really," Casey is fond of saying. "There's the guy who makes the product. There's the guy who sells the product. There's the bean counter, or scorekeeper. And there's the administrator."

That's how he determined he wanted to manage things at American, and, in fact, that's pretty much how American already was organized when he came aboard. All Casey had to do was to make sure the right person was in each of those four slots.

The "guy who made the product" or, in American's case, the guy who produced the service, was Donald Lloyd-Jones, senior VP for operations. An economist by training, Lloyd-Jones had worked his way up through American's finance department to become VP of corporate planning by the time Spater took over as chairman in 1967. Two years later Spater promoted him to senior VP for finance and CFO. In 1970 he was given a seat on American's board of directors. Then, in 1972, Spater asked him to move over to operations. On paper it was a lateral move. But Lloyd-Jones recognized it for what it really was, the biggest promotion of his life.

Lloyd-Jones saw the move as a way to broaden his understanding of the business, to increase both the scope of his responsibilities and the number of people who reported to him, and to position himself to become president of the airline in the not-too-distant future. As head of operations, the flight operations, maintenance, purchasing, corporate facilities, and real estate departments all reported to him. George Warde, American's president under Spater, and several of those who served as president under C. R. Smith had gone to the presidential suite through the senior operations VP's office. In short, by the time Casey came to American, Lloyd-Jones was the single most powerful person inside the company.

In stark contrast to Lloyd-Jones's powerful presence, there was no one fitting Casey's description of "the guy who sells the service" when he came to American. Otto Becker, senior VP for field sales and services, one of the most widely respected men at American and a thirty-four-year veteran of its vaunted marketing division, was the highest-ranking member of the marketing department, but only by default. C. R. Smith's decision to fire senior VP-marketing John Andersen, to whom Becker had reported, left Casey with a hole to fill. But because he had little knowledge of American or of the airline industry, Casey had no idea of who even the most obvious potential candidates for the job were. So he decided that, for at least a few months, he would do double duty and manage the marketing division himself. Doing so, he figured would give him a better idea of the job's demands.

Filling the administrator's position was easy. Gene Overbeck, a corporate and securities attorney, had come to American in 1959 from Wall Street to be the company's first in-house lawyer. While the airline always had had a general counsel on staff, it never had an internal legal department before Overbeck's arrival. Prior to that, even something as simple as filing the regularly monthly and quarterly documents required by the Civil Aeronautics Board had to be done by outside counsel, at considerable expense compared to what it would have cost if the airline had been able to do that work with in-house lawyers.

In 1967, when Spater was named vice chairman in anticipation of his replacing C.R. as chairman, Overbeck moved up to general counsel. A few years later he took on the larger title of senior VP for legal and public affairs. Casey quickly came to value Overbeck's in-depth, lawyer's knowledge of the inner workings of both American Airlines and Washington's regulatory process, his organizational skills, and his ability to provide objective advice on otherwise emotion-packed issues. He changed Overbeck's title to senior VP for administration and gave him oversight of all of the company's personnel and administrative functions—except for the hiring and training of pilots—in addition to his legal and public affairs responsibilities.

Then there was American's scorekeeper.

Robert Crandall had come to American in April 1973, ten months before Casey arrived, as senior VP for finance and CFO from Bloomingdale's, the top-of-the-line chain of department stores then owned by Federated Stores. According to an agreement reached when he was hired, he was in line to replace Marvin Traub as Bloomingdale's president when Traub moved up to the chairman's job. But Crandall left Bloomies after only six months. Two days into his new job with the big retailer, Crandall said he remembers thinking, "I made a terrible mistake."

After graduating with his MBA degree from the University of Pennsylvania's prestigious Wharton School of Business—which he'd attended on a full scholarship—Crandall had gone to work for Eastman Kodak, and then for Hallmark, the privately owned greeting cards company based in Kansas City. At both he worked primarily in the credit and collections area of the finance department. He also worked for a while in Hallmark's data processing department. The understanding not only of what computers could do but also of what they *should* be able to do that Crandall gained there proved immensely valuable to him later on.

From Hallmark, he had moved to Trans World Airlines, where he was named assistant treasurer for credit and collections. It was at TWA where Crandall seemed to find his life's calling. Whether it was as assistant treasurer for cash management in the airline's New York office, as VP of data processing at TWA's financial operations center in Kansas City, or as VP and controller back in New York, Crandall somehow just seemed to belong in the airline business. He thrived on its hectic pace and its big numbers. Still, when the people from Bloomingdale's came calling, Crandall left, in part because of the attractive financial offer they made and the promise that he soon would move up to president, and in part because he had wanted the senior VP of finance job but didn't get it.

Once he got to Bloomingdale's, however, he recognized that he had become addicted to the airline business's frenetic pace.

George Warde and George Spater hired Crandall for American in April 1973. When he came, he was well aware that the airline had problems. On top of the big losses the company had run up in recent years, there was the Juan Homs/Walt Rauscher affair, and several smaller scandals. The illegal contribution to the Nixon reelection campaign had not yet become public. The extremely ambitious Crandall, who was then just thirty-seven years old, might well have seen the airline's problems as opportunities. But what Crandall did not know—and could not have known—when the CFO's job at American was offered to him was that some of the most powerful members of American's board already had lost faith in Spater.

TOM PLASKETT moved to New York in March 1973, about one month before Crandall took the CFO job at American. Plaskett had worked for General Motors since he graduated from high school in his hometown of Kansas City, Missouri. And thanks to the automaker's cooperative education program, Plaskett was able to gain practical experience working for GM while attending the General Motors Institute and, later, the Harvard Business School. He moved to GM's New York offices from Detroit to be staff assistant to Dave Collier, General Motors' treasurer. Plaskett, who was only twenty-eight at the time, knew that he probably was fifteen years away from getting an assignment with the kind of major responsibilities he wanted. He also realized that even if he somehow was able to distinguish himself above the hundreds of other bright MBAs at GM, moving into the upper echelons of management meant eventually having to settle his family in Detroit.

"That was one of the last places in the world I wanted to live," he said, explaining why he was already looking for a way out of GM when Tom Parker, one of his Harvard classmates, called in September 1973. Parker had heard through a friend that Plaskett had recently moved to New York, so he was calling with an invitation to lunch. Plaskett gladly accepted.

Over lunch, Plaskett expressed some of his concerns about his future with GM. At the same time, he learned that Parker was involved with a venture capital search firm that also did some executive search work.

Two weeks later, one of Parker's partners called Plaskett with word that he had a major corporate client who was looking for someone to come in and put in a new budgeting and financial controls system. Would Plaskett be interested? Plaskett said yes, and a meeting was arranged with the chief financial officer at the client corporation— Bob Crandall of American Airlines.

"I walked over from GM's New York offices and met with Bob one evening in his office at American's old headquarters on Third Avenue in New York. I think we immediately took a liking to one another," Plaskett said.

Like nearly everyone who has had a serious discussion with Crandall, the first thing Plaskett noticed was Crandall's intensity. Though he stands just over six feet tall, Crandall, who was slightly built even in those days before he took up running and got really skinny, is not physically imposing. Just the same, he can dominate a room with the sheer force of his personality the way an All-Pro defensive lineman can dominate a room filled with average-size humans merely by standing up.

"I don't think Bob was significantly different then in terms of his motivation, or in terms of his intense focus on issues and problems. He was as intense then as he is today," Plaskett said years later.

"Bob, for as long as I knew him and worked with him, was always focused intellectually on the problem and the issues. As gruff and as blustery and argumentative and combative as he is, his focus is on an issue, is on a problem, is on solving it. When Bob attacks he doesn't attack individuals . . . he attacks the issues, the results. It's a form of intellectual honesty that I found refreshing. You may not agree with his managerial approach, but once you understand sort of how it works with him, you can appreciate it better.

"I guess I'd have to say that I decided to come to American principally because of Bob. I was most fascinated by Bob's presence and his . . . his . . . his intensity," Plaskett said.

Plasket joined the company in January 1974 as assistant controller.

His initial assignment was to install a new variable budgeting and financial controls system. Crandall had deemed the old one to be totally inadequate for a company of American's size and with such far-flung operations.

"I think the problem with the old budgeting and controls system was principally a function of the regulatory mentality that existed in the industry in those days," Plaskett said. "Your prices were controlled. You passed your costs through to the passengers. There wasn't any great need for acute analysis of costs and revenues, or of profits and losses."

As a former GM executive, Plaskett knew the value of having a budgeting and controls system that could give management reams of detailed information useful in making critical decisions on how and where to allocate corporate resources most effectively.

But he quickly learned that American had nothing comparable to GM's system for tracking production costs and sales figures for each of its car models on a region-by-region, city-by-city, and dealer-by-dealer basis. The airline had no reliable way of knowing on which routes it made or lost money. Station managers could provide some data on the number of passengers who typically flew on a given flight. Monthly revenue production figures from a single city could be compared on a year-over-year basis. But there was no statistically accurate method for determining, for example, whether American's New York–Los Angeles route was responsible for 5 percent or 50 percent of the revenue the airline generated in the New York market, or whether the costs associated with, say, operating out of New York's LaGuardia Airport were in line with revenues generated there. Senior management could rely only on experience and intuition in making such judgments. Yet, given the extent of American's schedule, no one had anything close to a clear picture of exactly where the airline made money or where it lost money.

"It took ten years to develop a flight profitability system that made sense," Plaskett said. "Ten years! It required a massive, total restructuring of the whole accounting system, the revenue accounting system, the way you add up the pennies and the nickels. There was an enormous amount of computing software development, applications software development that had to be done."

Launching the effort to develop that new budgeting and financial controls system signaled the beginning of the transformation of American Airlines into a modern business organization. No longer would American be managed in the seat-of-the-pants, entrepreneurial, and intuitive style established by C. R. Smith.

For forty-nine years, C.R. and a handful of his trusted aides had managed American largely on the basis of their instincts and experience. That they had been successful for so many years is a tribute to their innate skills and natural business acumen.

But once Plaskett, working under orders from Casey and Crandall, began installing his new budgeting and financial controls system in 1974 it became clear that American never again would be managed that way. There would continue to be room for and, indeed, a need for intuition and experience in decision-making. But from 1974 on, the vast majority of decisions made at American Airlines would be by the numbers.

4

Unleashed

IF KNOCKING down the wall between the chairman's office and the president's at American's headquarters was supposed to send a subtle message to the troops, Casey's next message after arriving at American had all the subtlety of a right hook to the chin.

"Al called and said he wanted to tell me personally that he'd picked someone else for the job"of senior marketing VP, Otto Becker recalled.

"I was a little surprised he called me. Some people in the company apparently had thought that because I was senior vice president of field sales and services, I was the heir apparent for the senior vice president of marketing job. But I never really considered myself to be a candidate. And I don't think Al did either. He was just informing me out of courtesy, I think. It was thoughtful of him, but I wasn't upset or anything.

"Besides, when he told me who he'd picked I instantly thought it was an inspired choice. I knew it would shock a lot of people, especially those lower down in the company or who didn't work at headquarters and therefore hadn't seen what we had seen. But I thought it would be great for the company," Becker said.

After deciding that he could work well with the team of Don Lloyd-Jones, Gene Overbeck, and Bob Crandall as the senior vice presidents of operations, administration, and finance, respectively, Casey began to look for the fourth member of his senior management team, his marketing guy.

He asked Lloyd-Jones and Crandall to submit names of people they knew, both in and out of the airline industry, whom they thought might do a good job. He also asked them to assist him in interviewing the candidates for the job. Typically, the candidates would meet alone with each of American's top officers for a while. Then Casey would join those sessions in progress, hoping both to size up the candidates and to get a better read on Crandall and Lloyd-Jones.

A number of strong candidates were interviewed. Initially, Casey believed American needed a very consumer-oriented marketing executive. First he went after Edward Gelthorpe, a consumer marketing expert who then was president of The Gillette Company. Later, Casey began to lean toward hiring Charlie Bucks away from Continental Airlines, where he had developed a reputation as the airline industry's most consumer-oriented marketing man. But something gnawed at Casey. Throughout the interview process, one person stood out from the rest in his knowledge of what American needed and how the new head of marketing could provide that. The problem was, that fellow wasn't one of the candidates for the job.

"Crandall asked the best questions," Casey said. "It dawned on me that from his questions, Crandall, who'd never had a marketing job in his life—he was always off doing something in data processing or in finance—instinctively knew more about marketing in general and about what American needed from our marketing department than all those other guys we'd interviewed, most of whom had been in marketing jobs their whole careers."

Whether Crandall ever actually asked Casey for the job remains unclear. Crandall said it was just "one of those things that the thought process evolved. . . . Somewhere along the way it became very clear to him and to me that I knew much more about marketing and the tasks that we were interviewing people for. . . . But I honestly don't remember whether he first raised that question or if I did."

Likewise, Casey can't recall which of them first mentioned moving Crandall into the marketing job.

"In those days he and I met every single morning at seven-thirty in New York. It became obvious he was interested in the job," Casey said. "He wanted to broaden his base of experience. And he was absolutely right for the job. He could do it better than anybody we had talked to. And I could run finance for a while myself until I found someone else to run it permanently."

"I knew some people in the company would be shocked by it, that they would see him as a bean counter. But I knew him to be a very creative guy and one of the best managers I'd ever seen. I had every confidence in the world in him," he said.

Crandall had at least three reasons for wanting the job that Casey eventually offered.

For starters, the extraordinarily ambitious Crandall correctly recognized that moving over into the senior vice president of marketing's chair—technically a lateral move—presented him the biggest opportunity of his career. In those days, well over half of American's 40,000 employees fell under the marketing department's jurisdiction. American's marketing chief was responsible for such obvious things as advertising and selling airplane seats, and for a host of other aspects, including the hiring, training, and supervising of flight attendants; the packaging of vacation tours; the planning of in-flight meals; and the supervision of the airline's cargo and charter flight operations. American's general managers in each city the airline served reported up through the field sales and services unit, which was a part of the marketing department. The senior VP of marketing also either was directly responsible for or had a strong voice in two key aspects of managing any airline; strategic planning and the selection of new aircraft. And, to the extent possible in a tightly regulated industry, the position Casey offered Crandall also had responsibility for setting fare prices and determining what routes American would fly, and when it would fly them. Because of those broad responsibilities, American's head of marketing effectively was responsible both for the company's revenues and a large portion of its costs.

In other words, what Casey offered was exactly the kind of opportunity—the kind of control—that the thirty-eight-year-old Crandall had been looking for all of his life.

"As long as I can remember, I wanted to lead whatever group I was a part of," he said. "If I didn't make the best grades in the fifth grade, I got very cross. This is something that's absolutely true. And if I didn't come out as the platoon leader when I was in the army, it made me cross. I've always wanted to be the leader of any group I've been a part of.

"I always knew that I wanted to be the chief executive officer of a major corporation. Even as a kid, I knew that's what I wanted. And a long time ago I made the determination that if anyone ever offered me a better job, or a job that enabled me to learn more about the business I was in, I would accept that offer, figuring that would help me reach my goal of being a CEO."

Crandall's high school classmates recognized that ambition way back in 1953. During his senior year at Barrington High in Barrington, Rhode Island, the staff of the school's yearbook, *The Arrow*, wrote a whimsical essay about what members of the class of '53 would be doing in 1963. The essay predicted that Crandall, described elsewhere in the yearbook as the class's best student, would be "the great P&A grocery store tycoon." It may have been a weak attempt at humor and a juvenile play off the A&P Grocery name, but the authors certainly understood just how ambitious their hard-driving classmate was.

So did Ted Tedesco, Crandall's Phi Mu Delta fraternity brother at the University of Rhode Island. Tedesco, who thirty years later came to work for Crandall as American's VP of governmental affairs, said: "I always thought Bob was destined for greatness because he was just more focused than the rest of us. We were in college, having a good time. We figured if we got a job, we'd be happy. Not Bob. He knew what he wanted."

And it wasn't money. It was success, as he defined it.

A second reason Crandall wanted the job Casey offered was that he honestly believed he was the best candidate. Though he'd never had a job that by definition was a marketing job, Crandall had approached every job in his career with the attitude of a marketing man.

In the early and mid-1960s, a not-yet thirty-year-old Crandall "was at that time recognized as one of the real innovators in using computers and technology in finding new and better ways to do things," said Bob Bolen of Forth Worth, owner of the largest chain of Hallmark card shops in Texas. Bolen, who served as Fort Worth's mayor throughout most of the 1980s and therefore came to know Crandall well, actually met him back in the early 1960s, at an annual meeting for Hallmark franchisees.

"I really only met him once or twice, but I sure heard a lot about him back in those days when he was at Hallmark. He was in the credit department and I dealt with the sales department people mostly. But they always talked about him.

"Even then, the reason people remembered him and talked about him was that he was recognized as being very, very innovative as far as finding new ways to use computers to improve the business; not just keeping records, like most firms do now, but how to manage inventory, track sales, process orders quicker, analyze sales results. From what I know of him back then, the whole object of what he was doing at Hallmark was to find ways to use computers and technology to lower costs, improve sales, and increase profits," Bolen said.

A few years later, as head of data processing at TWA, Crandall's marketing instincts again were evident. Throughout the 1960s and into the 1970s, most airline managers saw computers simply as machines that could do repetitive tasks quicker and more efficiently than people. Crandall, however, was among the first to understand that an airline could use advanced technology not only to sell its service more efficiently but also to increase its market share and, in theory, to improve its profitability.

Dick Pearson, a top Crandall lieutenant at TWA in the late 1960s and early 1970s, who became that carrier's president in 1985, said, "It's clear to me that there's always been a sense in Bob's mind of the value . . ." of being able to use computers and technology to improve his company's share of the market and its profits.

Even during his brief stint as American's CFO, Crandall had demonstrated his marketing instincts. In the fall of 1973, six months after he had joined American, interim chairman C.R. Smith sent him to negotiate a route-swap deal with Pan Am whereby American would trade its money-losing routes in the South Pacific for a package of Caribbean routes the globally minded Pan Am had been flying with something less than great enthusiasm and success.

Crandall had championed that idea from the time it was hatched for three reasons. First, American was losing its shirt in the South Pacific, mainly because it lacked the domestic and North Pacific route networks needed to attract enough passengers to profitably serve the long-haul South Pacific routes.

Second, Crandall believed that because American already was the most preferred domestic carrier among businesspeople in the Northeast—and especially in New York—the airline probably could leverage that loyalty to market leisure-oriented service to the hot Caribbean destinations those same customers preferred.

And, third, because the high season for tourism in the Caribbean is winter, American's weakest season, Crandall believed that expanding there would help improve the airline's first- and fourth-quarter financial performances and give some needed balance to its highly seasonal operations.

The final—and perhaps the biggest—reason Crandall jumped at the chance to take over American's marketing department was that doing so would give him the chance to return SABRE, American's pioneering computer reservations system, to preeminence within the

industry. Working with IBM, American had created the airline industry's first computerized reservations system in the late 1950s. But,
during the Spater years, SABRE had been allowed to fall behind the
competition. During his data processing days at TWA, Crandall had
watched with amazement as American passively let Eastern Airlines,
operator of the SystemOne CRS, become the industry's leader in
computer technology. United's APOLLO system and TWA's PARS
system also caught up with and passed SABRE in terms of technological sophistication during the Spater years.

But Crandall believed he could regain for American its lost reputation as the industry's technology leader by turning SABRE into the
powerful competitive weapon he thought a computer reservations
system should be.

So, by the time he and Casey began talking about changing Crandall's assignment, the self-assured Crandall was certain that he could
manage the airline's large, sometimes unwieldy, and far-flung marketing operations. He was convinced he knew how to squeeze more
costs out of the department's huge budget. And he was confident
he could come up with a way to increase American's market share
and revenues.

Doing all that was a tall order. But those who know him now and
those who knew him back then agree that the single most striking
thing about Bob Crandall is his supreme self-confidence. His is the
kind of confidence that often is mistaken for arrogance. Even back
in the mid-1970s, long before he became a living legend in the airline
industry and one of the most highly regarded leaders in all of corporate America, Crandall was, in some ways, the business world
equivalent of Chicago Bulls basketball star Michael Jordan. In his
arena, Jordan, in effect, says to the unfortunate player assigned to
defend him, "I don't care what you do, you can't stop me. You know
what I'm going to do just as well as I do. But you still can't stop me."

Just so, in the arena in which he competes, Crandall rarely bothers
with subtlety. Instead, like Jordan, he has the kind of confidence that
allows him to say flatly what it is he will do. Then he does it, no
matter what his opponent does.

Hooks Burr, a prominent Boston attorney and an American board
member from 1958 until 1987, had met hundreds, maybe even thousands of smart young business school grads climbing the corporate
ladders. But he'd never met one as confident as Bob Crandall was
even in his early days at American in 1973 and 1974.

"I remember thinking 'This guy is very, very bright . . . and he's

pretty damn brash too,' " Burr said. "But it didn't take very long
after that to say 'Not only is he bright and brash, he's also coming
up with an uncanny string of right answers.' "

The reaction to Crandall's appointment as head of marketing was
mixed. Just as Otto Becker had anticipated, many of those in American's vast field organization initially saw Crandall's move as a bad
omen of belt tightening and micromanagement ahead. Stories—some
of them exaggerated—about his hot temper and foul mouth, his
intensity, his extreme impatience, the incredible demands he made
of the people who worked for him, and the unbelievably long hours
he put in at the office already had made their way throughout the
airline. Some middle managers in the marketing department quickly
began to worry about their own futures and what new, and perhaps
unreasonable, expectations their new boss might have of them.

Meanwhile, around the rest of the industry, where Crandall still
was not very well known, his move into the marketing slot was seen
as further evidence that the Spater regime both had screwed up
American and had left the cupboard somewhat bare of managerial
talent. Most industry old-timers felt that if Casey, an outsider new
to American, had to turn to Crandall, essentially another outsider
who also had no marketing experience, to run as critical a department
as marketing then the once-great American was in a state of serious
decline.

WHILE AIRLINE industry insiders watched the changes at American
in 1974 with skepticism, casual observers might have thought that
Al Casey had the magic touch. Despite a rather listless U.S. economy
throughout 1974, American somehow managed to earn a $20.4 mil-
lion profit in Casey's first year there. That equaled a $68.5 million
turnaround from 1973, the worst year in American's history to that
point.

But Casey knew there was nothing magic about what produced
the seemingly positive 1974 results. Whether it was beginner's luck
or the luck brought to the company by its new Boston-Irish chairman,
American indeed had been lucky in Casey's first year at the helm.
Had it not been for two events over which Casey had little or no
control, and for one tough decision that was criticized around the
industry and lamented by some of the airline's best customers, American might have lost money in 1974 too.

First, early in the year American, like all other carriers, was forced to reduce its flight schedule in response to the national fuel shortage caused by the Arab oil embargo. American cut its service by 24 percent in terms of available seat miles. Doing so helped it pare its first-quarter loss to just $10.5 million, down from $28.8 million in the first quarter of 1973. But Casey had little to do with that. Lloyd-Jones had spent most of the fall of 1973 in Washington, negotiating the schedule reduction with the Federal Aviation Act (FAA), Civil Aeronautics Board (CAB), and competing airlines that were being asked to cut their schedules as well. The plan was pretty much complete by the time Casey arrived at American.

Then, the CAB granted some fare increases just as the peak summer travel season began. As a result, American's revenues rose 10.75 percent in 1974 even though capacity—measured in available seat miles—declined 9.6 percent and passenger traffic—measured in revenue passenger miles flown—dropped 0.8 percent.

Casey had little or nothing to do with either of those developments. But his finger was on the trigger when American decided to ground eight of its sixteen Boeing 747s to reduce the huge operating losses they were causing. (Eventually all sixteen were sold.)

The idea grew out of a study done by the headquarters staff that showed that American could consistently make money with the 747s on only one route, New York to Los Angeles. While there had been plenty of resistance within management to grounding the 747, a plane with which both passengers and the media had fallen in love, Casey quickly recognized that the 400-passenger jumbo jet had become an expensive marketing gimmick American could no longer afford. In fact, if Casey had not been both an industry outsider and a financially oriented manager more concerned about the bottom line than the average airline CEO of the day, American probably would not have made the tough decision to get rid of its 747 fleet. Most airlines and their managements had put so much into the glamorous 747, both financially and emotionally, that they could not turn their backs on the exotic but extremely unforgiving behemoth of the commercial skies. But Al Casey could. And he did.

While critics said the 747s were too glamorous and too well liked by passengers to be grounded, and that parking its 747s would hurt American more than help it, Casey didn't hesitate in doing what he believed had to be done.

"It was the only practical thing to do. They were the least fuel efficient airplanes we had because of their large capacity and because we were flying them with very low load factors. We had no other choice," he said.

Still, despite the seemingly positive results of the modest turnaround in 1974, Casey worried that his first year had been nothing more than a temporary cease-fire in a financial war of attrition that American could not win. He knew that in 1975 the airline couldn't trim its schedule much further without risking the permanent loss of its most loyal customers, business travelers. Casey also knew American stood little chance of convincing the CAB to give it additional fare increases in 1975. And, most bothersome of all, he knew that substantial fuel price increases were on the way. In fact, Casey's message to shareholders in the company's 1974 annual report included a thinly veiled warning not to expect a similar performance in 1975. His concerns later were proved to be well founded when American announced a loss of $20.5 million for the year.

Of course, Casey did more than issue warnings to shareholders. Frustrated by the seeming intractability of American's situation, he commissioned Tom Plaskett, Crandall's top lieutenant, to study the positive and negative aspects of merging with Pan Am. Plaskett— who ironically became chairman of Pan Am Corp. in 1988, too late to prevent the historic carrier from sliding into bankruptcy and, ultimately, into liquidation in 1991—presented his report in early 1976. He eagerly recommended that American acquire Pan Am, wipe out the Pan Am name, and reposition the new, giant American as the industry's first megacarrier serving both the U.S. domestic and international markets.

Based on Plakett's recommendtion, Casey called Pan Am Chairman Bill Seawell—the man who had been C.R. Smith's first choice to replace Spater as American's new chairman—to initiate merger discussions. But those discussions and the technical process of sharing specific operational and financial data caused Casey to become increasingly concerned that not only would merging fail to solve American's problems, but that combining two financially troubled airlines would produce only bigger headaches for the surviving company. In addition, when the carriers shopped the idea of an American–Pan Am merger around Washington, only the Transportation Department favored it. The White House, the State Department, and most important, the Justice Department—which had blocked Spater's plans for American to merge first with Eastern and then with Western— opposed the deal.

Ultimately, Casey called the whole thing off. Pan Am then implemented many of the proposals—especially those having to do with
cutting costs—proposed in Plaskett's study.

Casey, meanwhile, continued to believe that American was ill-
positioned for long-term survival on its own, especially if the deregulation movement then gathering steam in Washington succeeded in
opening up the airline industry to unfettered competition. So he went
back out on the mergers and acquisitions road. He and Plaskett visited
with Ryder Corp. officials in Miami about a merger, but nothing came
of those preliminary talks. Casey discussed a friendly takeover of
American with both Trans-America and American General, two of
the nation's largest insurance companies. He particularly liked the
idea of merging with an insurance company.

"With the deep pockets of an insurance company you could ride
out the recessions," Casey explained. "And you wouldn't have to
take the drastic measures most of us [airlines] did when we didn't
have available cash."

Casey also argued that buying an airline "would give an insurance
company a big kick. Insurance companies' stocks sell at very low
multiples. But with the leverage that an airline would give to an
insurance company, the insurance company's earnings should be just
terrific."

Casey also believed that such a merger would not have faced the
kind of opposition in Washington that a deal with another airline
would have.

But neither insurance company's management could convince their
boards or their largest shareholders that teaming up with American
would be a good deal.

By mid-1976 Casey had run out of options. A merger or an acquisition was very unlikely. And he was convinced that American,
unchanged and on its own, could not make it much longer. So,
though he knew it would be an extremely difficult undertaking and
that the chances for success were not very high, Casey decided that
American had to be transformed, completely restructured both financially and operationally.

"I said 'Screw it. We'll sell the hotels and fix the damn thing ourselves.' But I really wasn't sure at the time that we could do it," Casey
admitted.

One major stumbling block was cash or American's lack of it, to
be precise. If it was going to stand on its own, Casey figured American would need lots of cash to order new aircraft, upgrade SABRE,

make the other investments in facilities he thought would be necessary, and withstand any economic or labor-induced storms in the future.

That's where selling the Americana chain of hotels the airline had acquired came in. By selling the money-losing hotel division, Casey thought he could both rid American of a big cash drain and raise some sorely needed capital.

American had already been trying to sell its hotels before Casey decided to try to reposition American for long-term survival.

"We were in deep trouble and the hotels were a terrible drag on us. We were losing our fannies in that business. So I wanted someone to get rid of the hotels. It took me eight deals to get rid of twenty-one hotels," he said.

Yet even that effort started out poorly. American owned only nineteen hotels when Casey made the decision they had to go. But before he could dispose of even one of those nineteen properties, two more hotels bought by Spater in 1972 in one of his last major acts as president joined the American chain.

Don Carty, a young Canadian with a Harvard MBA and a few years experience at Air Canada, was recruited away from Celenese Canada, where he had been a division manager, to help straighten out the financial mess in the hotel division so that American could dispose of them.

"The hotels were a real mishmash," recalled Carty, who remained with American after the hotels were sold and eventually became executive vice president for finance and planning.

"We had wanted a high-end hotel company. But what we had collected over twenty years was a real mishmash of everything from almost-hotel-level kinds of motels, to the Chosun Hotel in Korea, which was the absolute lap of luxury in Korea. We had the whole gamut. And we had the Americana in New York, which originally had been built as a Hyatt Hotel. It was the biggest hotel, with more rooms than any other hotel in North America for many years. It's now the Sheraton-New York. And it was impossible to manage. Automation really hadn't come to hotels at that stage, and running a 1,800-room hotel with seven food and beverage outlets was all paper shuffling. It was unbelievable."

Carty recalls his first trip into the Americana New York's accounting department—"which is always in the basement in hotels, you never waste valuable space on the accountants.

"It was just full of paper. I mean stacked up high, everywhere. Just full. And no one knew where anything was," Carty said.

AL CASEY never concealed his personal preference for the financial and strategic side of the airline business. To be sure, he quickly grasped the fundamentals of airline operations and marketing. And, as a man who prides himself on being able to manage any kind of enterprise, Casey made sure he knew enough about what was going on in American's marketing and operations departments to provide the proper oversight and to make sure those departments were in tune with the company's strategic plan. But he focused most of his efforts on developing that strategic plan and on restructuring American's balance sheet so that the airline could do the hefty financing that the strategic plan required in the late 1970s and early 1980s.

With Lloyd-Jones, Crandall, and Overbeck in place as American's senior VPs of operations, marketing, and administration, Casey was free to turn his attention to financial issues and "The Big Picture." The decision to make Crandall senior vice president of marketing made that possible. Had he selected someone else to run marketing, Casey probably would have had to remain directly involved in the department much longer while the new man learned the business. It is also difficult to imagine how anyone else might have been as successful as Crandall in that job; and that success gave Casey the room he needed for his financial maneuvering.

Two men probably can't be more different in style than the jovial, personable Casey and the intense, sometimes overbearing Crandall. Casey's disdain for large staff meetings is renowned. And, to the amazement of business professors everywhere, he never wrote a memo in his eleven years at American. Casey preferred to gather his information and deliver his orders in a never-ending series of one-on-one meetings with his top managers, meetings that sometimes could turn into psychological grill sessions.

Conversely, Crandall is an acknowledged master corporate bureaucrat. His use of the large staff meeting—in which he picks up incredibly detailed knowledge on every aspect of the company and drives his people toward creative problem solving—is a textbook illustration of how to run fruitful business meetings. And his people treat his thoughtful, detailed, and precisely—and often sharply—worded memos almost as if they are scripture.

Yet Casey and Crandall share the ability quickly to comprehend a broad range of subjects and to motivate people to do the best work of their lives. That is why they are good people managers despite their very different approaches. More important, Crandall and Casey share a willingness to break the mold of past practice, to change whatever needs to be changed to achieve a goal. Perhaps more than anything else, it was that quality that led Casey to select Crandall to run American's marketing department. Likewise, it was that shared willingness to challenge convention, to do whatever was necessary, that allowed the Casey/Crandall team to so profoundly change not only American but the whole airline industry.

Still, even Casey admits that he did not fully understand just what it was he unleashed on an unsuspecting company and industry the day he made Bob Crandall senior vice president for marketing.

"I never doubted that Bob would be very successful. He was a very bright guy, one of the most intelligent guys I've ever been around. And he was a natural-born leader," Casey said.

"But no, I didn't know how successful he'd turn out to be. He just kept learning and growing as a person and as a manager. He never stopped learning. He never stopped getting better. He's done a superb job; far beyond my wildest dreams."

5
Rescuing American's Ox

TULSA, OKLAHOMA, hardly seems like the kind of place that would be foremost in the mind of the new chief financial officer of one of the nation's largest and oldest airlines. But that squeaky-clean city in northeast Oklahoma, near where the Great Plains begin their climb into the Ozarks, was one of the first places Bob Crandall went after joining American in 1973.

A year earlier, the heart of American's SABRE computer reservations system had been removed from its original home at Briarcliff Manor, New York, to a state-of-the-art facility built on the back side of the Tulsa airport, where American's major aircraft maintenance base had been located since shortly after World War II. American's data processing center housed two of IBM's huge, powerful 7090 mainframe computers, the brains of the SABRE system.

Max Hopper, a thirty-seven-year-old, soft-spoken Texan, had first worked on computer reservations systems in the late 1960s at billionaire Ross Perot's Electronic Data Systems, where he was a consultant and member of the team that developed United Airlines' APOLLO reservation system. Then, when EDS lost its contract with United in 1970, Hopper had gone to work directly for United.

Two years later, in March 1972, frustrated by problems that he felt would prevent APOLLO from being what he thought it should be, Hopper jumped to American to manage the transition of SABRE's computer brain from Briarcliff to Tulsa. He hoped to achieve with

SABRE what numerous technical problems inherent in United's data processing setup had prevented him from achieving with APOLLO. Yet, in his first year and a half at American, he had become just as frustrated as he had been at United. This time, though, the source of the frustration was not technical.

During the George Spater years, American had lost its lead on the rest of the industry in data processing and computer technology. Part of the problem was that Spater himself did not understand computers and discounted their importance. Therefore he had little enthusiasm for spending the kind of money necessary to upgrade and modernize SABRE so it could keep up with the rapid developments in computer technology.

Also, marketing and finance, the two areas of the company that might have been expected to be the driving forces behind development of computer technology, had failed to provide the leadership necessary to keep SABRE on top. The finance department was directly responsible for American's data processing operations. But the marketing department, which during C.R. Smith's waning years, and during the Spater years had developed a false sense of self-sufficiency and had become perhaps too inbred, actually determined the extent to which SABRE would or would not be developed through its control of marketing technology research and development funds.

In fact, rather than being the focal point for cooperation, SABRE for years had been a pawn in the feudal war that had raged between American's marketing and finance departments.

"It was never a happy relationship, going back ten years before I got there, about who was going to run SABRE," Hopper said.

Much to Hopper's chagrin, SABRE got next to no support from the marketing department, largely because of the futuristic beliefs of Rod King, American's assistant VP of marketing at the time. King was the antagonist in a long-running internal argument over the role of SABRE which he called "Big Mother." King "believed you really didn't need to have a reservations system at all, that is, a central reservations office," Hopper said.

Crandall recalled that King's was a "very advanced vision of the world as it might be someday—and it still isn't quite that way yet."

King thought that computer terminals soon would dot the landscape like pay telephones and that they would be readily available to consumers in a retail shopping kind of environment. Each terminal would be able to communicate with all the other terminals, allowing consumers to purchase travel on all airlines from any one of thousands of locations. Such a development would do away with the need for airline-owned reservations systems. All the carriers would have to do would be to provide their schedules to the network of computer terminals and watch as travelers sold themselves airline tickets.

Clearly, no one else at any other airline shared King's vision. Indeed, carriers with reservations systems poured millions of dollars into improving them. And nearly all of those airlines that did not own a CRS at least thought about building one before deciding against it, usually for cost reasons. Still, perhaps because they so misunderstood the role of technology in selling their service, Spater and the rest of American's management had allowed King's inherently flawed vision to hamstring SABRE's maturation process.

That's why Crandall, in one of his first acts as senior VP of finance, flew to Tulsa in the summer of 1973. His aim was to override King's skewed vision and to put an end to the petty fighting between the finance and marketing departments regarding SABRE. Crandall went to Tulsa specifically to get American's ox of a computer system out of the deep ditch in which it had been stuck for years.

Hopper was nearly beside himself with excitement when Crandall called and said he wanted to fly out from New York. He knew exactly where he intended to take Crandall first upon his arrival.

The basement.

HOPPER'S PREDECESSOR as director of American's reservations operations was Fred Plugge, a widely respected data processing manager who in the 1970s developed The Wizard computer reservations system for Avis Rent-A-Car. In the late 1960s and early 1970s, Plugge had tried in vain to keep American on track with the rapid changes then occurring in the field of computer technology. To that end, Plugge had ordered 1,000 custom-made CRTs—cathode ray tubes, or terminals—for use by American's own reservations staff. Other carriers were ordering similar CRTs. Prior to the advent of CRTs, airline reservationists had been forced to rely on high-speed IBM Selectric typewriter-style terminals. They took up a lot of space and were noisy, difficult to use, and, most important, quite slow in comparison with even the earliest CRTs. But Plugge—and later, Hopper—had been unable to get the CRTs installed at American's reservations offices.

"Plugge bought the 1,000 CRTs, but he couldn't get marketing to fund the installation. So they got put in the damn basement," Hopper said. "It was absolutely crazy, but the guys in marketing wouldn't take 'em even though they clearly were an improvement over the typewriter-style terminals we were then using. We'd already bought and paid for 'em, but we couldn't use 'em. It didn't make any sense at all."

Crandall had heard the story of and had been amazed by those 1,000 unused terminals gathering dust in the basement at Tulsa even during his days as head of data processing at TWA.

"It was quite a laughing matter around the industry in the other companies that American, a leader, was falling behind and the fact that those CRTs were sitting in a basement," he said.

Sadly, by the time Hopper finally showed Crandall those 1,000 CRTs in the basement in Tulsa, they had been in storage so long that they had to be refurbished before being installed. But they were installed, thanks mainly to Crandall, Hopper, and Jim O'Neill. O'Neill had followed Crandall from TWA in the summer of 1973, becoming vice president of data processing and Hopper's boss in New York.

"Bob wasn't going to put up with the kind of nonsense that had been going on that led to something like that happening. It's been said that he got mad about those computers being stored in the basement, but I don't remember him being mad so much as he was just dumbfounded that anyone could have allowed that kind of thing to happen. He couldn't believe that people had been so blind," Hopper said.

By the time O'Neill joined American, Crandall had already visited Tulsa. He made O'Neill his lead blocker on an end run around the marketing department to get those CRTs out of the basement in Tulsa and into use.

"One of the very first assignments he gave me at American was to get those damn CRTs the hell out of the basement," O'Neill said. "He told me to find out if it was economical to do so, and then put together the appropriations request to do it. Well, that's what I did.

"It was pretty clear that since we'd already bought and paid for them, getting those CRTs to work was the smart thing to do economically. But it wasn't just that simple. We had a lot of bastardized connections between the computers we were using back then, and figuring out how to make everything work together required more money than it should have."

As important as the decision to put those 1,000 CRTs to use was, Crandall insists that there were some far more important results of his first trip to Tulsa and his other early conversations with Hopper.

"At that point, Max and I set out to not only get American caught up with respect to SABRE, but to rectify the sort of laggard position that American had assumed in all of data processing.

"He and I reached agreement very early on that automation was going to be tremendously important to the airline," Crandall said.

Little did they know.

JIM O'NEILL had first met Crandall in 1967, when O'Neill was working as a consultant for Arthur S. Kranzley & Co., a small but highly regarded firm that had been behind the creation of the first regional bank card credit systems back in the 1960s. As head of TWA's credit and collections department, Crandall was the company's primary contact with Kranzley & Co., which had been hired to help straighten out TWA's problem-plagued travel card operations.

TWA originally had contracted with American Express to develop a travel credit card, but the pairing didn't work out very well. While American Express wanted to make money by charging members a small fee for the convenience of using a credit card, TWA was hoping to make money by enticing people who otherwise couldn't afford to fly to do so on TWA. The result was that American Express was left with too much exposure to people who were likely to fall behind on their credit bills. Meanwhile, because of American Express's concern about credit worthiness, TWA didn't get as much incremental business from its credit card system as it had expected.

Crandall and O'Neill worked together on bringing TWA's travel card operations in-house. They made a good team. By 1967 O'Neill already had a dozen years of experience in the world of information systems. That alone qualified him as one of the field's pioneers and top practitioners. But O'Neill was more than just another plastic pocket protector–wearing technology geek. He possessed the mind and instincts of a businessman. While he understood technology far better than most businesspeople, he understood business much better than the average technocrat. As a result, he had a reputation for coming up with innovative ways of applying computer technology to solve real-life business problems. Crandall, on the other hand, was a businessman who had developed extensive knowledge of and an intuitive feel for what computers could do for a large business. His understanding of and faith in computer technology was a rarity among businesspeople in the late 1960s and early 1970s.

Not surprisingly then, when O'Neill and Crandall found themselves thrown together at TWA, they quickly came to have a high regard for one another's rare combination of abilities. They also became close personal friends.

In 1970, when Crandall was selected to be TWA's new VP of data processing, one of his first moves was to hire O'Neill away from Kranzley & Co. and make him assistant VP of reservations data processing.

Throughout the late 1960s TWA had worked with the Burroughs Corporation on development of a new computer reservations system code-named GEORGE. Myriad technical and budget problems had hampered GEORGE's development. In fact, there was growing concern within TWA management that GEORGE might never work the way it was supposed to. In 1970 TWA chairman Charlie Tillinghast gave Crandall the job of analyzing the whole GEORGE project to determine whether TWA should continue with it or write it—and the more than $50 million already spent on the project—off as a failure.

"We had to definitively come up with a conclusion on whether GEORGE was ever going to supply TWA with the kind of results the company had hoped for going into it. We determined that it would not, but we had to make sure we were right and that Crandall could convince the board to cancel the whole project," O'Neill said.

"I helped Bob put that presentation together. It was over the Thanksgiving weekend in 1970. He took it to Tillinghast and the board early the next week. It was a hard call to make because we'd put so much into GEORGE already. But it was the right call and the board killed GEORGE."

Consequently, TWA determined that it then had to pour all of its resources into updating the computer reservations system it already had, known as PARS, which is short for Passenger Airlines Reservations System. That meant buying—and then modifying—Eastern's IBM-based programming language, which itself was a greatly enhanced version of the original programming language IBM wrote in the mid-1950s for the very first computer reservations system, SABRE.

Dick Pearson ran the commercial side of TWA's data processing department for Crandall in 1970 while O'Neill ran the reservations side.

"Once Bob convinced Mr. Tillinghast and the board that GEORGE was not the right way to go, we subsequently made the decision to install PARS in Kansas City. We committed to have an on-line re-servations system within twelve to fifteen months, which was an unheard of time frame at that time. But Bob made it work," said Pearson, who went on to serve as TWA's president in the mid-1980s before moving to American as senior VP for domestic field services.

"We had already begun building an administrative center in Kansas City to house the commercial side of data processing before the decision to scrap GEORGE was made," Pearson said. "The administrative center was only designed to hold the commercial data processing people. The building was half the size it ought to have been to put the reservations system people in there too, but we did it anyway. Bob wasn't going to let something like that stop him.

"We added a larger computer room to the building's design after they already had begun construction. And we took occupancy of the building when there wasn't even a road to it and there were no steps to the building. You kind of had to climb in the door on some boxes and planks somebody had set up. We had to walk through mud and construction debris and all sorts of stuff, but we had that reservations system on-line within the time frame Bob had laid out.

"Even back then, Bob was what I would call a great leader," Pearson recalled twenty years later. "I've known him about as long as anybody in the business has known him. And his desire to get things done, or to make the business better than what it has been in the past, has not changed. Maybe his vision was narrower then simply because his job responsibilities were restricted a little bit. But the basic skills, leadership, tenacity, working long hours—he really was into that, working long hours.

"Bob creates an environment of 'can do' so much. When I first met him I was impressed because here was a young guy in the corporate world who was willing to go out front and clear obstacles. When problems arose that you needed to address or get fixed, he simply was out front doing it. Then he would let you go in and follow and do what needed to be done. He made you very positive. I always said that he made you better than you thought you could be. And you ended up wanting to be better than you ever thought you could be too.

"In a business sense, if you took the business environment and supplanted that with the sports environment, Bob's the kind of great athlete that makes his teammates better. And he was that way even way back when we were at TWA together," Pearson said.

*   *   *

THE SABRE system that Hopper ran for American in the early 1970s was hardly the sophisticated computer network it is today. Today's ultra-sophisticated SABRE, the largest of all airline computer reservations systems, has processed as many as 111.1 million messages in one day and as many as 11.17 million messages in one hour, which breaks down into 3,103 messages a second. A message is any request for information made when a travel or reservations agent touches the "enter" key on the terminal keyboard. Today SABRE can be found in more that 22,800 travel agency locations in fifty-seven nations on six continents. It is the world's largest privately owned computer network.

But, while SABRE circa 1973 was a relatively sophisticated computer system for its day, it and all the other airline reservations systems still were just simple internal corporate computer systems. Only American employees had access to SABRE. When a travel agent wanted to book a customer on an American flight, he or she had to pick up the phone and go through an American reservationist, just like the general public.

That, however, began to change after Hopper bumped into Crandall on a New York street corner one summer day in 1974.

"There had been a number of attempts to automate travel agents back in the '60s and into the early '70s. But because of financial, technical, and regulatory problems, nothing ever got off the ground," Hopper said.

"Still, ASTA, the American Society of Travel Agents, had a desire to do something along those lines. They had a guy named Don Sohn, who was head of ASTA's automation committee. Don was a Ph.D. out of Harvard who was teaching at the time at MIT and who also was running a big travel agency right there near the campuses of Harvard and MIT in Boston. He was a really bright guy, and a very nice guy. He was one of the first to really see the need to automate travel agents. He and another fellow named Ray Smith, who ultimately succeeded him in the job of heading up ASTA's automation committee, started talking through ASTA to a lot of other folks about doing something to automate the travel agents."

By early summer in 1974 Sohn, Smith, and ASTA had hooked up with a small but highly regarded consulting firm, Greenwich Data Systems. They had come up with what looked to be a promising plan for building a computer reservations system specifically for travel agents. Not long after Hopper got wind of ASTA's plans, he happened to be in New York attending to business at American's headquarters. At lunchtime he ran into Crandall. Because he had just recently been made American's new senior VP for marketing, Crandall no longer was directly responsible for the company's data processing units, even though he did control SABRE's marketing research and development budget. Hopper, figuring that his old boss would quickly grasp the serious impact ASTA's plans could have on American's ability to control the sale of its service, seized the moment.

"I stopped Bob on the street. I guess I caught him going to or from lunch. It was in New York, just outside American's headquarters at 633 Third Avenue, at the corner of Third and 41st. I'll never forget it.

"I said to him, 'Do you know this is happening?' And I said, 'I don't think we want somebody in the middle of our distribution channel without any airline involvement,' Our conversation didn't last more than a minute or two, right there on the street corner. But he agreed with me and immediately began to look into it," Hopper said.

Prior to that point, O'Neill said, American had been ambivalent regarding the issue of automating travel agents. And even after that street-corner meeting between Crandall and Hopper, American's management continued to be ambivalent about travel agents' involvement in ticketing

"We knew we could prepare tickets for about half the cost. Yet the travel agents represented a major distribution channel. At the time they wrote about 45 percent of all tickets. And the percentage was growing every year," O'Neill said.

Travelers increasingly were turning to travel agents to book their travel for several reasons.

First, customers perceived travel agents as experts who could help select the best routing between cities. In those pre-deregulation days, there were no true connecting hubs providing quick and easy connections several times a day to even the smallest of cities. Travelers needing to go from, say, New York to Oklahoma City did not have the option of running out to LaGuardia Airport to catch the next flight for Dallas/Fort Worth Airport with the knowledge that they could make a quick connection to Oklahoma City on either American or Delta, the two hub operators at D/FW today.

In 1974, the year the giant new D/FW opened, the New York passenger bound for Oklahoma City might be able to catch one of several daily flights to D/FW on either American or Braniff International. But there was no guarantee that he or she could make a quick and easy connection to an Oklahoma City flight. Two-, three-, and even four-hour layovers with a change of airlines were quite common at D/FW. And that's just one example. Similar situations existed literally on several thousand city-pair routings within the United States.

Accordingly, a good travel agent who could search through the voluminous *Official Airline Guides* book to find the most direct and quickest routing was considered a valuable asset.

Second, in many cases travel agents offered superior convenience to travelers. While airlines operated CTOs—city ticket offices—in the downtown areas of major cities, those CTOs weren't necessarily convenient. In many cases, travelers used travel agencies that were closer to their homes or offices, or agencies that would deliver tickets right to their door.

For their work, travel agents typically received a ten percent sales commission from the airlines. Then, as now, that ten percent was not added to the price of the airline ticket. Rather it was deducted from the fare price by the airline and forwarded to the travel agency on a monthly or quarterly basis.

To make matters worse for the airlines, because travel agents still had to call an airline reservationist to book a customer's travel, the airline's own direct costs associated with selling seats on its flights were not reduced. It still had to have a reservationist available to handle booking calls regardless of whether the calls came from individual travelers or from travel agents.

As a result, while it typically cost airlines about $5 to sell $100 worth of air travel through their own reservationists, it cost them about $15 to sell $100 worth of air travel through travel agents.

Yet travelers preferred dealing with travel agencies rather than directly with the airlines. No airline could afford to ignore the travel agents, because they brought the airlines nearly half of their passengers.

On the other hand, automating travel agents appeared to be prohibitively expensive and massively complicated. O'Neill said that the general feeling at American, which wasn't making much money and which was burdened by heavy debts, was that "we just couldn't afford to do it by ourselves."

Still, the option of *not* automating travel agents was growing more and more expensive too.

"Travel agents were growing very fast, but they still had to call the airlines and make reservations. So the airlines were having to put in the phone capacity and having to hire more and more res agents," said Tom Plaskett, who joined American's management team in January 1974, just in time to get in on the internal debate over automating travel agents.

"Somebody said 'Hey, why don't we just put the reservations tubes right in the travel agencies?' And the answer was always 'Well, you can't do that' for all these ten thousand jillion reasons, legal and otherwise. But as the situation developed we figured we were either going to get so swamped with paperwork or we were going to have to add so many res agents that our costs were going to go through the roof.

"So we said maybe we ought to look at our top travel agents and automate them and try to reduce our costs that way," Plaskett said. "But then we'd look at it and say 'How are we going to pay for that? Travel agents don't have any money. They're mostly small business-people who don't have that kind of cash to make a substantial up-front investment in equipment and technology. And we sure can't afford to pay for it.'

"So we were in a real quandary. There were good reasons to automate the travel agents. But not enough to offset the cost of doing it."

ASTA's DEAL with Greenwich Data Systems—which subsequently was acquired by Control Data Corporation—changed things. Just as Hopper had anticipated when he buttonholed Crandall at the corner of Third Avenue and 41st Street in New York, Crandall feared that allowing a third party to enter the sales loop would mean the airline's costs directly related to selling tickets would go up dramatically.

"Historically, the airlines have ended up paying for everything," Crandall said. "If somebody else owned the methodology, we figured it wouldn't be a shared expense, it would be an expense that the airlines got stuck with. We said 'We don't want that. We manufacture the product, so we ought to have something to do with the method by which it is distributed.' "

Coincidentally, ASTA's annual membership conference was slated to begin in Rio de Janeiro a few days after Hopper's encounter with Crandall.

"So I went to Rio and met with the ASTA board of directors and proposed to them that we go out and organize the airline industry to perform a feasibility study for a system that would be jointly owned by the airlines and the travel agents," Crandall said.

"And that's exactly what we did. We went out and got, if memory serves, $200,000 from TWA, $200,000 from United, and $200,000 from ourselves" to perform that study. The airlines also sought, and got, temporary antitrust immunity from the Civil Aeronautics Board to allow them to enter into such discussions.

Thus was born the Joint Industry Computer Reservations System Conference, or JICRS for short. Nearly all of the nation's major airlines participated, as did ASTA. Hopper, more by default than anything else, was put in charge of organizing the study and writing the final report.

"Max was our third choice to head up the actual work on JICRS," O'Neill said. "Not that Max was not terrific. He is. That's not my point. My point is that officially I was the guy who headed up the JICRS Conference. But I was not going to be involved in the nuts-and-bolts work. We needed somebody who could do that, who could really be the operational head of the study. And we didn't think it was right for two American guys to be in the top two positions. Besides, we didn't really want to give up Max for that long a period. He was too valuable.

"The first guy we went to was Don Pusey at Eastern Airlines. But Eastern said he wasn't available. The next guy we went to was Ed Gehrlein. He used to work for me at TWA and was another good man. But TWA said they couldn't spare him.

"So I said, 'Jesus! Let's give 'em Max and get on with it.' So I asked Max to head this thing up in Chicago. He did and he did a superb job of it. He spent the better part of a year on it. He and his people in Chicago collected an incredible amount of data and did a really good job of analyzing it. Then they put it all in a huge report. I wrote a summary of the report, which was really a summary of the various summaries Max had already written for each section of the report. Max just did a hell of a job cataloging this stuff," O'Neill said.

IT WAS not a coincidence that the first travel agency in the United States to go on-line with an airline computer reservations system was Heritage Travel in Boston. Its owner, Don Sohn, had been the catalyst behind ASTA's plan in 1974 to build a system owned by the travel agents. And, when Crandall persuaded ASTA to hold off on that plan and to join with the airlines in the JICRS Conference, the visionary Sohn became sort of an unofficial, unpaid consultant to Hopper and the JICRS team.

As a reward of sorts, Sohn's agency got to be the first one in the nation to receive computer automation. But the system Sohn switched on in his Boston offices in May 1976 wasn't the JICRS system. It was SABRE.

Fifteen years later Hopper still scratches his head in amazement at the turn of events that allowed SABRE—which had been almost comatose when he arrived at American in 1972—to become the world's first commercially marketed computer reservations system.

"I'm firmly convinced that JICRS would have worked had it not been for United Airlines," he said.

"The JICRS Conference began in December of 1974. The study came out in late June or July of '75. Then we spent the next six months trying to get people to buy into it. The study said three things: that [building a single computer reservations system for the whole industry] was technically feasible, that it was financially feasible, and that from a marketing point of view it would work," Hopper said.

American, TWA, Eastern, and Braniff all supported the plan, although Eastern and Braniff ultimately backed out because of financial considerations. Continental, Western, and Frontier airlines were fence sitters.

"I think we could have convinced all of those guys to get in if United had gone along with us," Hopper said.

"But United was the problem. They felt their reservations system, APOLLO, was the most advanced in the industry. They had poured a lot of money into APOLLO in the three years or so since I had left them. Since I had helped lay out the plan and was there when they brought APOLLO up, I think I've got pretty good insight into what they were thinking at the time. They had spent a lot of money trying to take a lot of the ideas they had in their old Unimatic system to enhance APOLLO. . . .

"Meanwhile, American, because of all the internal problems, hadn't spent an awful lot of money on SABRE. Until Bob [Crandall] got here, I had a tough time getting commitments out of the marketing department to spend an awful lot of money on installing equipment. And by the time the JICRS Conference broke apart I still didn't have the same number of people working on SABRE as United had working on APOLLO," Hopper said.

Dick Ferris, then United's senior VP of marketing, had insisted to

Crandall that Hopper and his team at JICRS rewrite their initial report to tone it down.

"[United] just thought the report was too optimistic," Hopper said.

"But . . . I think they really . . . did not want to level the playing field. That was just their view of the world on everything. They were big, bad United, the biggest airline there was. And they just thought it was not in their best interest from a marketing point of view to have a level playing field in computer reservations that made everybody equal. They thought they had an advantage that would sustain them."

O'Neill said: "United had always distrusted the hell out of American. Since it was American that had pushed for the JICRS study in the first place, and since the biggest supporters of JICRS—Max, me, and Bob—were all American guys, they never really supported the JICRS concept."

The ink was barely dry on Hopper's JICRS study when, in the fall of 1975, American officials began hearing reports that United was placing APOLLO terminals in the offices of some big corporations that generated a lot of air travel. Hopper was deeply concerned.

"When [United] started automating corporate accounts that fall, we took it to mean that they were testing out their philosophy of what they were going to do in terms of automating travel agents, which, it turned out, we were right about," he said.

"That's when Bob gave me the go-ahead to start creating our own concept of what we were going to do to compete with them if they did break off from JICRS and go their own way with APOLLO. We didn't want to do that with SABRE. But we had no choice. If United was going to do that—and at the time it sure looked to us like that was what they were planning—we had to be ready."

The plan American's data processing brain trust came up with closely followed the one Hopper had laid out for developing the JICRS system. American identified its two hundred largest travel agency clients and set a goal of placing SABRE terminals in many of them.

"Having led JICRS, I knew what the market needed. I knew where the people were. I'd done all that work, which United had access to. But I don't know to what degree they used it."

O'Neill recalls how "We had sent out to everyone involved in JICRS copies of Max's report. It filled up two or three boxes. And I'm convinced now that we must have been the only guys to read through all that stuff. Everybody else must have pushed those boxes into a closet or something, because we did pretty much what Max's report said JICRS should do. And nobody else followed that path."

Still, Hopper, O'Neill, and Crandall held on to the hope that United might come around and support development of the JICRS system.

"We kept an eye on them, but we didn't want to have to go and do it ourselves," O'Neill said. "We were ambivalent about automating the travel agent community to begin with. And second, to do it ourselves, we felt, was going to be one hell of a big job. And we still didn't think we could afford it.

"We really had no idea how much it would cost to automate the travel agencies by ourselves. And that worried us. I was the guy who put together that first appropriations request. It was for $5 million. I carried it to Bob Norris, who was our chief financial officer at the time, and explained to him what we were doing. I told him, 'I don't know if the cost is really $5 million, or $50 million, or $500 million, and I'm not sure any of your guys can figure out how much its going to cost either. But you'd better sign this.' And he did sign it. We had no choice. We had to be ready to do it," O'Neill said.

The JICRS Conference finally fell apart in January 1976 after a big meeting of the senior executives from all of the participating organizations at the American-owned Flagship Inn in Arlington, Texas, near Six Flags Over Texas. With United opposed to going ahead with the implementation plan and American strongly supportive of implementation, the rest of the industry was caught between the largest, most powerful carrier (United) and the industry's intellectual leader (American). In addition, the cost of implementation was so high without United's support, most of the smaller carriers had to drop out because they simply couldn't afford to stay in the game.

Two weeks later United announced with much fanfare that it would begin placing APOLLO in travel agencies later that year.

But much to United's surprise, American was ready. The very next day American said it too would begin placing its computer reservations system, SABRE, in travel agencies.

To get around regulations that prohibited airlines from giving travel agencies anything of real value, American decided to sell or lease the SABRE terminals to travel agents on long-term contracts designed to keep the monthly charges affordable. The selling point for the agents was that using SABRE allowed them to sell more tickets in less time. Agencies then could chose to reduce their staff to save on costs or to generate even more business with their existing staff.

Three months later Sohn flipped the switch on the SABRE terminals in his Boston travel agency. The first travel agency equipped with APOLLO would not go on-line for nearly six months.

"We moved very quickly. Now, what we turned on was not a good network. It was a real burden on our communications system. The reliability of it was not something that we would tolerate today. There were a whole bunch of things that weren't good about it," O'Neill said.

"For instance, once we got SABRE out there we learned that in our own environment we could control things. We could tell our own reservations agents not to put too many entrys into it at once, or to count 1-MISSISSIPPI-2-MISSISSIPPI-3-MISSISSIPPI all the way to eight after hitting the 'enter' button before trying to type anything else. We were really worried in those days about overburdening the system. We could tell our own people 'do this' and 'don't do that.' But once we put it out there in a travel agency environment, we lost that control. We had travel agents playing with the system, learning what SABRE could and could not do, learning how to find out all sorts of stuff they had never been able to find out before because they simply couldn't look up all the information in the OAGs [the massive books published by Official Airline Guide each month that listed every flight to and from every city, and their fare prices]. But every time they hit 'enter' it sucked up resources that we didn't have to spare."

American quickly went to work to rectify that situation.

"What we did was we made a major commitment to SABRE at that time. We went out and got the best guys from United and TWA and Eastern and brought them in and put them to work on how to build a system that could handle the demand we were getting," O'Neill said.

SABRE's electronic brain—the data base on which the system is based—rather quickly was transferred up through a series of increasingly powerful—and increasingly expensive—mainframe computers. Finally American hit on the idea of teaming up four of IBM's largest mainframe computers in a network. That configuration, though expanded to a network of twelve even more powerful IBM units, continues to be centerpiece of SABRE today.

All of that took money, and lots of it. And American really didn't have a lot of extra cash to throw around in the mid- and late 1970s.

"That's where Crandall really did a hell of a job," O'Neill said. "That's where his vision really started to prevail. Everybody, both in the company and on the board, began to see that if we didn't do it, we would be facing a major problem in terms of losing market share."

ALLOWING AMERICAN to beat it to the market with a computer reservations system was, as Crandall today puts it, "a classic business mistake" by United.

"It was based on advice that Dick Ferris was getting from his people that APOLLO was a better system. They just made a misassessment. They thought that they had a lead, that they had a system which was superior to SABRE. But they did not have a system that was superior to SABRE.

"I think that was the genesis of it. Nothing more or less than the assessment that their system was superior and, therefore, that they ought to go out and take advantage of their superiority," Crandall said.

Hopper said: "I have had people on the United side tell me that they thought they had a three-year advantage over us in systems. But in six months they fell behind and they've never caught up since."

Clearly, United did underestimate American's ability to come up with a technologically advanced product. United also not only failed to follow the road map for marketing computer reservations systems that Hopper himself had drawn up in his JICRS report, it did not anticipate that American would follow Hopper's road map.

"[United's] product essentially was their internal reservations product. When we came out we were able to top them with the product that the travel agents really wanted. We had multiple carrier listings. We had real-time information. We had the ability to sell tickets on the other airlines. They had none of that initially. It was just their internal reservations system," Hopper said.

"Plus, we followed the road map. We went at it from a top-down point of view. We took the top travel agency accounts around the country and we focused our initial efforts on those accounts; as opposed to what United did, which was to kind of open it up to their local sales guys to decide who they were going to sell APOLLO to in each local market.

"We also did something for roughly the first three months that they didn't do. Every weekend we brought to our learning center at D/FW travel agents from all over the country. We promised them an education session. What it was was a very soft-sell message telling them 'Don't do anything until you understand what you're buying.' That combination of the soft-sell approach and bringing them in worked for us. United did none of that. And that's what enabled us within such a short period of time to get a big lead on them," he said.

O'Neill said he believes that like Spater nearly a decade earlier at American, Ferris and the rest of United's senior management failed to see how incredibly important computer technology would become in the airline industry of the 1980s and beyond. Therefore, he said, they did not completely think through the question of how to bring a computer reservations system to the travel agency market.

"Bob and I met with Ferris and one of his top guys in Chicago in a hotel bar after one of the JICRS meetings. And when we would talk about what this thing could do for all of us, you could just see Ferris's eyes glaze over. He had no appreciation whatsoever for information systems," O'Neill said.

"I think what happened was that they said, 'Hey, let's do something,' but had no idea how to do it. By the time they had gotten ready, we were already out there. I just don't think they had any idea of what it would take. And they just didn't have any appreciation for how powerful this could be."

Even Crandall and Hopper admit they were surprised at how quickly computer reservations were accepted in the marketplace and how big they grew to be.

"Clearly, we didn't expect that kind of response, because the forecast we put together for SABRE when we went out and decided to sell it to travel agents was that we felt we might sell 200 installations," Crandall said. "Now we've got 20,000 locations today around the world. So clearly we didn't see it.

"But we knew it was going to be important and we were far more persuaded of that than our colleagues at other companies. . . ."

Indeed, SABRE's development is perhaps the one thing in Crandall's career of which he is most proud.

"I think that is one thing where we clearly saw—and where I clearly saw—that this was going to be very important to us and to our industry over the long haul," he said.

6
The Legend of Fang

AMERICAN IN the early and mid-1970s could hardly be described as a lean and mean machine, even by the industry's now-laughable standards for cost controls. While managers throughout the industry gave lip service to worries about the airline business's notoriously high operating costs, they knew surprisingly little about where they actually spent their money. They didn't have to, thanks to the Civil Aeronautics Board and its regulation of fare pricing.

Though it is akin to a debate on the relative merits of one-and two-hump camels, American could argue that its cost controls weren't that much worse than those of its more successful competitors. Nor were they significantly better than those in place at worse-performing carriers. The real problem with cost controls at American was that the whole thing was as much a matter of attitude as it was of methods and procedures.

The years of inattention and turmoil in the highest ranks of management had contributed to a pervasive sense of apathy toward cost control. Not only did most American managers fail to fully understand where they were spending money, most of them didn't really care, or at least so it seemed.

In the summer of 1974, when Crandall moved over to become senior VP of marketing, he did not suddenly lose his concern about controlling the airline's costs. Indeed, if anything, that concern was intensified. And in his new position Crandall actually had more power to impact significantly the way American spent its money and how much it spent than he had had as chief financial officer.

However, before he could use that power effectively, Crandall decided he needed to learn everything there was to learn about where and how the marketing department spent money. And, just as important, he wanted all of his subordinates, from the highest-ranking corporate staff member down to the lowliest station manager, to know where they were spending the company's money, and why.

To make that happen, Crandall brought Plaskett over to the marketing department with him. Plaskett began installing essentially the same annual budgeting and review process he originally had been brought in to establish in the finance department.

Then, in 1977, when Plaskett became senior vice president and CFO, Crandall recruited yet another young turk to be his chief henchman in controlling the marketing department's costs. This time, however, he didn't have to look very far to find his man.

Robert W. "Bob" Baker, who, like Crandall, earned his MBA degree at the University of Pennsylvania's Wharton School, had been with American since his graduation in 1968, when he signed on as part of the airline's management trainee program. In fact, had it not been for American's management trainee program, Baker almost certainly would not have been available when Crandall called.

His father, Dick Baker, spent forty-one years at American in sales management positions. As American's district sales manager in San Francisco in the late 1940s, he hired Dave Frailey, who went on to serve ten years as the airline's VP of public relations in the 1970s and early 1980s. In 1950 the elder Baker was made district sales manager in New York, then American's biggest and most important market. That was followed by a stint in a senior sales staff position at American's New York headquarters. Dick Baker then wound up his career with a fourteen-year run as general manager of American's station in Philadelphia.

It was in Philadelphia where the young Bob Baker got his start in the airline business—sort of.

"I actually worked for United for six years when I was in college and graduate school," said Bob Baker. "When I started college my dad got me a job in Philadelphia for the summers and holidays with United, working as a cargo handler."

Somehow, between growing up as the son of an airline executive and working part time in the industry, the younger Baker got kerosene in his blood, as the industry old-timers say. Coming out of Wharton, he knew he wanted to make the airline business his career. But while he readily had accepted his father's assistance in getting that part-time job with United, he wanted to land a management job with some airline based on his own merit, not on his kinship to a well-known and respected industry executive.

"When I started looking for jobs coming out of Wharton in 1968, I purposely tried to stay away from American because my dad was there," he said. "I talked to TWA and United. But the other carriers didn't have anything to offer in the way of a well-thought-out program or an organized way to deal with new people coming into the company. American had a full-blown program, which had been going on for a number of years, in which they tried to hire ten MBAs a year."

While Baker wanted to avoid any appearance of nepotism in his hiring, when it came time for his final, formal interview to join American's management trainee program, he drew both on the almost intuitive understanding of the industry he'd gained growing up in an airline family and on his acquaintance with some of the executives with whom he interviewed.

"The interview process was . . . a meeting in the board room in New York, with the candidate on one side of the table and about twenty vice presidents on the other side," Baker said. "They asked you the typical kinds of questions like 'Why do you want to do this, that or the other thing?'

"Because I had a lot of knowledge about the company and, in fact, knew a lot of these people and kind of how things worked, I decided I would attempt to do something very different from most MBAs. Most MBAs in those days wanted no part of the field organization. That was where you got your hands dirty. They wanted to come into a staff job and on the Monday after they arrived become the decision-maker on advertising, or pricing the product or on food.

"I knew that this type of thing was really rubbing people wrong across the industry. The majority of senior managers in those days, if they had any college at all, that was saying something. So, when I went through this process I turned the tables on tradition."

When the executives interviewing Baker got around to asking what area of the company he wanted to start off working in, Baker said: " 'I think my preference for a number of years will be to be in field management because I don't think you can properly design procedures or make decisions about what the product ought to be if you haven't got a good understanding of how the product is delivered and what the customers are really like.

"I said, 'I really think I want to stay in the field four or five years. Then, of course, I'd like to climb the ladder and come into staff. But I really think it is inappropriate to start in staff'; at which point, guys like [then VP of field services] Otto Becker go 'Oh, yeah, he's my kind of guy.'

"One by one I was picking off these guys voting me in. Then they said, 'What area do you think you want to get in?' Well, I knew that the relative competitive lay in an airline like American was that most of the talent was in passengers, and not a whole hell of a lot was in cargo, and that the cargo guys were kind of different and kind of looked down upon by the rest of the airline. So I said 'I'd like to start out in cargo'; at which point the vice president of freight on the other side of the table said, 'He's my guy.' "

Baker's manipulation of the emotional and professional biases of his inquisitors worked, but it had its price.

"They were running these six-month programs in the field in Los Angeles, San Francisco, Chicago, Dallas, New York, and Boston. So I told my wife that we were going to go somewhere good. So guess where I ended up? In Newark, New Jersey, in air freight, working 10 P.M. to 8 A.M.," Baker said. "I end up in air freight at Newark Airport, working midnights, with a master's degree? But I thoroughly enjoyed it. I mean, I learned a lot and I'm glad to this day that I did it."

When Crandall first approached him about taking over for Plaskett, Baker was director of ramp services in the passenger services department, which in those days was a part of the company's marketing organization. It was not a position ambitious executives typically used as a springboard into the ranks of upper management. But Crandall, who had observed Baker's performance in several meetings and budget review sessions, had been impressed by the easy way he handled numbers, by how prepared he was, by his depth of knowledge about the airline and its operations, and, most of all, by his ability to stay cool and think clearly under pressure.

"I looked at it as a tremendous opportunity to get involved in the numbers," Baker said. "Understanding numbers and capital budgeting and yield management are kind of essential tools in this business. And I knew the job Bob offered me would allow me to learn a lot of this business, about how and why we spent money and about what things were really important to the bottom line and what things really weren't very important at all."

The most distinctive aspect of the annual budgeting and control process Crandall established in the marketing department was that he personally reviewed, at least once a year, the budget for every manager responsible for even a tiny section of the department's budget. It didn't take long for middle managers to begin equating Crandall's budget review sessions with the Spanish Inquisition.

Those sessions, which usually took place between August and October at the airline's Learning Center in Fort Worth, near the entrance to Dallas/Fort Worth Airport, spawned dozens of stories—some true—about Crandall's ruthless cost cutting and sometimes menacing behavior. For many middle managers, those budget review sessions were their only up-close-and-personal exposure to the chain-smoking, lip-curling, fire-breathing Crandall, whose vocabulary could make a sailor blush. Those who worked with him regularly at headquarters quickly grew accustomed to his infamous, profanity-filled fits of rage. They learned that those outbursts were simply manifestations of his extreme frustrations with various problems he encountered and that he rarely directed his anger toward an individual. But those who had little exposure to and understanding of him typically were shocked and frightened for their jobs when Crandall went into one of his tirades. The emotional climate Crandall created with his intense, impassioned and meticulous personal reviews of every manager's budget, and the very real and heavy pressure he put on them all to improve their job performance created a kind of corporate mythology about both Crandall and the budget review process.

It was mostly from those sessions that Crandall earned his many unflattering nicknames: Atilla the Hun, Bob the Butcher, Darth Vader, and Fang, which is the one that sort of stuck, in large part because it referred not only to his cost-cutting tactics but also to his personal appearance—specifically, slightly jagged teeth that he did not have fixed until his ascension to the chairman's office in 1985. Crandall, who has a well-developed and sometimes self-deprecating sense of humor, bristles at the suggestion that he's some kind of ogre. Still, he's been known to jokingly refer to himself as "Fang."

Like most legends, the Legend of Fang is based on truth, with liberal doses of hyperbole and some downright fiction sprinkled on top for flavor. One widely circulated story, which falls into the fiction category, was that one young station manager suffered a nervous breakdown after enduring a particularly rough budget review session.

Otto Becker, who despite his status as senior VP of field services still reported to Crandall when he was senior VP of marketing, participated in many of those budget review sessions.

"He gave my general managers absolutely horrible times. They were coming out of those budget meetings practically falling apart at times," Becker said. "He'd chew on them so badly at times that I had several sessions with him where I'd say 'For chrissakes, Bob, you're teaching these guys a whole new way of life. Back off and give 'em a break and let's teach 'em. Let's not beat the shit out of them!'

"And he would do things that would drive me crazy. I'll never forget one session in which we were debating a problem in the field organization. It was a budget session and he swung into one of his own guys saying 'Why can't we find these figures and prove this?' about whatever it was we were debating. The staff guy said, 'Bob, we're up to our ears and it probably would take another man or two to get that kind of detail.'

"And Bob told him, 'Well, put him on then. Let's go!' Then he turned around and started beating the hell out of my general manager over half a flight service clerk position he was trying to get put into his budget.

"That kind of thing set up some resentment," Becker said. "It ticked me off too because my service level depended on fleet service clerks, not some damn numbers boy in the general office. Those kinds of things annoyed me and annoyed my guys and just generally built up this kind of resentment. But I think over the years Bob has learned and toned down that kind of thing."

Baker, who took over for Plaskett as Crandall's chief numbers cruncher in the marketing department in 1977, admits that "Yeah, at times they were pretty tough. These weren't all yelling matches. But they were difficult sessions.

"It was like going to a test. They knew their assessment as managers was, to a great extent, riding on their performance. So as time went on and these stories of difficulty started to materialize, people started to get quite uptight about it. And some guys lost their jobs because of repeated poor performances in those meetings. They just never showed a real command of what their jobs entailed."

Baker's role was to develop the marketing department's budget, analyze it for ways to save money or to put money to better use, and serve as the department's internal controller. In effect, he provided the ammunition for Crandall's budget review gun. Sometimes that ammunition was lethal.

"We used to go through these dances at the Learning Center with Crandall and me, where we would bring in each city's general manager and sort of hold kangaroo court," Baker said. "My job really was to feed Crandall all the data and information he needed to pick apart those poor guys' budgets."

For a brief time, Baker even had the uncomfortable task of supplying Crandall with information for his review of American's Philadelphia station, headed by general manager Dick Baker, Bob Baker's father.

"I was responsible for developing the analytical data for all of the station reviews, including for my dad's station. But when it came time to review my dad's budget, I excused myself and let Bob handle it alone."

The younger Baker did so because he was concerned about the ethical problem presented by sitting in on his father's inquisition, not because he was afraid of what the volatile Crandall might do or say to his father. However, had Dick Baker, one of the company's most senior and well-respected station managers, not been so good at his job, his son might have had reason to worry on that score too.

"Bob was pretty tough on them sometimes, especially in the first few years," Baker said. "And sometimes we, in essence, played a version of good cop-bad cop on them."

Crandall, of course, was perfectly cast as the bad cop.

"But he had a good reason for doing it that way," Baker said. "The purpose of these reviews was, one, to try to understand our costs at the city level, and two, and more important, to serve as a teaching tool to the general managers about what they ought to be keeping an eye on: about the importance of costs; about knowing how many people you had and whether they were productive or not.

"It was an opportunity, particularly for Bob, to see people under some pressure, to see if they could handle numbers, to see if they knew why they were asking for a particular amount of money, to see if they really knew what was going on at their station. It was as much a management analysis as it was anything else. And it was a way people could demonstrate whether they were good managers in a broad sense, one element of which is the ability to understand how you're spending money," Baker said.

Crandall, however, claims his original motives for launching the budget reviews were more simple than that.

"Certainly in the early days when I first began the process of reviewing every station budget, the objective was very simple. It was to get the excess costs out. It was just as simple as that. In the early years, it was nothing more and nothing less than hammering on excess costs," he said.

"Now, as the years went by, and as the company began to grow, there were ancillary objectives, one of them being to teach people what sort of approach we expected them to take toward cost control and financial responsibility," Crandall said.

One of the station managers who survived Crandall's budget reviews in the early years was George Elby. In the mid-1970s he ran American's relatively small operations at St. Thomas in the Virgin Islands. Crandall's review of Elby's budgets then produced what is perhaps the definitive Bob Crandall budget-cutting story.

"I was in on that one," Baker said, a broad grin spreading slowly across his face as he recalled the events.

During one of Elby's first budget reviews, Crandall questioned a relatively small item labeled "services purchased." Elby explained that among other things, one of the services American purchased locally was the use of a guard dog to protect the airline's freight terminal at night.

"George explained that one of the accounts that we had had for years, flowing cargo traffic in and out of St. Thomas, was Timex," Baker said.

"Timex used St. Thomas to assemble their cheap watches. So we'd get in a box full of Timex innards worth a lot of money, and we'd have to store it in the freight terminal overnight. Thieves figured this out; they would go in there and try to hit that.

Elby told Crandall: "Bob, when we close the freight terminal at night we need a guard dog in there to chase away the bad guys."

"How often is the guard dog in there?" Crandall asked.

"Every night, Bob, from nine at night until six in the morning, when we reopen."

"Why don't you reduce that to three nights a week and do it randomly so the robbers never know when the guard dog's really in there? Then we can cut the bill," Crandall suggested.

Elby returned to St. Thomas and did as he was told.

Then when he returned for his next budget review, Crandall found a "services purchased" line item in Elby's budget, albeit for a smaller amount than before.

"What's this for, George?" Crandall asked.

"The guard dog for our freight terminal. You remember, Bob?" Elby said.

"Oh, yeah," Crandall said. "That's the guard dog we had in there randomly last year. You did do that, didn't you, George?"

"Yes, Bob. And we didn't have any problems with robbers," said Elby.

But Crandall wasn't satisfied.

He told Elby, "Why don't you go get a tape recorder and tape the dog barking. Then put it on a timer. Every ten minutes the tape recorder will play and the dog will bark and it will chase the robbers away."

"Funny thing is," Baker said, "when George got back to St. Thomas, he went and got himself a tape recorder and a timer and did just what Crandall said. And it worked."

ANOTHER OF Crandall's ancillary motives for personally performing the time-consuming, emotionally draining budget reviews each year was to learn for himself, in intimate detail, just how the airline really operated.

"Over the years the budgeting process certainly was an educational tool. But it was a two-way educational tool," he said. "I was never a fleet service clerk or a gate agent. I really learned the airline business through the budgetary process.

"You can't really do anything meaningful with cost control unless you understand the job that's being done. So this notion that Atilla the Hun can look at a budget and can chop out 20 or 25 percent on first sight makes good copy, but it's absolute nonsense.

"You really can only make a contribution if you understand the business. People don't always understand this, but a budget is really nothing more than a quantification of a business plan. If you are really going through a budget on a bottom-up basis, you're really going through a business plan. What are you going to do? What's driving this cost? This cost is being driven by this event, but why is that event occurring? Because I planned to do this. Why are you planning to do that? et cetera, et cetera, et cetera," he said.

"So that very detailed review of a station's budget really allowed me to learn the business."

No industry produces more statistics than the airline business. Professional baseball may be the only field that rivals an airline's ability to produce so many numerical expressions of performance although before Crandall began his budget reviews it is not at all clear that anyone in the business really knew or cared what these statistics meant. Carriers' quarterly and annual reports are littered with statistics. There's revenue passenger miles flown; available seat miles; revenue yield per passenger mile flown; cost per available seat mile; and dozens more. Internally, airlines keep detailed statistics on every route and every individual flight, on the performance of both people and machines, and on sales and financial performance.

But, if anything, Crandall's use of the budget review process compelled American to increase its use of statistical data as a way of quantifying all sorts of activities and problems. While Crandall's compulsive attempts to quantify nearly everything about the airline business at times borders on managerial overkill, it also has over the years yielded significant cost savings.

"And we couldn't always control the costs as we would have liked," Baker said. "But we at least wanted to know where the dollars were being spent."

For example, Baker remembers coming up with what easily qualifies as one of the more esoteric statistics ever created, kilowatt-hours per departure. But that weird ratio turned out to be an effective way of judging whether the airline was being fairly billed by airport managements for its use of electricity and of how tightly station managers ran their operations.

"We had a format, a preplanned budget review format, which changed a little bit every year depending on what we were interested in," he explained.

"For instance, we'd go through a city [station] and we'd stumble on to something, some cost that seemed out of line. So we'd start to adopt a convention. That's how one year we figured out how much we were spending on electricity per passenger boarding and per departure, systemwide. It was all because we discovered that the electricity budgets at our stations at the New York airports were very, very high."

"From then on, as a way to find out which of our cities [stations] were in line and which weren't, we'd compute the kilowatt-hours per departure or per available seat miles. It gave us a standard against which we could judge our performance," Baker said.

Also, in investigating why its electric bills at New York's three airports were so high, American discovered that the Port Authority there received one bill, then used a simplistic formula to charge the airports' tenants for their presumed electricity use. An airline that conscientiously practiced energy conservation was not likely to receive any financial benefit because the formula did not take such efforts by individual tenants into account. American subsequently learned that a similar situation existed at many other airports. Where possible, the airline had its stations put on separate electric meters so that it could exercise more control over its power usage.

"If we found a high [electricity]-cost station we'd initiate projects to see if we could reduce the kilowatt-hour usage. And when we found those airports that used Mickey Mouse allocation methods, we'd go try to get them to change. So that was an important exercise," Baker said.

Yet the most important product of the budget review process Crandall installed at American—which, over time spread to all departments—can't be measured, quantified, or expressed as a statistic. In less than a decade Crandall and his accomplices managed to do one of the hardest things to do in the corporate world. By focusing American's attention more intently on controlling costs than any airline manager before him, and because other carriers copied all or part of Crandall's new budgeting system, Crandall succeeded in changing not only American's own free-spending corporate culture; he also was the prime mover in bringing to an end many of the profligate ways of his entire industry.

7

A Big Mistake

JUST AS he reached out in 1973 to acquire the services of experts such as Jim O'Neill and Tom Plaskett when he was American's chief financial officer, when Crandall took over the airline's marketing department in the summer of 1974, he picked up the phone and called the man reputed to be the best strategic planner in the airline business.

Wes Kaldahl flew navy fighters off the wooden decks of carriers in World War II. After the war he got a job in Detroit with Pennsylvania Central Airlines, the predecessor of Capital Airlines, as a ticket agent, not a pilot. Though he didn't want to do any more flying, Kaldahl was fascinated by the commercial side of aviation. He spent nearly fifteen years at Penn Central/Capital, in the '40s & '50s, at first working in operations-related jobs. Later he discovered his true calling when he worked in the airline's planning and scheduling department.

Airline planning and scheduling often is referred to as the industry's black art because it requires the ability to synthesize empirical and subjective data, a rare combination of skills. While on the surface what planners and schedulers do appears to be relatively simple, it actually is anything but. Even with today's high-speed computers, airline planning is as much art as it is science. And in the precomputer days in which Kaldahl learned the business, the scale clearly was tipped to the art factor. Learning how to quantify the many variables that go into the overall travel profile of the hundreds of communities an airline serves takes years of experience. Understanding the intricate historical and social relationships that explain that travel profile takes a special "feel," almost a sixth sense. For instance, a planner trying to develop a flight schedule for a modern hub at Dallas/Fort Worth Airport must know about Austin's growing role in the computer and high-technology business in order to provide convenient connecting flights at the hub for travelers from Austin to California's Silicon Valley. That same planner must also understand that while Little Rock, Arkansas, and Jackson, Mississippi, are roughly the same distance from D/FW, people in Little Rock have far more business, social, and cultural ties to Texas and the Southwest than do those in Jackson, a city of the old Deep South that looks more to places like Memphis, New Orleans, and even Atlanta for its primary business relationships. That knowledge could mean that while the D/FW–Little Rock route can support eight flights a day, the D/FW–Jackson route can support only five.

In his years at Capital, Kaldahl earned a reputation as one of the brightest young planners and schedulers in the industry. But in 1960, when Capital was merged into United Airlines, Kaldahl jumped to a job in the planning department at American's headquarters in New York.

At American Kaldahl worked for and learned from Mel Brenner, widely regarded as the progenitor of modern airline schedulers. Brenner was the first to figure out how to schedule the expensive new jetliners that were joining commercial fleets in the late 1950s and early 1960s so that they could actually make money. He did that by linking the time-honored concept of high aircraft utilization—keeping the planes in the air many hours each day—with a more scientific, less intuitive approach to market planning than the industry had used previously.

Though it seems basic now, making sure that an airplane didn't have too many seats for the markets it served was not a major consideration before the jet age. Because piston-engine planes typically were half the size of the 100 to 125 seat jets that replaced them, the same plane that served New York profitably usually could serve much smaller markets without taking a financial penalty for having too many empty seats. The problem in those days immediately preceding jets was having too few, not too many, seats on the airplane in.

But when the bigger, more expensive jets went into service, Brenner quickly realized that their high operating and ownership costs relative to piston-engine planes demanded that jets be flown with more than half their seats filled all day long, every day. Otherwise the airline would be unable to generate the cash flow necessary to pay for the expensive new planes, let alone make a profit. Yet the demand in some markets was not strong enough to support the use of the bigger jets.

So for the first time, airlines had to begin carefully matching the size of their aircraft to the size of the markets those planes served. And that required planners to learn a lot about the size and travel habits of every market the airline served or hoped to serve.

Kaldahl, who was a key member of Brenner's team during the transition to bigger jets, left American in 1964 to be Eastern's planning vice president. Later he moved to Pan American World Airways in a similar position. He didn't meet Crandall until 1973, when both men testified before the Civil Aeronautics Board. Though there was more than a ten-year age difference between them, Kaldahl took a liking to the bright, intense, but still rough-around-the-edges young executive.

"He was young, and I think that was perhaps his first testimony," Kaldahl said. "Today he'd do an exceptional job. But in those days he was pretty new at it and a little nervous on the stand. In any case, we had a lot of time standing around outside the hearing room or whatever, to talk and get to know one another. I thought he was a nice guy. We got along real well. It was readily visible to me that he was the kind of guy I could get along with and communicate with."

Once the CAB hearings were over Kaldahl did not hear from or see Crandall again until he called in the summer of 1974. Crandall, who had just been made senior VP of marketing, said he knew that American's planning department—which reported to him—wasn't performing the way he thought it should be. Was Kaldahl interested in coming back to American?

"I had to reassess my estimation that he was the kind of guy I could work with and communicate with," Kaldahl said. "Was that really true?

"And one of the things when you're in my kind of job that you really worry about is will they let you do your business, your job? Or is somebody higher up going to decide what the airline is going to do and you just become the leg man? That's not a very pleasant position to be in."

That reassessment confirmed in Kaldahl's mind his original estimation of Crandall. As the two discussed the move further, Kaldahl concluded that he would have the kind of freedom to do his job he felt was necessary. So he accepted the offer and joined American in late 1974 as VP of marketing resources. The curious, ambiguous title stemmed from the fact that American already had a vice president of marketing planning, Randall Malin. Malin was shifted in 1975 to VP for passenger sales and advertising, a position he held until he left in 1980 to become senior marketing VP at USAir. But Kaldahl retained his peculiar job title until 1982, when he was promoted to senior VP of airline planning.

MOST OF those American shareholders who bothered to read Casey's first chairman's message in the company's 1974 annual report probably encountered for the first time the concept of airline deregulation. It was to be a subject they would hear and read about much, much more over the next decade.

Cornell University economics professor Dr. Alfred Kahn, author of a 1970 book entitled *The Economics of Regulation*, passionately embraced the view that government intervention in markets, however noble its intentions, always produced a negative result. While government regulation of a business obviously helped set standards for such things as technical specifications and product or service quality, Kahn believed that the market could and would set those standards more efficiently as people chose one brand over another. He further argued that the effect of such consumer decision-making would be lower prices on goods and services, since people instinctively choose the less costly of goods or services, provided that quality and convenience factors are relatively the same.

Kahn and other Ivy League economists and theorists whose ideas gained popularity in Washington in the early and mid-1970s also recognized that government regulation of certain businesses clearly protected the jobs of employees of companies already established in regulated businesses. They also recognized that deregulating industries would likely put some weak or inefficient companies—and their employees' jobs—at risk. But Kahn and his fellow deregulators countered that free competition ultimately would create even more jobs than it eliminated because competition drives prices down, increases the overall demand for any product or service, and, therefore, leads to the creation of more jobs designed to meet that rising demand.

Nearly every airline in the nation opposed deregulation. The lone carrier to support the idea happened to be the largest, United Airlines.

"They thought that with their size they could absolutely rule the world if the industry was deregulated," Kaldahl said.

American, on the other hand, feared that its size—it was still the second-largest carrier—would be a detriment in a deregulated environment. Because it was a big, relatively mature company with entrenched market positions and an older, heavily unionized, highly paid work force, American's management feared that the company would be a sitting duck for the low-cost, highly maneuverable start-up airlines that deregulation almost certainly would spawn. So American took the lead position among those airlines arguing in Washington against deregulation.

It wasn't unusual for American to be the leading voice on any issue affecting the airline industry. C.R. Smith's statesmanlike approach to industry issues and American's sheer size had put it in that position on hundreds of occasions over the years. But this time there was a new eloquence and a new passion to its leadership. Both were the products of fear.

"We were somewhat concerned about our well-being," Kaldahl said. "We were a relatively high-cost carrier, with a lot of old, expensive airplanes at that point. And at that point we had very limited cash and financial capability to go out and get efficient new ones. That was the really big reason.

"The second reason was that we were afraid that the people who were doing this didn't understand what it really meant, that they would be dissatisfied with it in a year or two and reverse the whole course. That would really be a big loss to the airlines, the process of having to shift back and forth."

AMERICAN, AND most of the rest of the airline industry, argued loud and long that while the free marketplace in theory would be a better regulator than the government, in actual practice deregulation would lead to huge losses for airlines and their stockholders, massive job losses, and a serious deterioration in the nation's only comprehensive intercity transporation network.

American also argued that those who wanted to fix the deficiencies in the existing air transportation system understood neither the real problems affecting the industry nor what the real results of deregulation would be.

Opponents of deregulation made essentially three major points—though discussions of minor points filled voluminous reports and hours of Congressional hearing time. First, they said the notion that traditional regulation had led to unnecessarily high air fares simply was wrong. Second, they warned that deregulation at that point in time would add stress to carriers' precarious balance sheets and threaten workers' jobs. And third, opponents argued that deregulation would lead to a shortage of capital for financing new aircraft purchases.

The airlines opposed to deregulation conceded that dramatic increases in the price of fuel following the 1973 Arab oil embargo and strong inflationary pressures had combined to push up fares. But fares did not rise nearly as much as the cost of most other consumer goods and services, they argued. One reason for that was that airlines had been quick to take advantage of technological developments that increased worker productivity and therefore helped control rising costs. A second reason why fares had not risen as much as other goods and services, they argued, was that the CAB was aggressively using its authority to reject proposed fare increases that it believed were based on costs related to the industry's excess capacity problem. In other words, opponents argued that because the CAB already was disallowing fare hikes that airlines attempted to institute solely to cover the cost of operating too many planes with too many seats, the regulatory process already was doing a good job of keeping prices low.

As evidence that fares, in fact, were not too high, the airlines argued that their profits were too low. The CAB's stated intent was to allow airlines to set prices at levels that allowed them a reasonable return on stockholders' investment. But deregulation opponents noted that the CAB's rate-making formula did not consider many cost items. As a result, airlines' actual returns on investment usually were far less than their theoretical returns computed for rate-making purposes. In fact, no airline since 1965 had actually earned what the CAB defined as a reasonable rate of return. Indeed, from 1966 to 1976 the difference between the airlines' combined actual profits and the amount the CAB said was reasonable was $3.6 billion, a huge amount of money even in today's inflated dollars. As an example of how aggressively the CAB was using its power to keep fare rates too low, deregulation opponents pointed to the agency's denial of two different proposed fare increases in 1975, a year in which the U.S. airline industry lost a total of $67 million.

The second major argument against deregulation made by American and most other carriers was that changing the ground rules just as the industry approached a major reequipping cycle threatened thousands of airline jobs and jobs at other companies that supplied or fed off the airlines. The workhorses of the U.S. commercial airline fleet in the mid-1970s were the Boeing 707, which American used and the Douglas DC-8, preferred by Delta and United. Both aircraft were introduced in the late 1950s and represented a rather primitive application of jet power and other new technologies. Besides being relatively old and in need of more costly and more frequent maintenance, they also were less comfortable and safe for the flying public.

Also, while the Boeing 727, which essentially was a 707 hull equipped with three tail-mounted engines, and McDonnell Douglas's DC-9 series of small twin-jets were improvements over the 707s and DC-8s in terms of performance, comfort, and safety, they still represented 1960s technology and, as such, were gas guzzlers that left airlines vulnerable to rising oil prices and therefore needed to be replaced.

On top of all that, demand for air travel clearly was growing at a steady clip. Airlines not only needed to spend money on replacements for their aging jets, they also needed to buy additional new aircraft.

The argument, then, was that substantially changing the competitive environment just as carriers needed to begin spending an estimated $40 billion over a decade would put unbearable financial pressure on the industry and force some carriers out of business. Some carriers, opponents said, would be forced to lay off employees or impose drastic cost-cutting measures that would negatively affect workers' paychecks and working environments. More ominously, some opponents went so far as to suggest that the economic pressures created by deregulation would produce an environment where the industry's high standards of safety would be compromised.

Third, and last of the major arguments against deregulation advanced by American and its allies, was that airline financing would dry up totally if deregulation occurred. Airlines already were having a very hard time attracting the kind of major investors, such as insurance companies, needed to finance the purchase of new airplanes and other equipment. The investment world had grown leery of the airlines since the late 1960s because even in their successful years, their profits were too slim to justify further or even continued investment. Opponents contended that the competitive forces unleashed by deregulation would drive profits even lower and likely would result in substantial losses at some airlines. Investors already concerned about the industry's inability to make reasonable profits simply would stop lending money to or investing in the airline industry. And if the airlines' access to the capital was cut off that way, they would be unable to stay in business.

No one on either side of the argument mentioned it in public much, but any clear-headed analysis of the deregulation proposal would have concluded that if the airlines were left alone long enough, a semi-oligopoly eventually would emerge in the industry as weaker carriers failed or were acquired by stronger competitors. The airlines didn't talk about that much because, except for United, none of them was at all sure they would be among the survivors.

Proponents of deregulation did not dwell on this scenario. First, doing so clearly would have hurt their case, because oligopolies tend to drive prices higher, albeit with the twin disciplining factors of consumer resistance—price elasticity in business school terms—and the existence of some degree of competition. And second, most deregulation supporters believed that strict enforcement of Federal Aviation Act safety regulations and antitrust laws would prevent the possible negative side effects of deregulation—such as the formation of an oligopoly—from affecting consumers or the nation's intercity transportation network. Indeed, Alfred Kahn believed that while a few traditional airlines might be forced into mergers or even out of business, deregulation would foster the establishment and growth of many smaller airlines that would create far more jobs and benefits than might be lost through some degree of consolidation among the old-line carriers.

DOWN IN Texas, proponents of airline deregulation said, there already was a perfect example of the good that could come from unregulated competition. Little Southwest Airlines began flying in 1971 with three leased Boeing 737s. It began by serving only three cities, Dallas, Houston, and San Antonio. It added service to a handful of other Texas cities in the following years, but it did not venture beyond the Lone Star state's borders until 1979. And it was a huge success, earning a profit in only its second full year of operations, 1973, and attracting an incredibly strong and loyal following with its low fares. The original one-way fare on Southwest's flights between Dallas and Houston, for example, was a ridiculously low $20. Still, Southwest was profitable.

Southwest could charge such low fares because it was not subject to CAB regulation. Herb Kelleher, a San Antonio lawyer who co-founded Southwest in 1968, argued that because Southwest did not operate outside the borders of Texas, it should not be subject to the rate and route regulatory aspects of the Federal Aviation Act. It took Kelleher three years and nearly every dime he had to prove his point, but the U.S. Supreme Court finally ruled that as a federal agency, the CAB could regulate airlines that participated in interstate markets only. Thus Southwest, which still had to comply with the FAA's safety regulations, was commercially regulated only by the do-nothing Texas Aeronautics Commission. In effect, it could fly anywhere it wanted, when it wanted, as often as it wanted, and charge whatever price it liked, so long as it stayed within Texas.

To a slightly lesser degree, Pacific Southwest Airlines (PSA), a low-fare intra-California carrier, provided another example of what deregulation of the airline industry might produce. Both PSA and Southwest approached the job of carrying passengers from one city to another with a lightheartedness never before seen at the self-important traditional airlines. PSA painted smiles on the noses of its aircraft. Southwest featured hot-pants–clad flight attendants and free liquor for passengers. But everyone understood that it was the low fares that really brought in the passengers and fueled the unprecedented growth in air travel in the markets they served.

American itself inadvertently contributed yet another good example of what benefits could be derived from deregulation. In the summer of 1976 the CAB authorized what were called air charter operators. For the most part, these companies weren't airlines at all. They were the forerunners of what today are called travel consolidators, or "bucket shops." They organized charter travel for groups, some of which were true tour groups, and some of which were just individual travelers who hooked up with the charter operators to save money. The charter operators bought large blocks of seats wholesale from the regularly scheduled airlines. In exchange for assuring an airline that it would have enough revenue to cover its operating costs on the flights involved, the charter operators got big discounts on the price of the seats they bought. That enabled them to resell those seats to their customers at prices below the airline's posted fare but above the wholesale price.

Crandall correctly saw that kind of thing as a potentially huge threat to his airline and the rest of the regularly scheduled industry. The charter operators were making money by playing off the scheduled airlines' own insecurity. That meant two things. First, the airlines were losing revenue because they weren't willing to accept the kind of risk the charter operators accepted regularly. And second, the scheduled airlines were missing what must be a significant market out there for discounted air travel.

The problem was that airlines traditionally believed that discounted fares diluted revenue: That is, discount fares typically were used by people who absolutely had to fly—such as business travelers—and who willingly would pay more if necessary. Unlike grocery stores that advertise bread or milk at very low prices in the expectation that shoppers will spend more money on other items they otherwise would not have bought or would have bought elsewhere, airlines had never been able to generate more revenue per flight by offering discounts.

American was the first scheduled airline to solve that problem. Crandall's marketing team came up with the industry's first restricted discount fare, called Super Saver fares, in 1977. If passengers were willing to buy a ticket a month or more in advance of travel, and if those passengers were willing to stay at their destination at least fourteen days before making the return-trip home, then American would sell them a ticket at a huge discount. By putting those restrictions on the discounted fares, American prevented business travelers, who rarely can schedule trips a month or more in advance and who almost never stay at their destination for two or more weeks, from using them. And, by offering huge savings, American was able to tap into a new market: price-conscious leisure travelers who previously would have gone by train, bus, or car or who would not have traveled at all. Super Savers, therefore, did not dilute the amount of revenue American got from a given flight. In fact, they generated incremental revenue.

The CAB approved the Super Saver fares, which other airlines quickly copied to remain competitive, and American enjoyed great success with them. But, unfortunately for American and others who opposed deregulation, supporters of deregulation pointed to the Super Saver fares as a good example of what would happen in spades if the government got out of the business of setting fare prices and awarded domestic air route rights.

They noted that American introduced Super Savers only in response to low-price competition from charter operators. They also noted that other airlines quickly followed suit, meaning the benefits spread to many markets, not just those served by American. Deregulation's supporters also pointed out that Super Savers were pro-consumer. By making air travel more accessible to middle- and lower-income people, American Airlines had demonstrated that there was a potentially huge demand for air travel that could not be fully met without deregulation.

MONEY WAS at the heart of American's opposition to deregulation.

In early 1974, when Al Casey arrived, the company was short on cash. American ended 1973 with $74.6 million in cash and short-term investments, against $587.4 million in long-term debt. Much of that debt was associated with the recently acquired Boeing 747s and McDonnell Douglas DC-10s that American was losing a fortune on by flying them less than half full. Indeed, by the time Casey arrived, two 747s already had been sold and buyers were being sought for the others.

At the same time American also had one of the oldest average fleet ages in the business. Ninety-three of its 231 aircraft were Boeing 707s dating from the late 1950s and early 1960s, including some of the very oldest and least efficient copies of the plane to come down Boeing's assembly line. Fifty-eight of its 100 Boeing 727s were the earliest -100 models. While they were only about ten years old, the 727-100s seated 25 percent fewer passengers than the -200 models, yet they burned more fuel. Thus they were obvious candidates for replacement.

Even worse, 131 of its aircraft were 707s, 747s, or DC-10s, long-range planes that could not be operated economically or profitably on short- and medium-haul routes. And because the 747s and DC-10s had so many seats and flew long-haul routes, well over 80 percent of American's available seat miles were deployed in long-haul markets.

Yet Casey's management team believed that if deregulation occurred, carriers that hoped to survive would have to concentrate most of their resources on short- and medium-haul routes. And with their short supply of cash and high debt, they doubted their ability to finance the kind of major fleet and route structure overhaul they believed would be necessary.

"It's very simple, very easy. We opposed deregulation because our biggest and best routes were the transcons and semi-transcons," Casey said, referring to American's many transcontinental routes in those days. "They were the first routes that were going to be attacked if deregulation came about.

"Now United wasn't like us at all. They were in the New York–Los Angeles market, sure. But they had taken Capital over and they had a lot of 727s, 737s, and DC-9s. So they were equipped to do a lot of what in those days we called traffic gathering. We weren't. We had all our planes in long-haul markets, or at least the majority of them.

"So United was the first to support deregulation. We never did. We opposed it all the way. We had the wrong route structure. We had the wrong aircraft for it. We weren't equipped right. We had very unfavorable union contracts. We were going to get killed. And we would have been killed if we hadn't changed our whole strategy. But at the time we weren't sure we could do that."

American's decision to oppose deregulation was not made easily or without some serious debate, both among management and the board of directors. Longtime board member Hooks Burr was among those who philosophically was inclined to favor deregulation. For that matter, Casey himself was torn between the realities he faced in running American and his own Republican philosophical bent. Reducing government involvement in the marketplace is, after all, about as Republican an idea as there is. Ultimately, however, Casey, Burr, and the other board members agreed that deregulation was a major threat to American's survival.

"I think Al was very much afraid of having everything he'd managed to do at American unravel on him. He was afraid that just as he was getting the thing straightened out and was getting the airline's head above water, deregulation would release the competitive thing and people would start cutting fares like crazy, and that we'd be seriously damaged by that," Burr said.

And Casey did, in fact, seem to be getting American straightened out during the four years that the deregulation debate was ongoing. The company lost $34.3 million in 1975, but then rode a strong national economy through three of its most profitable years to date, earning $47.1 million in 1976, $61.3 million in 1977, and a record $122.4 million in 1978. More tellingly, the company's cash and short-term investments nearly quadrupled, going from $115 million at the end of 1974 to $537.2 million at the end of 1978. Meanwhile American's long-term debt rose just 21 percent, from $474.3 million in 1974 to $578 million in 1978.

"I think you've got to give a lot of the credit for that to Al," said Tom Plaskett. "Al believed in liquidity, in maximizing liquidity when you are going into a period of uncertainty. And certainly in this business we were looking at deregulation and what the impact might be of deregulation and wondering if the old adage 'He who laughs last is the one who still has cash left' might be what we were looking at. So we consciously set out a policy of maximizing liquidity in 1976 that lasted virtually until the time I left.

"In fact, we probably paid a penalty because we would choose to finance something, to borrow money, when we had the cash in the bank to pay for it. If you have $500 million in the bank, you have a choice when you buy an airplane. You can finance it with general debt obligations and put 25 percent equity in it yourself and borrow 75 percent. Or you can lease it where you get virtually 100 percent financing. But we had made a conscious decision to maximize liquidity, which meant we would choose leasing to get the 100 percent financing and maybe pay a premium over what it would cost in terms of the pure cost of capital in a traditional debt financing. That was one reason we adopted the liquidity program.

"The second reason we adopted the liquidity program was that we wanted to build a large war chest if we had to take the unions on in a strike. If you've got $1 billion in the bank, you can say to your unions 'We can stay out longer than you can,' " Plaskett said.

Still, neither Casey nor anyone in American's senior management was convinced the company's financial picture had improved enough to do all that they believed would be necessary to survive in a deregulated environment.

"Plain and simple, American wasn't ready," Plaskett said. "Our view was that others could move more quickly, others with smaller planes, especially United. That we had all these long-haul airplanes and a relatively small fleet of short-haul airplanes concerned us if, in fact, the U.S. market was going to open up. We knew that they could move more quickly to grab markets than we could and that once they did that, we would be in a hole we might not be able to climb out of."

*   *   *

SENATOR HOWARD Cannon was perhaps the biggest proponent of airline deregulation in Congress. A Democrat from Nevada, Cannon's main interest was getting more air service for his state, which he believed would lead to increased economic development and more jobs. With the attraction of gambling casinos in Las Vegas and Reno, Cannon believed a lot of tourists would love to visit his state if only they didn't have to spend all their money to get aboard one of the relatively few airplanes that landed in either city each day. So, believing that deregulation would drive airfares lower and lead to expanded air service, Cannon authored a bill calling for the government to extricate itself gradually from the business of allocating domestic air service route rights and of setting the price of airfares.

But Cannon's bill went nowhere until Senator Edward Kennedy of Massachusetts threw his support behind it in early 1976. Kennedy had removed his name from consideration for the 1976 Democratic presidential nomination, but he was still considered an odds-on favorite to run in 1980, especially if the Democrats failed to knock off President Gerald Ford in the 1976 elections.

Kennedy, whose wealth and position made it possible for him to fly almost exclusively aboard private jets, represented a state with excellent air service. Boston was one of the most well-served markets in the nation, especially considering its size and near-the-end-of-the-line geographic location. So Kennedy had neither a personal nor a political stake in the airline deregulation issue. But with the war in Vietnam over, Richard Nixon out of the White House, and the economy rocking along pretty good, Kennedy was searching for an issue that would stir the masses. He believed he needed such an issue to champion in order to continue being taken seriously as a potential occupant of the White House.

Michael Levine, a Yale-educated lawyer and former Civil Aeronautics Board staff counsel, and Phil Bakes, a former Senate Judiciary Committee staff attorney who was the CAB's general counsel at the time, provided Kennedy with what they thought was just such an issue. Levine, who had left government to teach at the California Institute of Technology, and Bakes were ardent believers in airline deregulation. Both also had strong ties to Kennedy. It was at their suggestion that Kennedy joined Cannon's cause. Thus Cannon's airline deregulation bill came to be known as the Kennedy-Cannon Bill.

In June 1976 the Aviation Subcommittee of the Senate Commerce

Committee, on which both Kennedy and Cannon sat, held hearings in Washington on the issue. Airline executives lined up to rail against the idea. Economists such as Kahn, consumer activists, and even some business leaders testified in favor of deregulation. Nothing was decided as a result of those hearings. And, while the matter did gain some national attention and some degree of support among average Americans, it did not turn out to be the kind of burning public issue for which Kennedy had been hoping.

But the movement did gain the support of a certain peanut farmer from Plains, Georgia. Jimmy Carter, the toothy former governor of Georgia, came out of near-total obscurity to win the Democratic nomination for president that same summer. A remarkably intelligent and well-educated man—he was trained as a nuclear engineer but was well versed in the humanities, business, law, and finance as well—Carter had read Alfred Kahn's writings and was in philosophical agreement with him. In fact, one of Carter's featured campaign issues was reducing government regulation of free enterprise. The only question was what industry Carter would try to deregulate first if he got lucky and won the election.

Well, he did win. After his inauguration in January 1977, Carter didn't wait for Kennedy or Cannon to rebuild the momentum that had been lost when Congress went into recess the preceding fall. Early in his first year in office he named several members to the CAB, including a new chairman; each supported deregulation. In fact, Carter named none other than Alfred Kahn as the CAB's new chairman. The idea was to put Kahn, the leading intellectual light in the whole deregulation movement, into a position of power from which he could both direct Congress's discussion of deregulation and take the executive actions needed to set the stage for it.

Kahn initially balked at accepting the appointment because, he said, he knew nothing of the practical realities of the airline business. All of his work on the subject of deregulating airlines had been done on the basis of abstract theory. But Carter convinced Kahn that by heading up the CAB he could blaze the trail for deregulating other industries in the years to come.

When Kahn took over as CAB chairman in June 1977, five months into Carter's presidential term, the dye was cast. Ten months later, in his letter to shareholders in American's 1977 annual report, Al Casey wrote: ". . . we are gravely concerned by some of the problems we see ahead. One of these is the inexorable rise in the costs of fuel and another the apparent inevitability of substantial changes in the form of government regulation of the airline industry."

While American and other carriers continued to resist the deregulation movement, they recognized that it was only a matter of time before it went into effect.

According to Barbara Sturken, a reporter for the trade journal *Travel Weekly* and co-author of a book on the history and impact of airline deregulation, "Timing, as they say, is everything. The idea of airline deregulation happened to come along at a time when Watergate was still pretty much a fresh memory. The mood in the country and in Congress was for reducing government regulations and getting politicians out of the process, not just in the airlines, but in the savings and loan industry, in trucking, and in lots of other regulated industries. The only really curious thing is that they decided to go after the airlines first, because deregulating the trucking industry would have had a much bigger impact on the average person's life because trucking is such a big business and it touches nearly every product there is.

"And, while a lot of people think that Jimmy Carter's election was really the key thing behind deregulation, it probably would have happened had Gerald Ford won the election. Ford supported deregulation. People forget that. It was one of those issues where the candidates and both parties happened to be in agreement. The Republicans liked it because getting government off the backs of business is a Republican issue. The Democrats liked it because it was promoted as being pro-consumer," she said.

In October 1978, a little more than two years after the Kennedy-Cannon hearings on airline deregulation and more than a year after Kahn took over as head of the CAB, Congress passed the Airline Deregulation Act of 1978. The law actually went into effect in early December of that year.

American Airlines—and the entire U.S. airline industry—was never the same again.

8
Turf

AL CASEY first met Bob Crandall on February 20, 1974, shortly before it was announced Casey would be American's new president and chief executive officer. After exchanging pleasantries, Casey asked Crandall to come over to the apartment American had rented for him in New York. The new boss wanted to take his first look at the company's books.

A week earlier Casey had received a note from C.R. Smith in which the venerable old American chairman had offered his assessment of the key players on the management team Casey was about to inherit. Regarding Crandall, whom he had known a scant six months, C.R., in his typically terse style, wrote: "One of the brightest young financial men I've ever met. Formerly with TWA. Entirely competent." That was all Casey knew about Bob Crandall until his new thirty-eight-year-old chief financial officer appeared at his apartment door as instructed.

"I had a huge, thick book which had all the statistical data about the airline, and all the analysis, studies as to what we thought we ought to do. Strategy A. Strategy B. Whatever," Crandall said. "I went over and sat for several hours with Al and went through that book, which was really an educational process because, of course, Al came from outside the airline business. We had a very pleasant meeting, and thereafter went about our business of trying to fix this company."

But there was more going on in that meeting than just a CFO giving his new CEO a thorough briefing. The ambitious Crandall used that meeting, and his nearly daily meetings with Casey over the next six years, to move himself to the head of the line of succession to American's throne.

"Bob was running for office from day one. And I don't mean that in any way as a negative," said Tom Plaskett, who from his arrival at American one month before Casey until his resignation in 1986 to become president of Continental Airlines was viewed as Crandall's protégé. "Bob was an ambitious guy—still is—and he never made any secret of the fact that he wanted to run a major corporation someday, or that he'd like for that major corporation to be American. There's nothing wrong with that, so long as it doesn't get in the way of getting things accomplished that the company needs accomplished. And I don't think Bob ever allowed that to happen."

It's a good thing too. Executives who didn't perform up to the results-oriented Casey's considerable expectations were personally counseled by Casey, who in private can be as stern and gruff as he is jovial and gracious publicly. If they still didn't cut the mustard, Casey cut them. While over the years Casey and Crandall had their share of profanity-filled arguments over various issues, Crandall never was the beneficiary of that particular kind of career counseling. In fact, his performance, his understanding of the industry, and his passionate approach to management got him "promoted" only five months after Casey's arrival to senior vice president of marketing, even though he had never held a marketing job in his life.

Two years after that Casey was behind Crandall's election to American's board of directors, where he joined Donald Lloyd-Jones, the airline's senior VP of operations and a holdover from the George Spater years, as the only members of management besides Casey on the board. The move was more or less the first public indication of what those inside American's management had seen developing almost since the day Casey arrived. By the time Crandall was named to the board, everyone at American's general offices at 633 Third in Manhattan, and even some of those out in the field, already knew that he and Lloyd-Jones were the Thoroughbreds in a two-horse race. Though technically they were equal in rank to American's two other senior VPs, Plaskett and Gene Overbeck, Lloyd-Jones and Crandall clearly were the two most powerful forces in American's management other than Casey himself.

And that was pretty much okay with Overbeck, senior VP for

administration. He had given up the title of general counsel several years earlier to protégé Dick Lempert, who ran the day-to-day operations of the company's legal department. And Overbeck's managerial responsibilities extended well beyond that department. Still, it didn't take very long for him to become known as "Al's lawyer." That's because Casey came to rely heavily on the even-keeled Overbeck's calm, impartial counsel on sundry matters, legal and otherwise. About the only thing Overbeck seemed to become irrationally passionate about was Michigan Wolverine football.

He also may have been best writer ever to work in American's senior management. Important legal briefs in major cases nearly always had Overbeck's personal stamp on them. Other senior executives often asked for his assistance or advice when they had to prepare a speech. And for the better part of two decades Overbeck personally wrote most of American's annual reports. Even after his retirement in 1989, Overbeck routinely was given a rough draft of the annual report and told to "make it sing, Gene."

A corporate and securities attorney by training and experience, Overbeck took a lawyer's careful approach to problem-solving. He understood the importance of history and could be counted on to remember critical details of route cases, legal proceedings, and all sorts of other events that happened both before and after he came to American. He also understood something that hard-driving, business school–trained managers often do not: that the price of victory sometimes is too high. That sense of perspective and his lawyer's ability to approach issues with a sense of detachment made him a steadying force in an organizational structure brimming over with strong-willed—some would say bull-headed—executives anxious to push their plans and ideas into action.

Yet, as valuable and as necessary as those qualities were to American, they also were the qualities that kept Overbeck out of the CEO derby. While every large organization needs someone adept at playing the role of devil's advocate, someone capable of saying "wait a minute" when others are rushing headlong with some bright new idea, such a person rarely possesses the kind of leadership ability necessary to actually lead a large corporation. Spater, who in 1959 personally had hired Overbeck as American's first in-house lawyer ever, is perhaps the best example of that. Spater was a solid, thoughtful general counsel and senior advisor to C.R. Smith. But after years of presenting alternatives to his boss, Spater was uncomfortable making decisions himself and totally ineffectual in getting his people to believe in the decisions that he did make.

Fortunately, Overbeck—who, like Spater, lacked experience in airline operations, marketing, and finance—always understood both his strengths and his weaknesses. Therefore, he understood and was satisfied with his role and never really sought the top job at American. Thus, while neither Crandall nor Lloyd-Jones saw Overbeck as a strong ally on whose unflagging support they could count on in every internal debate, neither saw him as a rival. And Casey always knew that Overbeck's advice, whether good or bad, was the product of professional sincerity, not of ambitious avarice or of office politics.

The fourth member of Casey's original team of senior managers was not quite as content with the treatment that Crandall and Lloyd-Jones got. Robert J. Norris was brought in from Martin Marietta Corporation in 1974 to replace Crandall as senior VP of finance and CFO. His personal management style was very different from Crandall's, who though he had left the finance department continued to keep a close eye on it. Not surprisingly, the two men quickly became serious rivals. Perhaps that conflict was inevitable, given the circumstances. But it proved to be Norris's undoing. Casey fired him in 1976, after he'd been with the airline only two years.

To some extent, Norris was the victim of his own traditional—some say plodding—approach to financial management, which prevented him from making the kind of rapid progress toward the impatient Casey's goal of putting American on a firmer financial foundation. But according to many who were in or close to American's management in the mid-1970s, Norris's case was hurt most by his turf warring with the more dynamic, harder working, and visionary Crandall.

"The biggest issue between them was their very different philosophical, conceptual framework about what role the finance department should have in scheduling and planning," Plaskett said. "If you ask Bob [Crandall], he'll tell you that Bob Norris wanted veto power over scheduling decisions. But if you ask Bob Norris, he'll tell you that's not what he meant at all. But that was the major dispute, and it got to be a real conflict."

Casey, in effect, stepped in between the two in 1976 when he had Crandall named to the board of directors. Casey, who rarely was subtle regarding how his lieutenants performed, certainly didn't do that just to send a message to Norris. But Crandall's elevation was an indication that Norris had maneuvered himself into a no-win position.

"Al has a view that when he brings somebody into a job he gives them two years. And if they haven't satisfied him in two years that they can do the job he wants done, he'll put someone else into it. So the Bob Norris era lasted just about two years. Sadly, it was a disruptive influence on the company. It created schisms, some real splits between finance and marketing," Plaskett said.

Casey's choice to replace Norris as CFO caught many in the industry and some in the company by surprise, not so much because of who it was but because of the message it sent. Plaskett's promotion to senior VP and CFO in 1976 was an indication not only of how talented he was, but also of how powerful Crandall had become at American.

"Norris's departure created a vacancy in the CFO's job in May or June of '76, if I remember right," Plaskett said. "Al then made the decision that he was going to go inside for a replacement. And there were two of us who were the candidates. Bill Twomey was the controller and I was vice president of marketing administration. Al subsequently chose me."

Shortly thereafter, Twomey was named president of Sky Chefs, American's in-flight catering subsidiary.

"The other senior vice presidents had a voice in that decision, at least in the sense of offering their opinion to Al," Plaskett said. "But it is my judgment that the strongest voice in that belonged to Bob Crandall. I feel sure that his influence mattered. He helped Al. He didn't make Al's decision for him. Nobody does that. But I'm sure that Bob had a significant influence on the decision."

ARMED WITH both a master's and a Ph.D. in economics from Columbia University, Donald Lloyd-Jones joined American Airlines in 1957 as a senior transportation economics analyst. By 1968, when George Spater succeeded C.R. Smith as American's chairman, he had risen to senior VP for finance and CFO. In that position, Lloyd-Jones negotiated the final terms for American's deals to acquire the 747 and DC-10 widebody jets. He'd also gained a reputation as one of the top financial managers in the entire industry. His ability to handle the technically complicated aspects of airline finance was unquestioned. And he was widely considered to be a smooth operator when it came to developing and maintaining the often-delicate interpersonal relationships that airline CFOs are expected to have both with the top people at the manufacturers and with stockholders, bond buyers, analysts, and investment bankers.

Lloyd-Jones never made much of the fact that he had an earned doctorate. His official company biography mentioned it only in passing, and he never used the "Dr." title. But his warm, friendly, and laid-back personal style, his contemplative and collegial approach to problem-solving, the pipe that perpetually seemed either to be in his teeth or in his hand, and even his English-sounding hyphenated last name all combined to give him a professorial air. Fittingly, Lloyd-Jones also generally was considered to be the leading intellectual light on Spater's overly large senior management team.

In late 1970, Spater had Lloyd-Jones named to American's board of directors. Then, in July 1972, the chairman asked Lloyd-Jones to move over to the operations department as senior VP, a key position in senior management that gave him responsibility over flight operations, maintenance, purchasing, corporate facilities and real estate, and aircraft purchasing and sales. Lloyd-Jones was not thrilled by the move. The job itself was not the problem. The head of operations, while technically equal to the head of finance, generally was considered to be a more senior executive. And over the years several of American's presidents had advanced from that job. Lloyd-Jones's problem was that he thought he deserved the presidency itself.

In 1972 Spater was under pressure from American's outside directors, whose disenchantment with his protracted—and ultimately failed—merger expeditions and his inattention to the airline's faltering operational and financial performance was growing. So he decided to elevate George Warde, executive VP and general manager, to the position of president. Even though Warde outranked Lloyd-Jones, Lloyd-Jones thought the job should have gone to him.

"Spater felt he had to have a president under him," Lloyd-Jones recalled. "Marion Sadler had become ill again and George had been using Marion kind of as his president, even though Marion's title was vice chairman. He was the public image guy. Marion was very good at that. But he came down with cancer. He was supposedly cured from when he'd had it back in '68. But it reoccurred.

"George decided he had to have a president and that it would be either me or George Warde. George [Spater] told me that he'd like it to be me, but George [Warde] mixed with the troops so well that he had to name him. I didn't like it one bit, but what could I do?

"Spater then made me senior vice president of operations. I didn't know anything about operations. But George said to me, 'You know airplanes, don't you?' Which was true because I'd been so involved in negotiating the 747 and DC-10 deals and also worked on the deal to acquire American's first 727s from Boeing. I'd done or directed all the economic studies on the last three airplane deals American had done. So, I accepted and became senior vice president of operations," Lloyd-Jones said.

Thirteen months later, when C.R. Smith was called out of retirement to hold things together until the board could name a permanent replacement for the fired Spater, Smith wrote Lloyd-Jones one of the pithy little notes for which he was famous. All it said was "What the hell are you doing running operations?"

Just before Smith went back into retirement, he wrote a follow-up note to Lloyd-Jones that said: "Whoever put you in that job knew what they were doing. You're doing a good job." Lloyd-Jones kept that note.

Old C.R. had gotten an eyeful of Lloyd-Jones during his short reprise as American's chairman. The two spent a lot of time together in Washington in late 1973 and early 1974. Lloyd-Jones was American's representative in the CAB-sponsored industry talks designed to cut back on the nation's air service schedule in response to the Arab oil embargo and the ensuing national fuel crisis. Lloyd-Jones also was involved in talks with the government on how to help the effort to transport war materiel and other goods to Israel in the wake of the second Arab-Israeli war. C.R. sometimes sat in on both sets of meetings. And he was involved in the hearings over American's proposed deal to swap its South Pacific routes to Pan Am for Pan Am's routes throughout the Caribbean. Those circumstances threw Smith and Lloyd-Jones together, usually alone, in Washington for the better part of two months. They frequently met for dinner to discuss the airline's problems, world events, and what American had been like in the old days. The old man had been impressed by Lloyd-Jones's understanding of both the industry's and American's problems.

IN LATE 1974 Lloyd-Jones lost another competition for a job he wanted, this time to Bob Crandall. Both men wanted the job as senior VP marketing, which they agreed would be the most important and influential of the four senior vice presidents' jobs called for in Casey's unique management theory. Neither one of them had a day's worth of experience in marketing at American or any other company. But both figured they had been around airlines and American long enough to run the marketing department effectively.

According to Lloyd-Jones, "The marketing slot was open. It came down to me and Crandall. And Al figured it would be easier to replace the finance slot than the operations slot."

Others saw it as a matter of Crandall, who had been with American only a little over a year, outmaneuvering a seventeen-year company veteran. Even as both men interviewed outside candidates for the marketing job, they knew Casey was evaluating them. Crandall quickly saw those interview sessions as a way to display his marketing savvy to Casey and seized the moment by more or less upstaging the candidates he was interviewing. It wasn't that he was out to put the screws to any of those candidates. Nor was he putting his own desires ahead of the company's best interests. It's just that he was convinced he could do the job better than anyone alive, and he was determined to demonstrate that fact for Casey.

Lloyd-Jones clearly had the ability to run the marketing department. And had Crandall not convinced Casey to pick him, Lloyd-Jones probably would have been a good choice for the job. His logic-based approach to problem-solving is similar to Crandall's, though somewhat less passionate. His understanding of American's problems was very similar to Crandall's. And the amiable Lloyd-Jones was well liked throughout the company and highly regarded around the industry. Crandall, on the other hand, was not yet particularly well known among the troops or around the industry.

In any event, Lloyd-Jones was only mildly disappointed at not getting the marketing job. Crandall may have gotten the most influential of the four lieutenants' jobs, but the job of senior VP of operations was still critically important. If the flights didn't arrive on time, or if the passengers' bags kept getting lost, the marketing guy could dream up all sorts of innovative ways to sell tickets and it still wouldn't matter. Besides, Lloyd-Jones continued to be the only member of management other than Casey to have a seat on American's board.

However, that changed too in 1976, when Casey put Crandall on the board. And while that action effectively put an end to the Crandall–Bob Norris turf war, it launched a new one between Crandall and Lloyd-Jones. But this time the stakes were much, much higher. Casey made it clear that he almost certainly would select one of them to become the airline's president, which, in turn, should lead to chairmanship upon Casey's retirement.

Both participants worked hard at keeping their battle low key and out of the industry's gossip mill. Both also tried to keep their competition from negatively affecting the airline's operations or its reputation.

As the two senior vice presidents not involved in the succession derby, Plaskett and Overbeck were in position to watch the fracas unfold. Because he had been hired, promoted, and championed by Crandall, Plaskett, who tried to stay out of crossfire, was something less than neutral. An ambitious man, Plaskett figured that as Crandall's top protégé, he would be in line to succeed Crandall as president when Crandall ultimately moved up to chairman. Likewise, while he got along well with Lloyd-Jones, it stood to reason that if Lloyd-Jones became president, he might not want someone he perceived to be a Crandall loyalist on his senior management team.

"Bob was just the better choice," Plaskett said. "Bob had a broader perspective of the business."

Overbeck, on the other hand, was more impartial, sort of like the veteran sportswriter covering a game between two teams he respected and admired but did not love. Perhaps it was because he was older than either Crandall or Lloyd-Jones and did not want the president's job for himself; but for whatever reason, Overbeck's overriding concern was that the company would avoid being damaged by the competiton and that the best man would succeed Casey. Still, from time to time, he worried that the fight between Lloyd-Jones and Crandall for Casey's blessing would damage American or end up costing both combatants their jobs.

"They worked together pretty well, because they had to. But there was real tension there," Overbeck said. "Crandall would complain about something Lloyd-Jones had done in a long, long memo to Casey and copy Lloyd-Jones. Then Don would respond and accuse Crandall of something in another long memo to Casey and copy Crandall.

"I remember Al coming in my office one day and saying 'Gene, what am I gonna do? I got another one of those god-damned long memos [from Crandall] crying about Lloyd-Jones, and now I've got to get in the middle and sort it out. I hate those sons of bitches.' But Al didn't mind it enough to put a stop to it. He recognized that both men were talented enough to put up with that sort of thing. In fact, I think Al kind of enjoyed watching them match wits."

One of the biggest points of contention between Crandall and

Lloyd-Jones was over who would control negotiations with the aircraft manufacturers about the possible acquisition of new planes.

"The answer to that was that the manufacturers were careful to serve two masters, both Bob and Don," Plaskett said.

In any case, Overbeck said, it was sometimes fun watching, especially if you happen to like watching chess masters at work. For that's more what Crandall vs. Lloyd-Jones was: a championship-caliber chess match, not a fifteen-round heavyweight boxing match. It was a contest of subtlety and finesse as opposed to bravado and raw power.

"Don couldn't hold a candle to Bob in terms of intellectual debate. Not that Don doesn't have great intellectual skills. He clearly does. Don's a very intelligent guy. But not many people in this world have the intellectual skills of Bob Crandall," Plaskett said.

"So, often that forced the debate into the corner office, where Bob would work on Al for his point of view, then Don would come in and work on Al from his point of view. Then Al would have to play the role of arbiter and make the decision. But, really, there's nothing wrong with that. It happens in every organization."

The good thing about the competition, Overbeck said, was that it pushed both men to excel at their respective jobs. And, though it at times threatened to disrupt management of the airline, both combatants were too honorable and loyal to the airline to allow that to happen.

"It was about as gentlemanly as one could imagine given the situation," Lloyd-Jones said of his five-year face-off against Crandall. "Our biggest problem was controlling our people who were loyalists. Somebody in maintenance would squabble with somebody in marketing, and Bob and I would have to step in between them and separate them. We more or less had an agreement between us that that was something that we weren't comfortable with and wouldn't tolerate."

Crandall today also downplays the notion that he and Lloyd-Jones conducted some sort of epic struggle to be Casey's successor that made bitter enemies out of two colleagues.

"The literature of business tends to be much overblown," he said. "The media wants to make every succession competition into a lions-and-Christians war. It ain't that way. In most cases there is no clear-cut moment of victory. The fact of the matter is that there's a succession competition going on in every corporation in America. It goes on every day. It is a normal part of life.

"Don Lloyd-Jones and I had a friendly relationship. We were never warm personal friends, but we always had a friendly relationship, before I came to American, while I was at American, and since he left American. The fact of the matter is that we both knew that because we were the only two senior vice presidents on the board of the company, and because Al wasn't going to stay forever since he came to the company in his fifties, that one of us, if we proved to be adequate, could be a successor. As for it being a contest, it was a very inexplicit contest," Crandall said.

"I think from time to time at a particular corporation where the chief executive chooses to make a deliberately adversarial environment, then maybe that kind of warfare can happen. But I don't think that that ever happened here. Staffs tend to create imaginary contests to give themselves something to do. To the extent that any such things ever happened here, they never had any impact on the operations of the company."

BOTH CANDIDATES clearly had the managerial skills and leadership ability to succeed as American's next president and, ultimately, as chairman. As a result, Casey did not have to wait to see which one would prove to be incapable or unworthy. Rather, he had to somehow decide which of the two very capable executives could take American the farthest.

So why did he choose Crandall?

Never one to say publicly anything negative about a former colleague, especially one he fired or passed over, Casey was purposely vague when he explained: "The factor that tilted my decision toward Bob was Bob's understanding of the concept of marketing. I like Don. I think Don is a terrific guy. Highly principled. Informed. Intelligent. But I think Bob understood my style, which was to establish standards and programs—everything's done by a program—with incentives, leaving nothing to chance, with good, solid communication [with the troops]. Bob's a master at that."

"Al has the ability to take a very complex problem and break it down very succinctly," Plaskett said. "That's based on everything he learned or developed throughout his career in different situations. He even taught that at SMU after he retired from American."

Crandall also is renowned for his ability to dissect extremely complicated issues or problems and to explain them in the simplest terms. His analytical mindset is reflected in his heavy reliance on statistical and financial analyses of every aspect of American's operations and of every issue or problem the airline tackles. By the same token, Crandall regularly demonstrates his considerable communication skills in the numerous speeches he delivers around the nation and the world each year. Whether he is addressing a chamber of commerce group in one of American's hub cities, a group of Wall Street financial analysts, or several thousand American workers at one of his two dozen or so "president's conferences" each spring, Crandall's reputation as a hard-hitting, straightforward and candid orator typically draws packed houses.

That's not to say that Lloyd-Jones was significantly less analytical. He was not. Where Lloyd-Jones fell short was in his inability to communicate clearly what his positions on various issues facing the company actually were. And even then, it wasn't that Lloyd-Jones was not a good communicator. Rather, the more reserved Lloyd-Jones just could not muster the same kind of passion in advancing his arguments as did Crandall. With Crandall, every issue, no matter how small, is earth-shatteringly important, and every decision is a make-or-break proposition. Whether or not it is fair to downgrade Lloyd-Jones on that basis, he had difficulty generating that same sense of immediacy with his arguments.

Another big reason why Casey ultimately picked Crandall over Lloyd-Jones was that Crandall in the mid- and late 1970s was able to put together what now is widely regarded to have been the best and deepest management team ever assembled anywhere. By the time Crandall was named president in 1980, he had hired or promoted a veritable murders' row of executive heavy hitters. Not only were Crandall's team members good at what they did, most of them were multitalented switch hitters who gave Crandall two or three top people capable of doing every job well.

For starters there was Plaskett, who was always seen as Crandall's protégé. Plaskett replaced Crandall as senior VP of marketing upon his mentor's ascension to the president's throne. He left American in 1986 to become president of Continental Airlines, where he lasted only nine months in the shadow of overbearing Chairman Frank Lorenzo. Plaskett then joined Pan American World Airways as chairman in 1988, where he tried valiantly but, ultimately, unsuccessfully to save the feeble old carrier from its final collapse.

At American Plaskett hired John C. "Jack" Pope, who eventually became senior VP of finance and CFO before jumping to United. Today he is president and chief operating officer of the world's second-largest airline and also serves as chairman of the Covia Partnership that runs the APOLLO computer reservations system. United owns 50 percent of Covia.

Then there was Wes Kaldahl, the most respected strategist and planner in the industry for a quarter of a century and the man commonly, though only half correctly, referred to as the father of modern hub-and-spoke operations. One of the few senior Crandall advisors who was substantially older than his boss, Kaldahl retired from American in 1988 after developing its network of six domestic hubs and outlining its rapid growth plans for service to Europe.

Stephen Wolf, vice president in charge of American's western region, left the company in 1981 to become Pan Am's senior marketing VP. He then served briefly as president of Continental, before being named chairman of Republic Airways, where he engineered that money-losing carrier's successful acquisition by Northwest Airlines. Wolf then moved on to the financially ill Flying Tigers Line air cargo carrier, where he dressed the company up and sold it to Federal Express in 1987. That same year Wolf joined United as chairman, following the ouster of its unpopular and discredited longtime leader, Richard Ferris.

Randall Malin, who for a decade served as senior vice president of marketing and vice chairman at USAir, was one of Crandall's lieutenants in American's marketing department in the late 1970s. So was Mike Gunn, a University of Southern California football player who through hard work and dogged determination overcame the "dumb jock" stereotype that initially seemed to limit his career potential. Gunn today is American's senior VP of marketing.

Jim O'Neill, Crandall's buddy from his data processing days at TWA, moved over from the airline's information systems department to become president of the airline's catering division, Sky Chefs, in 1980. He continues to serve as CEO of Sky Chefs, which was spun off from American in a leveraged buyout in 1986.

Max Hopper, the visionary strategist behind American's redevelopment of SABRE as the industry's biggest and best computer reservations system, left American in 1982 to join Bank of America as executive VP of operations. Hopper returned to American in 1985 and took control of both SABRE, which had been more or less separated from the rest of American's data processing operations and converted into a quasi–stand-alone business, and of AMR Information Services, a subsidiary marketing computer and telemarketing services to companies outside the airline industry.

Don Carty, one of the brightest young financial minds in Canada, was hired in 1978 to assist in the cleanup of the financial mess at the Americana Hotels in preparation for their being sold off. When American moved its headquarters to Fort Worth in 1979, Carty moved with it and left the soon-to-be-sold hotel division behind. He spent a year helping Jim O'Neill put in place a new management system for the airline's rapidly growing information systems group, before being promoted to VP of profit improvement, a specially created position from which Carty managed the development and implementation of about two hundred specific cost-cutting and revenue enhancement projects. He also served as coordinator of all of the analytical work Crandall ordered done in association with the major strategic shifts that were in the works in 1980. As a result, Carty was a central player in the theoretical study that was used as a blueprint for American's dramatic growth in the 1980s. He then left American in 1985 to become president of CP Air in his native Canada, but returned two years later when CP merged with Pacific-Western Airlines to form Canadian Airlines International. Today Carty is American's executive vice president for finance and planning.

Bob Baker, the second-generation American executive whom Crandall promoted to VP of marketing administration when Plaskett was made senior VP of finance in 1976, moved on to run American's southern division and the cargo division. Then in 1982, when Hopper left to join Bank of America, Baker took over SABRE and managed the computer system through the period of its most explosive growth. When American was embarrassed by a $1.5 million fine imposed by the Federal Aviation Administration following a thorough inspection of the airline's maintenance operations, Baker was sent in to straighten out that mess. His performance as senior VP of operations was so impressive that Crandall promoted him to executive VP of operations, a new position that included the combined functions once managed separately by Crandall and Lloyd-Jones. As such, Baker is the airline's co–No. 2 executive along with Carty.

"With the exception of Kaldahl, who was older, and then Lloyd-Jones and Crandall in their forties, we were all in our thirties," Carty said. "I think it was kind of fun. There was a lot going on then, as there continues to be today."

The hyperactive Jack Pope, the youngest member of Crandall's kiddie corps of the late 1970s and early 1980s, recalls a moment aboard a flight bound for Tokyo when it dawned on him that "the night before I had been in Europe, and I'd called a guy on my staff and said 'meet me for lunch in New York tomorrow.' We had met and talked over lunch, where I gave him some important instructions on the bond deal I was putting together, and then there I was, headed for Tokyo that afternoon to sell more bonds. In about twenty-four or thirty-six hours I was conducting business worth several hundred million dollars in London, New York, and Tokyo. And I think I was like twenty-nine or thirty at the time and I was still single. Those were pretty heady times. And it was like that for all of us, whether we were in finance, or marketing, or SABRE, or whatever. We were doing some pretty amazing, creative things. And I guess most of us were too young and aggressive to realize we had no business doing what we were doing at that age. We just knew we had to get it done and we did it. And we all were having a blast doing it.

"Once Bob kind of put his initial team of young guys together it just sort of kept building on itself. We were all young, except Wes Kaldahl, and I think Wes enjoyed being around us because he was such a forward thinker that he really thought more and acted more like one of us than like someone from his own generation. I think we kind of kept him feeling young and energetic and we all learned a lot from his experience. But Crandall was the real glue. In the late '70s and early '80s Crandall really moved into control. And he's so good that he just attracts people who really want to work for the best."

Carty said: "I think all of us thrived on each other. It was not a heavily competitive environment because there was sort of nothing to compete for. We were all part of the senior group, and the leadership of that group for many, many years to come was pretty clearly defined for all of us. It was going to be Bob and that was it. So we weren't trying to nudge each other out of the way. We were working together and working quite sensibly."

Indeed they worked together well enough and effectively enough that even a veteran and somewhat jaded businessman such as Casey, who had pretty much seen it all, was impressed by the quality of the young Turks Crandall had surrounded himself with by the end of the 1970s. Casey told Robert Serling, author of *Eagle: The Story of American Airlines*, "These sons of bitches are the best there are."

By contrast, Lloyd-Jones had no such team of talented managers, young or old, working behind him. Today none of his top aides at American occupies a senior management position anywhere within the airline industry. It's not that Crandall purged them after he became president. Rather no one on Lloyd-Jones's staff in the 1970s showed the kind of energy and ability Crandall's henchmen did.

"Don Lloyd-Jones is a very smart, well-educated individual," Kaldahl said. "But he was just out of sync with the management team that was forming under Casey. His personality was just so different from the rest of the management team.

"He was indecisive, even in his own area, although when he was in finance I don't think he had that problem. I think that sort of developed as he tried to become the guy who saw the whole picture. He would not have been nearly as effective a president as Bob."

Otto Becker, who retired as American's senior vice president for field services three months before Crandall was named president of the airline, may have put it best when he said: "I think Casey understood Crandall's strengths better than anybody. I think his financial background appealed to Casey. I think he just had a sense, a feeling that Crandall was the right man for the job. I think that's why he picked Bob instead of Lloyd-Jones. I think he felt that Crandall was a real driver, and the fact that he ruffled feathers may have been good," Becker said.

ONCE AL Casey made his decision to name Crandall president over Lloyd-Jones, he called Dave Frailey, American's veteran vice president of public relations, and instructed him to prepare for a news conference to make the public announcement. Frailey and his staff prepared the news release and updated the corporate biographies of Casey, Crandall, Lloyd-Jones, and Tom Plaskett, who was to replace Crandall as senior vice president of marketing.

Frailey also arranged for a conference call hookup at the news conference that allowed aviation reporters from all around the nation, both from the general and the trade press, to listen in and ask questions.

Much to his credit, a dignified Lloyd-Jones, who privately was terribly disappointed but not too surprised by Casey's decision, faced the media with a smile on his face. When the reporters asked him the inevitable question about whether he could continue working for American and Crandall after having lost the competition for the presidency, Lloyd-Jones pledged to continue doing the best job he could for American Airlines. And he unequivocally gave his personal support to Crandall.

Lloyd-Jones stayed at American a little more than a year after Crandall became president. And when he finally left, it was not in anger but to become president of Air Florida, one of the start-up airlines everyone had predicted would be spawned by deregulation.

"We both had expected it to be an awkward situation," Lloyd-Jones said. "But, because of [Crandall's] ability to make good business decisions that I, for the most part, agreed with, it was not nearly as awkward as either of us had expected it to be. But I was a little older than Bob, and I wanted to run something myself. So, a little more than a year after Bob became president I felt it was time for me to move on. It was my decision. Bob did not force me out. He was very understanding and gentlemanly about the whole thing."

9
Coming Home

IN 1972 Mel Olsen, a young scheduler at the Los Angeles head-quarters of Western Airlines, decided to visit his brother, a medical student at Bowman Gray School of Medicine at Winston-Salem, North Carolina. In those days of regulated airlines, Western, true to its name, didn't fly within a thousand miles of Winston-Salem. So Olsen and his wife boarded a Delta flight at Los Angeles International Airport that would take them to Atlanta, where they would have to switch to another Delta flight for the short hop up to Winston-Salem. It was the beginning of an experience that profoundly affected both Olsen's life and, years later, the competitive balance of the entire U.S. airline industry.

"We left on a Friday night on Delta, flew all night, and got to Atlanta around 5 A.M. Saturday morning," Olsen said. "We had a little layover so when we got off the plane we went looking for a coffeeshop to get some breakfast. But I started noticing that Delta had every ticket position manned and lines were going clear across the lobby. Eastern, meanwhile, had one position manned and no customers.

"Then we went into the coffeeshop and we couldn't even get a seat it was so crowded. Being a scheduler, I couldn't figure out what was going on. It sure wasn't like anything Western had going on."

What was going on, as Olsen discovered once he got back to work and started looking into Delta's operations, was that Delta was operating something called a "hub" at Atlanta. It scheduled flights from more than a dozen cities to arrive at Atlanta all within a relatively brief window of time. Then, once all of those flights dumped their passengers into the old Hartsfield Airport terminal, those going on to other cities, plus passengers originating from Atlanta would board outbound flights. All of the planes would leave at about the same time. This process happened about half a dozen times a day.

Olsen didn't fully comprehend just how powerful a hub operation could be in terms of building up passenger traffic and dominating a market. But the image of a terminal full of passengers at 5 A.M. on a Saturday was etched forever in his consciousness. Quite by accident, he had discovered why Delta had not reported an annual loss since shortly after World War II.

Unfortunately, Olsen also learned that Western could not duplicate what he saw at Delta's Atlanta operation. Like Western, Delta could serve only those routes that the Civil Aeronautics Board had given it the rights to serve. But Western could only dream of having rights similar to Delta's: rights to nearly all of the short-haul routes between Atlanta and other cities in the southeastern United States. To serve those routes effectively and profitably Delta had concentrated on flying relatively small aircraft a couple of times a day on each of those routes. Then, because it also had rights to fly from Atlanta to most major cities around the nation, Delta had discovered it could combine traffic from places such as Mobile, Jacksonville, Chattanooga, and Tampa to fill up larger planes bound for places such as New York, Los Angeles, and Chicago. In fact, Delta's Atlanta operations gave rise to Southerners' common lament that when they die, whether they're going to heaven or to hell, they have to change planes in Atlanta.

Western had no such near monopoly on the short-haul routes within its home region. And even if it had, geography and demography would have prevented it from operating a hub like the one Delta ran in Atlanta. Atlanta, about 250 miles inland from the Atlantic, is in the center of the densely populated southeastern region of the nation. Los Angeles, on the other hand, is located on the western edge of the thinly populated western region. So while southern California's huge local population made Los Angeles a terrific "O&D"—origination and destination—market for nearly every airline in the business, it was poorly situated as a site for true connecting hub operations.

Still, Olsen filed away his understanding of the hub concept for possible use sometime in the future.

AT PRECISELY seven minutes after midnight on the morning of Sunday, January 13, 1974, Captain Vern Peterson of Valley View, Texas, fifty miles north of Fort Worth, brought the silver Boeing 727 gently down on Runway 17 Right/35 Left. He and the other crew members of American Flight 341 from Memphis and Little Rock—first officer Bob Barrett of Euless, Texas; flight engineer Anthony Ferrante of Irving, Texas; and flight attendants Joyce Shobe, Marjorie Stough, and Sharon Oshiro, all of the Chicago area—had just brought in the first commercial jet ever to land at the new Dallas/Fort Worth Regional Airport, the world's largest and best.

D/FW was designed by and built under the direction of visionary airport planner Thomas Sullivan, whom the Dallas/Fort Worth Interim Airport Board had stolen away from the Port Authority of New York and New Jersey. In New York, Sullivan had designed and built what became John F. Kennedy International Airport and had overseen the redesign and redevelopment of both LaGuardia and Newark airports to accommodate jets.

In keeping with the everything's-bigger-in-Texas approach, D/FW was a monster of an airport. Built on nearly 18,000 acres of Texas prairieland, it was roughly the same size as Manhattan. It opened with three runways, each 11,400 feet long. Each of the four passenger terminals had plenty of room to grow, and nine more terminals could be built in the future. The airport even had its own automated train system, Air Trans, to shuttle passengers to the different terminals.

But D/FW was a monster in one other way too. While its plush, modern facilities were a dramatic and much-needed improvement over the cramped, dingy old terminal at Dallas's Love Field—those new facilities did not come cheap.

"Suddenly you had a great new airport," Bob Crandall said. "But it was also a great new problem: tremendous costs. We were sort of thinking about multiple problems at that time. We were thinking about deregulation and that stuff in the background. And in the forefront we were saying 'My God! What are we going to do with these big new costs we've got down here at Dallas/Fort Worth with this huge new airport?' "

Fortunately for American, it was better situated to handle the move from Love Field to D/FW and the related big jump in operating costs than any airline except Dallas-based Braniff Airways. Partly because of its Texas roots and partly because of the influential Texans who over the years had sat on its board—Fort Worth's Amon Carter, Sr., and later Amon Carter, Jr., and Dallasite Jim Aston, plus C. R. Smith himself—American had managed to win a significant number of route authorities between Dallas and major cities throughout the Northeast. And partly because it had positioned itself as the businessman's airline, American had always done well in a pro-business, white-collar Dallas that forever was striving to gain recognition as one of the nation's most important cities. American, in fact, was the dominant carrier on the Dallas–New York, Dallas–Chicago, and Dallas–Los Angeles routes even though it competed against hometown Braniff on the first two routes and the courtly Delta on the third.

In an attempt to deal with the new, higher costs associated with operating out of D/FW, American, over about three years, established something that looked and operated a little bit like Delta's hub in Atlanta. Groups of flights were scheduled to arrive and depart relatively close to one another to allow for some connecting between flights by those passengers whose itineraries followed routes American flew. Then in late 1977, Wes Kaldahl began tightening up the D/FW schedule. Assisting him in that intricate and still somewhat novel task was a bright young scheduler who had been hired away from Western Airlines, Mel Olsen. Kaldahl and Olsen reduced the time between the arrivals of the first and last planes in a bank of incoming flights and cut the elapsed time between the beginning and the end of a departing bank of flights.

American also began to put more and more of its newer Boeing 727 tri-jets on routes served out of D/FW; they carried about the same number of passengers as the old 707s but at much lower costs on short- and medium-haul routes.

"We built the so-called looser hub gradually. There was no big decision to go out and do it as some sort of big project," Kaldahl said. "We were able to add service to some of the Florida cities because under the CAB in those days leading up to deregulation, it was already becoming easier to get new route authorities. But it was still a very limited hub operation when you compare it with the kind of hubs we run today."

Nevertheless, that loose hub served as sort of a proving ground for what would become a key element to American's plan for surviving deregulation.

"We started in late 1977 and early 1978 defining what it was we were going to do when deregulation came. We were still fighting it then, and it didn't happen until October of '78, but we were pretty sure something was going to happen in the way of deregulation; maybe it wouldn't be the full-blown sort of thing that it in fact turned out to be, but it would be some sort or form of deregulation of routes and of pricing," Kaldahl said.

"One of the things we sort of came to a quick conclusion on was that we had to have a strong base of operations where we would be big enough and strong enough to fight off any of the start-up carriers that we expected would be spawned by deregulation. We began rather quickly to see that the hub was the way we were going. If we could get the hub working at D/FW and at Chicago, those were the two big keys. If we could do that, we knew it would be very tough for one of these low-cost carriers to come in and upset the apple cart."

To an extent, the strategy worked. D/FW's location midway between the East and West coasts made it an ideal connecting point for people needing to travel to and from cities on either coast to smaller cities in the central United States. And by bunching its flights together, American was able to solidify its position as the number-2 carrier at D/FW. As a result, American was more than able to cover its higher operating costs at the big new airport.

Still, because of limited availability of new route authorities, a lack of aircraft to serve the hub, and space limitations at its D/FW terminal, American was never able to bring more than sixteen planes into its loose hub at any one time. And more than half of those passengers connecting to American flights outbound from D/FW did so from competing carriers' flights, not from arriving American flights. So, while American was somewhat stronger at D/FW by the end of the 1970s than it was when the airport opened in 1974, it was hardly invincible.

D/FW AIRPORT board Chairman Henry Stuart and Ernie Dean, the airport's executive director, flew to New York in April 1978 to meet with Al Casey, ostensibly about American's need for a new reservations center to replace the one then housed in a converted, dilapidated old hangar at Fort Worth's old, closed Great Southwest

International Airport, just south of D/FW. The old reservations center was one of four significant American employment centers in and around the area. Besides the reservations center and the airport itself, where American had more than one thousand mechanics and other ground workers plus several hundred pilots and flight attendants, the airline also operated its Flight Academy and Learning Center, the training facilities for its pilots and flight attendants, respectively.

Stuart was a well-known and politically influential Dallas businessman who had known Casey when he was president of the Times Mirror Corp. and had negotiated the acquisition of the *Dallas Times Herald* newspaper and what now is known as KDFW-TV, the CBS affiliate in Dallas. Stuart also knew Casey through his friendship with Jimmy Aston, chairman of Republic Bank Corp., Dallas's biggest bank, and a member of both the Times Mirror and American boards. Dean had come to North Texas with Sullivan, his mentor, as second-in-command during the construction of D/FW. Then, when the high-strung Sullivan finally gave in to his persistent heart problems and retired three months after D/FW opened, Dean was named to replace him.

Both Stuart and Dean, like nearly all well-connected business, civic, and political leaders in the Dallas-Forth Worth area, believed it was inevitable that American one day would move its headquarters to north Texas. It made sense. D/FW was at the heart of the airline's route network, and it was the world's best and biggest airport. American already had a substantial operational and corporate presence in the area. Its roots in Texas went all the way back to the late 1920s with Fort Worth–based Southern Air Transport, one of the little carriers that merged to form American and the one that gave the company C. R. Smith. And its two most senior directors, Aston and Amon Carter, Jr.—whose father initially had bankrolled Southern Air Transport and for years had been American's largest individual shareholder—were Texans. Indeed, Stuart and Dean knew that in 1972, under the direction of Chairman George Spater, American had quietly studied relocating to either Dallas or Fort Worth but the steady stream of economic and other problems that eventually forced Spater to resign nixed the deal.

Whenever they saw Casey, both men made it a point to ask him jokingly when he was going to move American's headquarters home to Texas. Casey, who never gave a serious answer to a question he didn't want to discuss, always answered with mock incredulity, claiming that he didn't have the slightest idea what they were talking about and that American would never think of leaving New York City.

But when Dean teasingly asked Casey that same question during his and Stuart's meeting with the airline chairman in April 1978, Casey surprised his guests. Instead of his stock reply, Casey asked what the airport, and the cities that owned it, might offer American to lure it there.

"American had to move," Casey explained years later. "We were out of money. We were out of everything. Everything was going wrong. Deregulation was just hitting us. We moved out in '79, but the decision was made a year and a half before we had to move. That was a time when everything was just going wrong for us and we knew we had to make some drastic changes."

Stuart and Dean were floored. But by the time they returned to Texas, they had the basic structure of a deal in place. American would move its headquarters to D/FW if the airport would build it both a new headquarters and a reservations center, financed with tax-free airport bonds, then lease the facilities to American at a sufficient rate to pay off the bonds.

A month later Dean delivered a formal proposal to American. D/FW offered to expand its boundaries south to include American's existing Flight Academy and Learning Center facilities—then owned by the city of Fort Worth and leased to the airline—and sufficient other land to build a new headquarters building and reservations office. In effect, American would get not only a new headquarters but a whole corporate campus. And because it would be on airport land and eligible for tax-free bond financing, the airline would be able to save millions—initially estimated at $200 million—on rent over the life of a forty year lease compared with what it was paying for expensive office space in midtown Manhattan. In addition, because of D/FW's central U.S. location, corporate staff members could fly to either coast for meetings and be back the same day. By the same token, field managers could come in for meetings and be back home the same night. All of that would save the company a small fortune in travel costs and improved productivity over the years.

IN JUNE Casey approached his board with the idea and got approval to launch a study of the economics of making such a move. He assigned Tom Plaskett, who by then had been promoted to senior VP for finance and CFO, to head up the study.

"He told me I was to do the best economic analysis I knew how to do as to whether it made sense, whether the numbers made sense to relocate the corporate headquarters," Plaskett said. "He told me just to concentrate on the numbers part of it. He said 'I will take care of the subjective and the political part, and I'll write that part of the study myself.'

"Now, Crandall and I had had several—in fact, numerous—discussions prior to getting to this point where it was going to be an official examination. Intuitively we both felt that it made sense to move the headquarters down here, given the direction where things seemed to be going and the growth of the company. But my job was to bring Al and the board the best economic analysis I knew how to do."

While American also toyed with the notion of relocating the headquarters in Chicago, St. Louis, and Atlanta, D/FW was the only site to get serious consideration. Chicago, where American had had its headquarters in the 1930s, was a major point of operations for the airline, but it also was United's home. Atlanta was a great city with a wonderful climate and life-style, but American had only a small presence there and it wasn't in the middle of the airline's route network. Besides, Delta was based in Atlanta. St. Louis was perfectly situated geographically, almost in the center of the country. But St. Louis, where American had a relatively small presence, was bracketed by two major markets for American, Chicago to the north and D/FW to the south.

"I think Chicago probably was the only other place that was seriously considered," Plaskett said. "But the fact that United was already there was a major negative. I think there may be something in Al's subjective paper, as I remember it, that asked the rhetorical question, do you want to be one of two big fish in a great big town or do you want to be a single big fish in a big town?

"Meanwhile, D/FW was a big operation. The growth was coming here. The new airport was open. It was obvious we were going to expand here. We had the training centers here. It just had a lot of the right 'feel' from a corporate perspective," he said.

But, while United's presence in Chicago was a major negative, Plaskett said far less was made of Braniff's stake in Dallas. United, of course, was the largest airline in the nation and American's biggest rival. It may have been a somewhat sluggish and sleepy competitor, but American was not eager to pick on the 900-pound gorilla. Braniff, on the other hand, was smaller and not well regarded, and not only because it had been mostly a regional airline until the mid-1970s. Few people in the industry respected Braniff's management under the flashy, domineering Harding Lawrence. A close examination of its finances showed Braniff to be running on one of the most heavily burdened balance sheets in the industry. And Braniff's reputation for poor customer service and management indifference made it an easy target for competitors.

ONCE PLASKETT and his team of analysts began doing their research, it didn't take long for word to leak out. Some of American's employees had to be informed about bits and pieces of what was going on in order to provide information that was needed. As a result, some were able to piece together the big picture. Also, airport, city, and chamber of commerce officials and upper-echelon real estate executives in the Dallas–Fort Worth area had to be made aware of American's study in order to develop proposals relating to such things as helping employees buy houses. But, as is usually the case, as the circle of people involved in the project grew, so did the rumors.

On August 2, the *Fort Worth Star-Telegram,* picking up on a report in American's own internal newspaper, the *Flagship News,* broke the news publicly that American was considering the move. Bob Baker, who a few months earlier had left his position on Bob Crandall's marketing staff to run American's D/FW operations, told the newspaper that it was "purely conjecture as to where the headquarters would be located, whether it would be Fort Worth or Dallas. It's a little early to comment as to whether we'll move at all."

Baker wasn't lying—precisely. The final decision to move had not been made. But Baker had good reason to believe that it was going to happen. As vice president in charge of American's southern division, he had been acting as liaison between the executives from headquarters studying the possible move and the handful of Texans trying to woo American. He arranged places for his out-of-town colleagues to meet with the locals. He supplied detailed information to the headquarters staff needed for its study. And he did his best to keep American's employees at D/FW from becoming too suspicious about all the high-level executives shuttling back and forth to New York that summer. Baker also was intimately aware of how American was planning to greatly increase its emphasis on and expand operations at D/FW. While the plans were far from complete, Baker knew management had already determined that the airline's success or failure in the future, to a large degree, would be determined by how well it executed its plans to grow at D/FW. Naturally, Baker did not share that knowledge with D/FW or city officials.

Still, as a veteran airport executive, Ernie Dean undoubtedly knew that American was going to increase the scope of its D/FW operations under deregulation. Also, members of the D/FW Airport Board, the two city councils, and the leading business leaders in Fort Worth and Dallas had a pretty good layman's understanding of the commercial airline business. Clearly they hoped that American would increase its operations at D/FW. But none of them, not even Dean, could have even conceived of what American already was planning in terms of expanding D/FW.

On August 3, the day after the *Star-Telegram*'s story appeared, Casey met at the Fairmount Hotel in Dallas with Mayor Robert Folsom. Later that day he met at the Century II Club atop the Fort Worth National Bank building with Fort Worth Mayor Hugh Parmer, the Fort Worth members of the airport board, and American board member Amon Carter, Jr., who still retained the title of publisher of the *Star-Telegram* even though he'd recently sold the centerpiece of the vast kingdom his father had built to Capital Cities, Inc. At those meetings, Casey informed the local parties that American almost certainly would be moving to the area. Only some major, unforeseen obstacle could derail the plan.

New York City Mayor Ed Koch tried hard to create just such an obstacle. He, his deputy mayor, Peter J. Solomon, and several other city officials met with Casey a few days later to find out if the reports they were hearing were true. Koch was particularly upset by the news. He felt personally betrayed by Casey, whom he had appointed to the city's Emergency Financial Control Board and Business Marketing Corporation. The former had engineered the city's recovery from near financial collapse. The latter was formed to encourage businesses currently in New York to stay put and grow and to entice other businesses to move to the city. Still, Koch tried to approach the problem as a business deal. He told Casey that New York would develop a counteroffer.

A few days later Koch and his party, this time including members of New York's congressional delegation, met with Casey and promised to match whatever was in the D/FW offer. They also offered American space in its choice of either the World Trade Center or a prime office building in midtown Manhattan, at rental rates comparable to whatever it would have to pay in Texas.

That's when Casey played his trump card. He told the group that he personally loved living in vibrant New York City, center of the financial world and overflowing with cultural delights.

But Casey spoke bluntly to the New Yorkers. Not only would American enjoy financial savings by relocating to Texas, the Texans would treat American like a trophy corporation and not just one of many big companies. More important, Casey told the New Yorkers that he had been impressed by the political muscle demonstrated by the Texas congressional delegation, especially when compared with the New York delegation's impotence in a recent international air-route authority case that had pitted them against Texas's team in Washington.

In late 1977, the CAB ruled that a new route between D/FW and London should go to Pan American even though the other applicant, Braniff, was based at D/FW and had much greater ability to "feed" a flight to London with passengers from around the Southwest and Great Plains regions. Pan Am had no such feeder network at D/FW. Thus the CAB's decision essentially meant that the new D/FW–London service would succeed or fail based almost solely on the strength of demand for travel between the Dallas-Fort Worth area and London. Infuriated by the decision, the political leaders in Texas went to work to overturn it. House Majority Leader Jim Wright, a Fort Worth Democrat, Senators John Tower, a Republican, and Democrat Lloyd Bentsen, and a host of other influential Texans in Congress were able to convince President Jimmy Carter to use his rarely exercised authority to overturn a CAB recommendation. When Carter awarded the route to Braniff, there was little more than a whimper heard from Pan Am's home state delegation from New York.

Casey told the New York delegation that American needed the kind of support from its representatives in Congress that Braniff had enjoyed from the Texas delegation. Such support was especially important, Casey said, because deregulation was threatening every airline's future.

Koch, obviously concerned about the damage being done to his own political future by New York's continuing fiscal problems, came unhinged. He accused Casey and American of civic treason and tried to intimidate the airline chief into staying put.

Dumb move.

While Casey hides the more tenacious, bulldoglike aspects of his personality behind his jovial exterior, once he's certain what he's doing is right, no one—not even Bob Crandall—can persuade him otherwise. Thus he was hardly the type to buckle under to Ed Koch's personal reproaches. The meeting ended with the New York City delegation all but being run out of Casey's office.

AMERICAN DELAYED announcing its move until after its November 15 board meeting, which was after New York's statewide elections that year, so that the move would not become a major campaign issue. But during that delay, the whole deal almost unraveled.

In the late 1970s Dallas insurance magnate Ben Carpenter was involved in one of the most unusual and adventurous real estate developments in the nation. Through his Southland Development Corporation, Carpenter was turning his sprawling ranch into a giant planned business and residential community called Las Colinas. Located entirely within the city of Irving, D/FW Airport's neighbor to the east, Las Colinas featured the "urban center," essentially a brand-new downtown area featuring a dozen or so high-rise office towers and hotels laid out along a series of canals and small lakes. Ultimately, Las Colinas would have more than half as much office space as was available in downtown Dallas. It also featured expensive neighborhoods, the kind airline executives would want to live in. Indeed, a number of American executives, including Plaskett, eventually bought homes along the fairways of the championship golf course at the Las Colinas Sports Club.

Carpenter was approached initially about providing American some space for a temporary headquarters until a new building could be built. But he came back with an attractive proposal to locate American's headquarters in the urban center permanently. In an uncharacteristic show of unity, Dallas and Fort Worth city officials stood together against Irving, which had always been something of a complainer about and less than a good neighbor of the big airport. Fort Worth officials said that if American went to Las Colinas, they would not support the bond package that was supposed also to fund construction of a new reservations office for the airline. Surprisingly, Dallas officials backed up their old rivals from Cowtown and said they too would not support an American move to Las Colinas. They also told Casey that it would not be in American's best interests to locate in one of the suburban cities if he expected to get either major city's political support on various issues.

Casey decided that the deal as offered by the two big cities and the airport was good enough. After all, it did include about $147 million in tax-free bond financing, and it would put American's headquarters less than five minutes away from its airport terminal. American found inexpensive and functional temporary headquarters space in a pair of office buildings owned by LTV Aerospace in south Grand Prairie, about ten miles south of the airport. The aerospace manufacturer was between major contracts and glad to have a paying tenant.

When American finally did make the announcement, North Texans were elated. Not only were there about 900, well paid, headquarters personnel moving to the area, most locals recognized that having the nation's second-largest airline headquartered locally could influence other businesses to move there or to expand the business presence they already had. American's corporate relocation also signaled that the airline in fact did have big plans for growth at D/FW, which would mean more and better air service and more business opportunities as a result. Landing the airline was considered a milestone event in the history of North Texas economic development, not only because of what American was, but because its move was seen as a harbinger of great things to come.

On the other hand, New Yorkers were outraged. Koch said publicly that Casey "should be ashamed of himself." Various city employees unions urged their members and fellow New Yorkers to boycott American's flights. Someone even suggested that New York's cabbies should not take passengers to or pick up passengers at American's terminals at any of the three area airports.

Casey tried to point out that while 900 people would be moving to Texas, another 8,000 American employees would remain in New York. But that didn't stop the hysteria. New York–based Warner Communications, which annually spent about a third of its $3 million air travel budget on American, announced that it had instructed its employees to use other airlines. Casey said he was disappointed, but added that he'd continue to show Warner Brothers' films on American's flights.

The *New York Daily News* published a survey in which New Yorkers said they believed American's decision had nothing to do with economic considerations but was the product of a "Sunbelt power play."

And New Yorkers weren't the only ones opposed to American's move out of the city. Many of the airline's own employees were against it too. Don Lloyd-Jones strongly opposed the move. Crandall, a Rhode Islander, personally didn't want to leave the Northeast, but he recognized the corporation's economic and cultural need to get out of New York City, for which he had no great love.

Don Carty almost was a casualty of the move to Texas. In 1979 he was given the choice of staying with the Americana Hotels and obtaining a handsome severance package upon their sale, or staking his claim with the airline—in Texas.

"I'd never been to Dallas and I wasn't at all sure I wanted to live there. But the opportunity with the airline was so exciting I couldn't pass it up, so I went even though I was not at all certain I would like living down here," he said.

Because Casey played the whole headquarters move game so close to the vest, not even Lloyd-Jones and Crandall really knew their boss's feelings about the move.

Many people suspected that the move was at least in part a payback to Jimmy Aston, who had played a key role in Casey's moving to American. There is, however, no evidence to support that suspicion, and Casey has denied it on several occasions.

More than a decade later Plaskett steadfastly maintains that the big reason—and, in fact, the only real reason—for the move was economics.

"Al was from Boston, but he loved living in New York. Bob Crandall's from Rhode Island. He wasn't necessarily wedded to New York City, but I think he prefers the East Coast, or at least he did in those days. Most of our corporate office people were either New Yorkers or easterners. There was no great desire among them to leave home and friends and family to go to Texas," he said.

"What really did it for us were the economics and productivity issues. In New York, people invariably would commute an hour or more each way, each day. Generally, at lunchtime people were gone for an hour. So we picked up at least half an hour to forty-five minutes of actual work time daily from every employee who moved to Texas, including the corporate officers. Al lived in New York. But Bob lived in New Jersey. I lived up in Connecticut. Most of the officers lived well outside the city. We were all captives of the train schedules," Plaskett said.

Plaskett said American had anticipated some of the negative backlash that occurred. After all, New York City was just emerging from its darkest hour financially and was still suffering from its negative image as a dirty, crime-infested city in decline. The city and its residents had something of a bruised civic ego, to which American's decision was certain to do further damage. But the personal vilification of Casey was totally uncalled for and unfair, Plaskett said.

"You learn about people as managers and as leaders through example, through what you see. Through that one event, I learned more about and gained a tremendous amount of respect for Al, simply by the way he handled that whole thing; more, I think, than anything else, than any other single event I can remember in my business career with Al," he said.

"Here was Al Casey. He served on the rescue board of New York; very active in the New York social and business communities; lived in New York; an easterner, born in Boston. Strong ties to the East. Still, I didn't know until the night before we were going to the board meeting whether Al Casey really thought it was a good idea and wanted to move to the Dallas-Fort Worth area or not. He never once sent any signals. He never said, even in passing, 'Gee, I really don't want to go,' or 'I really do want to go.' And if you look at the history of corporate moves what you find is that they are skewed to where the CEO wants to live. I must tell you that Al Casey conducted that corporate decision at the highest level of intellectual honesty. He really wanted to do what made sense for the company.

"That confirmed an awful lot of what I had come to know about Al Casey and his approach to business. I learned a lot from that," Plaskett said.

AS THANKSGIVING approached, New York seemed to give in. Koch, though he still was mightily peeved at Casey in private, said publicly that while he didn't like what American was doing, the boycotts were a bad idea because the company would continue to be a major local employer. In fact, the boycotts never really occurred, mainly because American was the dominant carrier in the New York market and had a huge following of businesspeople who weren't about to change their preferences over what clearly was a business decision.

But while American's flights in and out of New York were as packed as usual over the long Thanksgiving holiday weekend, traditionally one of the biggest travel periods of the year, there still was some fight left in the big city.

Prominent Dallas attorney Ray Hutchison, a former Republican state party chairman and D/FW Airport's bond counsel, was the first to stumble across what New York was up to. One of his best sources in Washington circles called one afternoon in early December, two weeks after American had announced its plans to move to Texas. The source told Hutchison that the Internal Revenue Service was about to rule that the $147 million worth of Dallas/Fort Worth Regional Airport bonds that would be sold to finance American's move would not be eligible for tax-free treatment. Without such treatment, the interest rate on those bonds would jump from about 7 percent to 10 percent or higher. And because American's deal called for it to pay rents in the amount necessary to retire the bonds, that three percentage point jump in the interest rate would cost the airline millions of dollars. The economic incentive for moving the headquarters would be lost.

Hutchison felt ill at the prospect of losing American this late in the game. He also knew that the timing of the IRS's impending action was too suspicious for it to be a coincidence. New York had to be behind it, he thought.

Sure enough, New York Deputy Mayor Peter Solomon, speaking at a dinner in early December, responded to a question about American's impending move by saying he wasn't so certain that the airline would be moving after all. He said he had heard that the IRS was going to overrule the bonds sold by D/FW to finance the move. Three days later an attorney who worked for the firm that represented New York City attended a conference in San Francisco. He spread the gossip he'd heard about the IRS's plans. A Dallas attorney attending the same conference overheard the report, cut his stay short, and hopped the next plane home to sound the alarm.

It took some doing, but Hutchison learned that a relatively low-level IRS bureaucrat was going to rule that because such things as airline headquarters and reservations offices don't really have anything to do with airport operations, bonds sold to finance them aren't eligible for tax-free status. The kicker was that the IRS wasn't going to make a new rule to establish that principle, it was going to reinterpret an existing rule and make it retroactive. That action threatened the tax-free bond status on existing facilities at airports throughout the nation, including even New York's three airports. Obviously, the New Yorkers behind the IRS's plan were so angry over American's decision they were willing to hurt themselves in order to stop American from moving out of town.

Besides Hutchison, Casey, and a handful of top American executives, the only people who knew about the threat to the status of D/FW Airport's tax-free bonds were D/FW's Dean, Jim Wright, and

Senators Bentsen and Tower. That small group determined that they had to work fast and quietly. They even kept the Fort Worth and Dallas city councils and the D/FW Airport Board members in the dark, fearing that the more people who knew, the more likely a news leak became. And a news leak would have the same effect as the IRS's proposed new ruling. No investor would buy the bonds if he or she knew they might lose their tax-free status.

Disaster was averted when Hutchison lied outright to a reporter for the *New York Daily News* who called asking about the situation. Hutchison told the reporter he knew nothing about the bonds. Luckily, the reporter believed him. He never called again and didn't write a word about it.

After two weeks of intense lobbying with top appointed agency and elected officials and with officials in Washington, Wright sent a sharply worded letter to Secretary of the Treasury Michael Blumenthal. Wright said his concern went beyond his obvious ties to D/FW. He told Blumenthal that in 1969 he had participated in writing the law that established tax-exempt financing for the nation's airports.

Wright wrote:

> If the Treasury Department feels a genuine need to examine this area of national policy, Mr. Secretary, then the investigation should surely be on a prospective basis, relating only to airport revenue bonds sold after the date of the first public notice of the intention to consider the question, and culminating only after full public hearings and debate—as was done in the case of the original regulations on these matters. I seek your assurance that this will be done.

It worked. On December 28, the IRS issued a notice of its intention to clarify the tax-free status of bonds used to finance facilities at airports that aren't directly related to air service operations. A hearing date was set for March 7. The IRS proposed a rule that would exclude airline headquarters and computer centers and other such facilities from being financed by tax-free bonds. That ruling eventually was made. American's D/FW headquarters was the last such building anywhere in the nation financed by tax-free airport bonds. American's bonds survived the attack because they were sold several days before the IRS issued notice that it was proposing to amend the rules.

*   *   *

AMERICAN'S HEADQUARTERS staff moved from New York to temporary offices in Grand Prairie, Texas, in phases during July and August of 1979. For months the company flew special charter flights between New York and D/FW on Fridays and Sundays to allow employees to go house hunting, to commute to D/FW until they moved their families to Texas or, once the move was completed, to return to New York to attend to personal business, such as closing down or selling a house. For several years after the move, headquarters personnel could be spotted every Friday evening at D/FW, milling around the gate from which the carrier's flights to New York departed, standing by to take any open seats so they could go "home" to visit friends and family.

But gradually, as the 900 or so people who made the move to Texas with their families established roots in Dallas, Fort Worth, Arlington, Richardson, Euless, Irving, Grapevine, Plano, and the dozens of other cities that make up the Metroplex, the demand for standby seating on those Friday afternoon and evening flights to New York trailed off. Today most of those expatriate Yankees root for the Dallas Cowboys and the Texas Rangers. Most of their kids either attend Southwest Conference universities or plan on doing so once they graduate high school. They host parties by the swimming pools in their backyards. They tell Aggie jokes, have picked up a slight twang in their speech, and can be heard saying "ya'll" occasionally. They would never think of buying a car not equipped with air conditioning. Many of them own a pair of cowboy boots, and a few sometimes even wear them to work with their business suits. A few who made the move to Texas are even buried there.

American is at home in Texas now, and so are they.

10

Grounded

WALT LUX released the brakes at 2:56 P.M. CDT, eleven minutes behind schedule. The ground crew forty feet below him began pushing the 379,000 pounds of sheet metal, fuel, bags, and people bound for Los Angeles back from Gate 5 in the K Concourse at Chicago's O'Hare International Airport. That's how American Flight 191 began on May 25, 1979; it was mind-numbingly routine.

Lux, a former Air Force pilot who had been with American twenty-nine years, taxied N110AA, the twelfth DC-10 jumbo jet ever built by McDonnell Douglas Corporation, out to Runway 32R. Six and a half minutes after pushing back off the gate, Lux radioed for takeoff clearance. He moved his big bird out onto the runway, pivoted it awkwardly to the left, and paused to make his final checks. On Lux's command, First Officer James R. Dillard pushed the throttles forward as the captain lifted his feet off the brakes. N110AA lurched forward and, in a matter of seconds, was swallowing up concrete at more than 100 miles per hour. Everyone on board was pressed firmly against his seatback as the jet hurtled down the runway. About 4,000 feet down the 10,600-foot runway, Dillard called out "V-1," meaning the aircraft was going too fast to safely reject the takeoff if something went wrong.

A moment later, about 5,000 feet down the runway, Dillard called out "V-R." Lux pulled back on the yoke, the butterfly-shape steering wheel. N110AA's nose came up and the silver behemoth stepped up into the air.

At that precise moment, there was a loud *thump* from the direction of the plane's left wing and a strange vibration. As all pilots are trained to do, Lux focused his attention on his gauges to discover what was wrong. They told him his No. 1 engine, mounted under the left wing, had stopped working. While that was neither normal nor good, Lux was not overly concerned. He had practiced for just such an eventuality many times during training "flights" in the simulator. He knew the procedure. He pulled the throttles back and brought the aircraft's speed back to V-2, the minimum speed needed to stay in the air—in this case, about 180 mph—and began running through the emergency check list. All evidence suggests that Walt Lux followed perfectly American's FAA-approved procedures for handling the loss of an engine on takeoff.

What Lux did not know, and could not have known, was that the No. 1 engine had not simply shut down. It had fallen completely off the plane just as he had pulled back on the yoke. In the process, the hydraulics lines in the left wing were damaged, rendering all of the movable control surfaces on that wing immobile and useless.

When the airplane decelerated to V-2 speed, the left wing went into a stall; that is, it lost the lift needed to continue flying and, in essence, became a falling object. The V-2 speed had been figured on the assumption that the plane's slats, devices on the leading edge of the wing that extend forward and down to produce more lift, would remain in the extended position. That proved to be a fatal assumption. With the left wing in a stall, and the right wing still flying, the DC-10 rolled hard over on its left side as if it were performing a tight banking maneuver normally done only by fighter jets and stunt planes.

Had that happened at 20,000 or 10,000 or even 5,000 feet, Lux almost certainly could have recovered by pointing the nose down and/or increasing the power in his remaining engines. Either way, the plane would have increased its speed enough to get the left wing out of its stall. But at 600 feet there was nothing he could do. There was no time to react, and not enough altitude to execute such a recovery maneuver even if Lux had had time to react.

American Flight 191 ended a little more than eight minutes after Lux had released the brakes back at Gate 5. N110AA slammed nose-first into the ground at 230 mph about a quarter of a mile northwest of Runway 32R. The 79,000 pounds of jet fuel—kerosene—on board exploded on impact, sending a huge red-and-black fireball hundreds of feet into the air. N110AA disintegrated into millions of pieces. Lux, Dillard, Flight Engineer Alfred F. Udovich, 10 flight attendants, 259 passengers and 2 people on the ground—274 people altogether—all died instantly. Thirty of those aboard were buried together—anonymously—six weeks later in San Pedro, California. Their bodies had been so badly dismembered and burned in the horrific crash that a frustrated team of crack forensic specialists brought in from around the nation could not positively identify them.

At the time it was the worst air crash in U.S. history in terms of human lives lost.

THREE DAYS after the crash, Federal Aviation Administrator Langhorne Bond ordered U.S. airlines to check the engine mount and pylon assemblies on the Nos. 1 and 3 engines—the wing-mounted engines—on all DC-10s in their fleets. The order was issued after investigators discovered that the critical bolt in the pylon—the structure that connects the engine to the wing—that gave way did not show evidence of metal fatigue. Something else, almost certainly some structural problem, caused or allowed that bolt to be ripped right out of the pylon.

That something else, crash investigators were able to figure out, was a ten-inch-long hairline crack in the pylon that had been created two months earlier when American mechanics had used a forklift to mount the engine and pylon to the ill-fated plane's wing as a single unit. That job originally was intended to be done with a crane, not a forklift. And the pylon and engine were supposed to be mounted separately. However, Continental Airlines had discovered that an engine could be changed faster and less expensively by using the forklift method. McDonnell Douglas and the FAA both approved the change in methods. And cost-conscious American was the first airline to copy Continental's "improved" method.

In his initial order, issued at 2 P.M. CDT on May 28, Bond gave the airlines until 2 A.M. the next morning to complete the inspections and make any necessary repairs. Any DC-10 not inspected and, if necessary, repaired by the deadline was to be grounded until those tasks could be accomplished. American, the launch customer on the DC-10 along with United, had twenty-eight DC-10s, each of which seated 264 passengers. Only United, with thirty-seven, had more. But United was just starting to rebuild its flight schedule and its

passenger bookings after a two-month mechanics strike. So, while
Bond's order was a major inconvenience for United, it was not affected nearly so severely as the heavily booked American.

American, like the other seven DC-10 operators in the United
States, complied with Bond's order, which in effect meant the temporary grounding of their biggest revenue producers. Each inspection
took about six hours. Repairs, if necessary, could double that. It took
American more than forty-eight hours to get all of its DC-10s ferried
to its major maintenance stations, inspected, fixed, and put back into
revenue service.

But Bond's edict fanned the flames of the firestorm of controversy
that already had begun to engulf the DC-10 in the wake of the crash.

Almost from the day of its first delivery, the big airplane had been
dogged by suspicions about its structural integrity. And, in fact,
several structural deficiencies had been discovered and resolved long
before Flight 191 crashed at Chicago.

The worst air crash in world aviation history, in which 346 people
died, involved a Turkish Airlines DC-10 that crashed into the French
countryside from a height of 13,000 feet on a flight from Paris to
Istanbul. A poorly designed cargo door blew off the plane in flight.
The resulting rapid decompression, coupled with the fact the plane
was carrying an unusually large number of passengers in an all-coach
configuration, caused the passenger cabin floor to buckle. That, in
turn, ruptured the central lines of the aircraft's hydraulics system,
which is used to manipulate control surfaces such as flaps and ai-
lerons. The crew lost its ability to control the aircraft, which then
went into a fatal spin.

In 1972 another American DC-10 was involved in a chilling but not
fatal incident. A rear cargo door blew off just a few minutes after
takeoff from Detroit's Metropolitan Airport. As in the case of the
Turkish Airlines DC-10, the American plane's cabin floor buckled,
again rupturing most of the central hydraulic lines, which ran just
beneath the cabin floor. By using asymmetrical thrust, the pilots,
Captain Bryce McCormick and First Officer Paige Whitney, were able
to bring the airplane back to Detroit without the rudder or stabilizers
and with very limited elevator control. By varying the amount of
thrust from the two wing engines—reducing power on the left wing
and increasing it on the right to turn slowly left, and vice versa to
turn right—they were able to steer their crippled airplane back to
Detroit and to make a landing approach. Then, as the aircraft moved
over the runway and came down to fifty feet, McCormick turned off

Bob Crandall in 1989, at the very height of his and American's success.

Mel Olsen, responsible for the study that led to the basis for American Airlines' entire hub and spoke system.

Wes Kaldahl, chief architect of the 1980's expansion of American's route network.

Don Carty, widely regarded as the second-best mind in the industry—behind Bob Crandall—and the most likely to succeed Crandall at American's helm.

Bob Baker, second generation American executive, Crandall's top troubleshooter and perhaps his most trusted lieutenant.

An American operations manager at the console on "The Bridge" of American's Systems Operations Control Center in Fort Worth. From here American monitors all 670 of its aircraft worldwide via voice and data communications links.

Top, left: Chairman Al Casey and President Bob Crandall pose for the 1982 annual shareholders report. *Bottom:* Bob Crandall and Boris Panyukov of Aeroflot sign a 1991 agreement calling for American Airlines to sell various management and operations services and technologies to the former Soviet state airline. *Top, right:* SABRE—A collection of IBM mainframe computers that make up the world's largest privately owned computer network. These computers are located in a super secure, high-tech underground facility on the backside of the Tulsa International Airport.

Top: American ordered fifteen 767-300 ERs from Boeing in
1987 on "walkaway" lease terms. *Left:* Four McDonnell
Douglas MD-80s being prepared for delivery to American
at the Douglas Aircraft plant in Long Beach, California.

Top: An exterior shot of the first permanent American Airlines head-quarters in Fort Worth, Texas. *Bottom:* Until Bob Crandall's arrival at American in 1973, the airline used outmoded IBM selectric-style terminals.

the No. 2 engine in the plane's tail and added a bit of power to the Nos. 1 and 3 engines. That caused the DC-10's tail to drop slightly and put it in a perfect "flared" attitude for landing. The airplane's main landing gear under the wings settled gently onto the pavement, followed a few seconds later by the nose gear. The landing was as smooth as if there had been no problem at all. It was a tremendous job of flying that netted McCormick and his crew the Distinguished Service Award, the highest honor given by American to its own employees.

In the wake of Flight 191's crash, newspaper and magazine stories and television news reports dwelled on those and other stories about various problems with the DC-10—most of which were not at all unusual for any commercial aircraft and did not occur with alarming frequency. Though steps had been taken to remedy the two most serious problems with the aircraft—the cargo door locking mechanism had been redesigned and the cabin floor had been reinforced to prevent buckling and a subsequent rupture in the hydraulics system—millions of people quickly came to believe that the DC-10 either was poorly designed or jinxed.

Amid, and perhaps in an overly sensitive reaction to, the public hysteria over the DC-10, Bond dealt a second, far more devastating blow to American and every other DC-10 operator. On June 6, against the advice of safety experts from the airlines and McDonnell Douglas, several airline's CEOs, and even some technical experts from the FAA and the National Transportation Safety Board, Bond suspended the DC-10's design certificate. Because airlines cannot fly planes that are not certified by the FAA, the order effectively grounded 12 percent of the nation's commercial jet fleet, aircraft that carried, on average, more than 70,000 passengers a day. Flight schedules were thrown into total disarray, and thousands of passengers were inconvenienced, especially in the first few days after the order.

The airlines protested vehemently. They argued that the cause of the Chicago crash was known; therefore, all that was needed was a frequent and rigorous inspection and replacement program until McDonnell Douglas engineers could come up with a permanent fix for the pylon bolt problem. But for thirty-seven days Bond—who prior to the Flight 191 crash had been heavily criticized by aviation safety and consumer protection organizations for being the airlines' lackey and for being too soft on enforcement of the FAA's safety rules—arched his political neck and refused to give in. Finally, on July 13, he restored the DC-10's design certificate and issued an order mandating frequent inspection of the pylons and engine mounting assemblies until a better solution was available.

Bond's second grounding of the DC-10 proved nothing. Everything that was to be known about what caused the crash on May 25 was known before the grounding order was issued. True, problems with the pylons and engine mount assemblies were found on nearly half of the 135 DC-10s in the U.S. commercial fleet during the thirty-seven-day grounding. But they would have been discovered and repaired under the same kind of frequent inspection and repair mandate Bond eventually put in place anyway. If the grounding hadn't taken place, nearly 3 million passengers would not have been displaced. Also, the nation's airlines, which already were sliding downhill toward the economic bloodbath that everyone expected to come from deregulation, would not have been damaged financially so unnecessarily.

Still, as a presidential appointee faced with rapidly escalating public concern regarding the safety of the DC-10, Bond's actions were both inevitable and predictable. The Airline Deregulation Act had been passed the preceding year in part because the FAA, under pro-deregulation President Jimmy Carter, had assured Congress that economic deregulation would not cause it to back off one iota from its responsibility to enforce aviation safety regulations. Therefore, Bond simply had to look as if he were doing something to address what was perceived to be the biggest airline safety issue in nearly two decades.

While every carrier that flew DC-10s was damaged by the lengthy grounding, American was hurt the most. Its twenty-eight DC-10s represented 11 percent of its total fleet. Moreover, because of their large seating capacity and because they were deployed on its most heavily traveled and profitable routes, American's DC-10s generated nearly a quarter of its total revenues. The airline diverted some of its smaller narrow-body planes to the routes normally served by its DC-10s. Yet, not only did the narrow-bodies fall way short of making up for the lost capacity of the DC-10s, American also lost revenue on the routes from which those smaller planes were diverted.

American's management, at the urging of several board members who feared the plane's reputation had been so badly damaged that passengers would avoid airlines that operated DC-10s, briefly considered trying to sell the big jumbos. But the idea quickly was rejected as one born out of panic. Despite all the bad publicity it had received, the 264-seat DC-10 was still the right plane for American. Besides its routes to the Caribbean and Mexico, American did not operate any international flights that could support the use of the larger Boeing 747. And, in fact, there was growing evidence that carriers that operated 747s were losing money because the aircraft was simply too big and cost too much to operate on all but a few very heavily traveled routes.

If the 747 was too big and the DC-10 too controversial, then the only jumbo jet left was the Lockheed L-1011. But the Lockheed plane, which was almost identical to the DC-10 in size and operating characteristics, had been hurt by its reliance on Rolls-Royce engines that fell short of the manufacturer's original fuel efficiency standards. In addition, whether American could have acquired the L-1011 in 1979 is doubtful. The financially beleaguered Lockheed had lost its shirt on the L-1011 program and was slowing its production in expectation of getting out of the commercial transport business altogether.

In any case, American simply could not have afforded to sell its DC-10 fleet. Had the decision been made to dump all of its DC-10s on the used aircraft market at once, as a couple of American's board members advocated, the company would have lost a fortune in the process. As one of the largest, most technically sophisticated airlines in the world, American, like United, was a trendsetter. Smaller airlines would have been very reluctant to acquire a plane shunned by a trendsetter, and would have done so only at bargain basement prices.

A CURSORY look at the year 1979 likely would lead to the conclusion that it was a pretty good year for American Airlines.

The company moved out of expensive New York City to the friendlier, less expensive prairie of North Texas and the Dallas-Fort Worth Metroplex. United Airlines, American's biggest rival, virtually was shut down for fifty-eight days by a mechanics strike in the spring, then spent the summer trying to rebuild its system. American's capacity, measured in available seat miles, rose a reasonably healthy 8.8 percent with the addition of nine new airplanes. And actual passenger traffic, measured in revenue passenger miles flown, jumped a whopping 15.1 percent.

But such an assessment would be dead wrong. The wheels didn't exactly come off that year for American in 1979. But the lug nuts did. And the wheels started wobbling.

The year 1979 was the first full year in which the U.S. airline industry was deregulated. And, just as Al Casey and company had feared and predicted, the industry's self-destructive tendencies were laid bare. The regulated environment had hidden those tendencies for a long time. While regulation prevented carriers from expanding in any market they wished, it also gave carriers many markets where they were protected from interlopers who, horror of horrors, might try to reduce fares. Unfortunately, the sense of security fostered by that kind of regulation also nurtured a profound laxness in the area of cost controls.

Prior to deregulation, airline managements were notorious for their free-spending ways. Airline employees, from pilots to bag handlers, were among the best-paid workers in the world, even though most of them—except for pilots and certified aircraft mechanics—had no special skills that they could transfer to other businesses and receive anything close to their airline pay. Regulated carriers' managements could afford to spend a lot of money on everything from their employees and equipment to lavish corporate offices because they knew that whatever trouble they got their carriers into, the Civil Aeronautics Board could be counted on to get them out. To prevent airlines from disemboweling themselves with the sword of stupidity, the CAB invariably allowed fare increases that otherwise would not have been necessary. Or it granted new routes to carriers that desperately needed additional sources of revenue to cover the huge debts run up by their undisciplined managements.

The CAB continued to exist for five years after the deregulation act was passed, but it had diminished responsibilities. The original idea was to phase in aspects of deregulation over that five-year period. But the reality was that from the moment the law went into effect, any airline could begin charging whatever fare prices it wanted on virtually any domestic route it wanted to serve. If two dozen carriers wanted to serve the very same route ten times a day and charge fares 50 percent lower than what had been the standard fare prior to deregulation, the CAB could not stop them. The government had gotten out of the business of saving airlines from themselves.

TWA was among the first airlines to exercise two of the new rights it got with deregulation: the right to set its own prices without government intervention and the right to display publicly just how inept and stupid its management really was. In February 1979, only three months into the deregulated era, TWA launched a winter ticket sale that featured deep discounts and a "Kids Fly Free" feature.

American was not opposed to discount ticketing. Indeed, even before deregulation American had devised one of the first, and perhaps the most successful and widely imitated, discount fare programs in industry history. American's Super Saver program, which was introduced in some markets in 1977 and expanded systemwide in early 1978, was a success because it stimulated discretionary air travel and did not cause an erosion in the full-coach-fare traffic. Thus the Super Saver discount program generated more revenue for American than it would have received had Super Saver fares not been available.

But TWA's 1979 winter sale fares strayed dangerously away from the principles that had made the Super Saver fares so successful. The TWA winter sale fares had far fewer restrictions on their use and offered substantially larger percentage discounts than had the original Super Saver fares. As a result, businesspeople who willingly would have paid, say, $800 for a round-trip ticket often were able to buy a ticket for less than half that price. Because American, like nearly every major airline, was forced to match TWA's winter sale fares to keep from losing market share and customer loyalty, it lost money on the offer right along with the misguided TWA.

The year 1979 would have been bad enough had TWA's fare sale been the only irrational and/or drastic pricing action of the year. But it was not. United, crippled by a two-month strike, had to take drastic action to attract passengers back to its flights once its mechanics' strike ended. So it took the drastic but not wholly irrational step of printing up thousands of coupons for 50 percent off the published fare. The coupons were distributed to United's best customers—business travelers—travel agents, and the general public in United's most important markets. Again, American had to match the fares or watch United steal market share.

Then there was the introduction of the first $108 fare for one-way, coast-to-coast travel by start-up carriers or older, smaller carriers trying to horn in on the glamorous transcontinental routes after deregulation. The price bore no relation whatsoever to the true cost of flying an airplane from the East Coast to the West Coast. Rather it was selected because some "marketing genius" believed that $108 was a figure that both would grab people's attention instantly and make them want to fly and would stick in their minds when it came time to buy their tickets.

In the airline industry, it's said that fare prices in any market will go only as high as the weakest—or, in some cases, the dumbest or most suicidal—participant in that market will allow them to go. As the single biggest player in the transcontinental markets, American was far more exposed to the irrational pricing decisions of financially ill or poorly managed traditional airlines and, a bit later, to the low-fare schemes of low-cost airlines spawned by deregulation. Thus American had no choice but to match the $108 one-way fare offers, at least to some degree.

Then, as a result of the FAA's decision to ground the nation's fleet of DC-10s following the crash of American Flight 191 in Chicago, American's intricately constructed schedule had to be torn apart. Basically, American missed out on half of the peak summer travel season, a key period when airlines traditionally make all or nearly all of any annual profits they report.

Mother nature was equally unkind. The first quarter of 1979 featured some of the worst winter weather on record in nearly every region of the nation. The first quarter typically is a difficult one for airlines, even in years with mild winters. But in 1979, nationwide ice and snowstorms forced thousands of flight cancellations. The costs associated with such severely disrupted operations can be staggering. And they certainly were in 1979.

On top of all that, fuel prices rose steadily throughout 1979. While automobile owners complained about gasoline prices that approached $2 a gallon in some areas, American saw its kerosene bill jump 55.7 percent in one year, to $801.5 million, even though it consumed only 5 percent more fuel in 1979 than it did in 1978.

That huge increase was the biggest factor in American's 24.1 percent increase in operating costs in 1979. Strong demand, especially during the United strike in April and May, and restricted capacity during half the summer while the DC-10s were out of commission pushed American's load factor—the average percentage of seats filled by paying passengers—to a company record of 67.4 percent. But the huge increase in operating costs drove the break-even load factor—the average percentage of seats the airline needed to fill to cover its operating costs—to a record high of 67.3 percent.

Another big factor in American's staggering increase in operating expenses was its inability to control labor costs. The airline's wages, salaries, and benefits costs jumped 15.2 percent that year, even though its total employment rose just 5 percent. Overall wages, salaries, and employee benefits represented a whopping 38.4 percent of American's 1979 operating expenses. As a regulated enterprise, American, like other airlines, always had been able to pass its outrageously high labor costs through to the passenger in the form of ever higher fares. But in the newly deregulated airline industry,

American could not pass its rising labor costs on; in fact, it had to cut fares in the face of new, low fare competition.

Moreover, the national economy, buffeted by almost runaway inflation and rapidly rising interest rates, began falling into a recession in the latter half of 1979. Airlines stocks are highly sensitive to national economic cycles. Indeed, many analysts and economists consider airline performance to be a leading indicator of an approaching shift in the nation's economy. That's because as the economy turns down, one of the first things people and businesses tend to cut back on is travel. And once a recession hits bottom and businesses complete the task of getting their costs under control, they usually want to capitalize on their new, lower unit costs by increasing sales. That often means they will put their people back on the road again.

Luckily for American, business travel remained surprisingly strong even as the national economy slowed down in the fall of 1979. That year fifty-three out of every one hundred people who flew on American's flights traveled on business. American's longtime status as the airline most preferred by business travelers proved to be a valuable asset. No competitors did as well in the business travel category that year.

Nevertheless, had the International Association of Machinists— representing United's mechanics—not gone out on a two-month strike, American would have reported only a minuscule profit, or maybe even a loss, in 1979. As it was, the company reported net annual earnings of just $87.4 million, down 34.9 percent from the record $134.4 million in 1978. American earned $95.3 million in the second quarter, of which $25.1 million came from the insurance payoff on the DC-10 lost in the Chicago crash. Without that extraordinary gain from the insurance payoff, and without the big second quarter profits earned at United's expense, American's 1979 would have been absolutely abysmal.

As it was, American was able to disguise most of its problems and hide the negative trends that began in 1979. Other than the very well known problem with high fuel prices, the average traveler, the average employee, and the average investor probably didn't suspect a thing was wrong.

Investment analysts and savvy investors, on the other hand, saw the problems coming. Many of them bailed out of American's stock, which began 1979 at $14.75 a share, but dropped to $9.13 a share in the fourth quarter. The company's preferred stock also fell, from $20.88 a share to just $16 a share during the year.

But Wall Street's concern about American's future was mild compared with that of Al Casey, Bob Crandall, Don Lloyd-Jones, Gene Overbeck, Tom Plaskett, and the rest of Crandall's kiddie corps of young, hotshot MBAs. They recognized how bad things already were and understood, probably better than anyone else in or out of the airline industry, just how bad things were going to get unless American took drastic action to save itself. They worked frantically, in some cases literally day and night, throughout 1979 to come up with a survival plan for what they all believed would be American's biggest test ever: the continuing transition to a deregulated environment, which looked like it would take place amidst a deep recession.

11

They're Likely to Do Anything

BOB CRANDALL became president of American Airlines on July 16, 1980, an accomplishment not altogether unlike being named captain of the *Titanic* shortly prior to its maiden voyage. Unlike the *Titanic*'s skipper, however, Crandall fully recognized his vessel's vulnerability and therefore was much more concerned about the dangers he expected to encounter on his shakedown cruise. The airline Crandall took command of already was sailing through icy financial waters, and he admittedly had no idea how he would get it through. Yet that did not lessen his determination to succeed.

While American suffered a lot of damage in the second half of 1979, it did report a profit that year of $87.4 million. But the wheels came off in 1980. The disappointing profit in 1979 turned into a record loss of $75.8 million, virtually all of which was sustained in the first six months. The negative numbers drove the folks at headquarters straight up the wall. During that time, those $108 coast-to-coast fares introduced in 1979 dropped to $99, and the number of competitors flying the transcontinental routes, particularly New York to California, jumped from three to seven.

Fuel costs shot through the roof in 1980. At American they went up $313 million, or 39 percent, compared with 1979—despite the fact that its fuel consumption rose by just 9.2 percent. To make matters worse, American's passenger traffic dropped 15.5 percent, forcing the company to reduce its capacity 5.8 percent in the latter half of the year. At the same time, American's labor costs rose nearly 10 percent from the previous year despite its decision to lay off more than 10 percent of its workers in the second half of 1980.

The first two years of deregulation were nightmarish for American. Casey and Crandall had been right when they predicted massive upheaval and financial devastation in the industry.

"I think if you look back at our deregulation argument," Crandall said a decade later, "you can fairly say that we were technically correct and philosophically incorrect. What we said was premised on what proved to be an accurate forecast of what would happen in the industry, and the presumption that we would do poorly. So, as I said, I think we were technically correct.

"But we were philosophically incorrect because it also is clear now that the free market works better than a government-regulated market."

Of course, Crandall and company took no comfort in being able to point to Congress, which had passed the Airline Deregulation Act of 1978, and say "We told you so." Indeed, though Crandall's emotional, profanity-filled outbursts were more than a common occurrence around American's offices even in the best of times, his fits of rage became even more frequent and venomous in 1980. Knowing some of the reasons why things were going so wrong did nothing to ease Crandall's extreme frustration. In fact, knowing why, yet being unable to do anything to change the situation immediately only compounded it.

As Casey and Crandall had predicted, American and other traditional, old-line carriers were ill prepared to make the transition to deregulation. Also, start-up carriers or financially nimble small airlines with the ability to grow at low costs could inflict serious damage on the industry's old battleships.

Still, even though American had done a good job of predicting all the bad things that would come from deregulation, it, like the other members of the industry's establishment, actually was slow to respond to the new economic environment.

"I think it is fair, probably, to say that the first year and a half or so [after deregulation] we were to some extent stuck in neutral," Crandall said. "We simply didn't know what would happen in the free market."

However, Crandall and his young turks were determined to figure out the answer to that question before anyone else in the industry.

"The airline had opposed [deregulation] to the best of our ability until it happened. Then, when it did happen, we all said, 'Okay, it's happened. Let's go to work thinking about how we can do as well as possible in this new environment,' " he said.

Crandall assigned one of his more analytical young lions, Don Carty, to the task of thinking almost full time. After spending a year helping Jim O'Neill put a new set of management controls on the SABRE business, Carty was named vice president of product improvement. In that position he served more or less as Crandall's defensive coordinator, monitoring more than two hundred different projects—some small, some huge—designed to reduce the airline's costs and generate profits. Because it was purely a management task force kind of assignment, Carty had no direct managerial responsibilities and, thus, no real authority to implement any of those projects. But everyone recognized that, in effect, Carty was Crandall's personal representative and was acting on the boss's authority.

Carty quickly moved on to become American's controller, managing all of the internal accounting functions. In that position he still had primary responsibility for controlling costs and reported directly to Crandall.

In both jobs Carty also participated in many of the deep, theoretical discussions aimed at finding a way to remake the airline into one capable of competing in the free market. While American made great progress in 1980 and thereafter in reducing its costs, those projects simply could not solve its basic problem: costs that were out of line with the new economic reality and its limited revenue-producing ability.

"While it's fair to say that in historical terms it looked like we turned things around pretty quickly, if you were there and felt it at the time, I see us as having done nothing to sort of turn it around," Carty said. "It took a year to a year and a half before we started to move. I think it was late 1980 before we had articulated the pieces, the first pieces of the strategy that we wanted to put into place [after deregulation].

"I think there's two reasons for that. One, I think there tends to be a letdown when you work so hard on something and it fails. We worked so hard at trying to derail deregulation; after Congress passed it anyway and the president [Jimmy Carter] approved it, we sort of said 'Those jerks! Now they're going to get what they wrought!' And there was sort of a letdown. Now that letdown in our case was sort of compounded by the fact that we were in the middle of a major corporate relocation and management's attention was sort of focusing on the implications of that move," he said.

But by late 1980, after the move to the company's temporary headquarters was accomplished, American's management was able to shift its focus back to finding some way to transform the airline into a company capable not only of surviving but of thriving under the new rules. In fact, the corporate move actually was an important factor in developing some of the major changes the airline implemented in the early and mid-1980s. It certainly helped foster a new mind-set among the company's 40,000 workers.

By moving the corporate flag from New York to Texas, Carty said, "We changed the whole culture of the company to a culture more willing to embrace change. We got to see the country differently, from a new perspective. I'm not sure we'd have seen it as clearly if we had been stuck in midtown Manhattan."

Crandall agreed. "Yeah, I guess it sort of sent the message that if we were willing to move the headquarters out of New York, we were serious about making whatever changes we thought were necessary for this company to survive.

"That certainly was not one of our reasons for moving the headquarters to Texas. But we did create an environment that was more open to change. Our people had to be thinking 'If they'll move the headquarters out of New York, they're likely to do anything.' And we sort of institutionalized a willingness to accept change and even an expectation that things should change and would change."

WHEN CRANDALL was named president, Mel Olsen, the airline's vice president of scheduling and route planning, and the rest of the marketing department got a new boss too. Tom Plaskett had spent a couple of years in marketing on Crandall's staff before being promoted to senior VP of finance and chief financial officer. And because Plaskett was one of Casey's "four guys," Olsen assumed he was up-to-date on what Wes Kaldahl's planning and scheduling unit were working on.

But you know what they say about assuming.

"Tom called me into his office one day and his basic question was 'Should we depeak D/FW?' His premise was that if we spread out our departures and arrivals, we could lower our manpower and our costs at D/FW," Olsen said.

"Well, I about fell out of my chair to realize that any executive in this company could possibly think that that would be a smart thing to do!"

Unbeknownst to Plaskett, Olsen had been trying to find a way to shoehorn even more flights into American's limited terminal space at D/FW. Plaskett's question, therefore, betrayed not only his newcomer's ignorance of what was going on in his own department but also his mistaken belief—which no doubt grew out of Crandall's extreme emphasis on cost cutting—that American could improve its financial performance by managing its costs better. Cost cutting was, in fact, part of the answer. But in the airline business, as in so many other pursuits, you can't save your way to prosperity. Thus Olsen and his small group of planners were working on ideas that they hoped would cause American's revenues to grow at a much faster rate than its costs.

"It never dawned on me that people higher up in the organization hadn't thought of what we in planning had been thinking about for quite a while. But at that point I realized that the higher-ups were not so much experts in their various fields but managers who encouraged and depended upon their staffs to come up with the good ideas we needed to solve our problems," Olsen said.

Olsen already had a reputation for having one of the sharpest minds in the industry in planning and scheduling. He could have confronted Plaskett then and there to show his new boss just how far off base he really was. But Olsen didn't know Plaskett well enough to do that immediately. And besides, such an action would have been out of character for the mild-mannered, bespectacled scheduling guru. That's not to say he was afraid of his superiors, or weak-willed. He just had a more clever way of making his point, a way that would not insult his boss or endanger their working relationship.

He used facts and logic.

"Tom asked me to do a study about the possibility of depeaking D/FW, so I went to work on a presentation entitled 'Should we depeak D/FW?' Of course, the answer I gave was 'No, we shouldn't.' I put together a graph that showed how the number of passengers grew geometrically when you added flights to the peak [of the connecting hub operations at D/FW] and another graph that showed how our labor staffing went up at a much more moderate rate," Olsen said.

There may never have been a more memorable series of charts developed by anyone in American's history than those Olsen showed Plaskett in the fall of 1980. For months Olsen displayed his charts to executives throughout the company. Every time he did, he would see the lights turn on. A decade later, many of those present at one of those meetings point to Olsen's presentations as their personal "Ah-ha" moments, the specific point when they first came to understand what they now reverently call "the power of the hub."

Through those charts Olsen was able to demonstrate the tremendous revenue and profit potential that would accrue to American if it were to drastically increase the size and scope of its hub and spoke network centered on D/FW. Within the company, even the most ardent opponents of the idea of cramming more flights into limited airport gates had to admit that Olsen's ideas made good sense.

Explaining the information contained in Olsen's chart can be tedious. But it is worth the effort in order to understand the fundamental operating principle of the U.S. airline industry today and how American pioneered it.

American's operations at D/FW already were set up to operate in a "loose" hub-and-spoke fashion. Five or six times a day, the airline would schedule sixteen planes to arrive at D/FW within thirty minutes of each other. Connecting passengers would change planes, then those flights would all depart around the same time. During the rest of the day, there was very little activity at the terminal. For that reason, American had to staff the terminal to handle peak demands and suffer the costs of inefficiencies during the slow periods.

Olsen proposed filling in the slow time between those peaks of activity with more peaks. Doing that would not reduce labor costs; in fact, total labor costs would probably increase slightly. But the workers would be far more productive because in essence there would be no slow time between the peaks. Labor unit costs—that is, how much the airline spends on labor per available passenger seat mile—actually would go down. If unit costs go down and revenue costs go up, profits should improve.

Everyone agreed that made sense. But nearly everyone in the industry just assumed that there wasn't enough demand for travel to fill that many more flights. Olsen thought otherwise. He believed that by operating more flights more efficiently, American could keep both its unit costs and fares go down to reasonable levels. The greater availability of low fares would lead to some increased demand. And, most important, by offering a superior schedule of flights to the hub airport and, ultimately, to the travelers' destinations, American could shift passenger traffic in the outlying, or spoke, cities away from other carriers and to its own flights. On top of that, not only could

American expect to take market share away from Braniff, D/FW's largest carrier in those days, and other carriers there, it could also expect to take market share away from carriers serving points on either side of D/FW with connections through some other city.

This belief was based in the knowledge that travelers, especially business travelers, value frequency of flights above all else. The businessperson in, say Lubbock, Texas, may not decide to go to Chicago until midday. But few people need to travel between Lubbock and Chicago on any given day, so the Lubbock traveler has to make a stop at some major airport, most likely D/FW, to make connections with a flight to Chicago. Historically, travelers from Lubbock or similar cities had the choice of a morning or a late-afternoon flight. If they were really lucky, a midday flight was also offered. Then, when they arrived at D/FW or some other major airport, they could expect a layover ranging anywhere from one to four hours before catching a flight to Chicago. And before deregulation the chances were better than fifty-fifty that such travelers would not only have to change planes, they would have to change airlines, which required leaving the secure terminal area, transferring by train, foot, or bus to another carrier's terminal, and going through the security checkpoint again.

Olsen figured that if American could offer that same traveler half a dozen or so departures a day to D/FW, and then convenient connecting flights to Chicago or a host of other cities, that Lubbock businessperson would be able to catch a midday flight to D/FW, switch planes, and be in Chicago in time for a business dinner. Or the businessperson could leave early in the morning, arrive in Chicago before lunch, conduct business, then catch the evening departure and be at home before midnight. That would make for a long day, but the traveler could avoid an expensive night in a hotel and would not be away from his or her family overnight.

Now, if the airline was trying to carry only those people traveling between Lubbock and D/FW, or even between Lubbock and Chicago, demand might be sufficient to support two Lubbock-D/FW roundtrips a day. But what if American could offer the people of Lubbock service to dozens of cities six or more times a day via connections at D/FW? Each of those D/FW-Lubbock flights likely would be filled with enough passengers to make money.

For example: The 8 A.M. departure from Lubbock on a 140-passenger plane might include twenty-five people destined for the Fort Worth-Dallas area. Another three passengers would be bound for New York, two for Washington, three for Atlanta, five for Chicago, one for Little Rock, two for Birmingham, and so on. If the airline could manage to fill eighty-five to ninety seats, that flight would break even or even make a little profit. What's more, those Lubbock-to-Chicago passengers who might have waited for a connecting flight on another carrier via some other airport almost certainly would take the 8 A.M. flight on American, because it offered a shorter elapsed time from start to finish, easier connections at the hub, a more attractive departure or arrival time, and all around less hassle.

At the time Paskett asked Olsen to study the possibility of de-peaking American's loose hub at D/FW, the airline could put no more than sixteen planes on the ground there at one time. That's all the gates it had. Typically, those planes came in from and were bound to major cities. Thus, American could accommodate the connecting passenger from Philadelphia going to Phoenix. But the Birmingham-to-Lubbock passenger most likely had to fly Delta from Birmingham to Atlanta and from Atlanta to D/FW, then switch to either American or Braniff for the final leg to Lubbock.

Olsen proposed opening up service to the Lubbocks and Birminghams in the southern tier of states (that is, medium-size cities that had very poor air service because their markets were too small to support much nonstop service to more than one or two large cities). The more cities American could add to its D/FW hub-and-spoke network, the more routes, or city pairs, the airline could sell to passengers.

For example: In those days the Austin-to-D/FW passenger had sixteen possible destinations on American that did not require a lengthy layover; the Fort Worth–Dallas area or one of the fifteen other places tied to the loose American hub, assuming that the sixteenth plane was going back to Austin. Each city added to the hub gave passengers from the other cities tied to the hub one more choice. In fact, Olsen was able to show that by adding many more cities to the hub-and-spoke network, the airline could create not simple arithmetic but complex geometric growth in both passenger traffic and revenues, while total labor and capital costs would rise much more slowly and unit costs actually would decline.

When Olsen went in to explain all of this to Plaskett, it didn't take long for the airline's new senior VP of marketing to see the point. After only a few minutes Plaskett was convinced.

"Tom picked up the phone immediately after I finished with my presentation and called Crandall to set up a meeting for him to see my presentation. We had a meeting, just the three of us, Crandall,

Plaskett, and myself, and Crandall saw it immediately. He picked up on what we were saying right off, that not only should we not depeak D/FW, but that we should build it even bigger and faster," Olsen said.

"I think Crandall bought the concept in the first thirty minutes I had with him explaining it."

"Mel did some analysis and ran an exponential chart that showed the number of city pairs you could serve with a hub, and the bigger the hub got, the greater the revenues," Plaskett said. "Then it began to unfold that 'Geez, if you could build a giant hub you could really control traffic and serve thousands of city pairs, and you wouldn't be impacted if a particular segment didn't do well because you had much more traffic to a lot more destinations on that one airplane.'

"The whole hub plan began to evolve from that," Plaskett said.

Within days, American had undertaken a major project to develop and, if possible, to implement the hub concept Olsen had proposed. Wes Kaldahl, Olsen's boss and one of Crandall's most trusted aides, was in charge. American took a little more than a year to move that concept from Olsen's charts to reality.

Initially, Kaldahl's team included Olsen, vice president of forecasting and research Earl Ditmars, and about a dozen of Olsen's and Ditmars's staffers.

"Also, Otto [Becker, senior VP of field services] had the field system, and all the station people had to report up through him, so he was involved because even if we could do marvelous things in operations at the hubs, we had to make sure everything worked right at the outlying stations or the planes wouldn't get back to the hub on time, which was an absolutely critical thing," Kaldahl said.

"The reason timing and the performance of the ground workers and field system was so critical was that we were changing the concept from the Delta-type hub concept we had been working on. We tightened it up greatly from what Delta had been doing. From the time of the first [plane] in to the time of the last [plane] out it was much, much tighter then, and still is today, than what Delta did."

Though it took more than a year to implement all the operational changes required to make American's new, tighter hub work, the company had to get over an even bigger hurdle to reach that point. It had to overcome its own employees' decades-old assumptions about what airlines could and could not do and about what travelers would and would not do. The initial resistance to the new hub concept was widespread. Bag handlers and ramp workers swore they couldn't do the job they were being asked to do without hundreds of additional workers. Airplane cleaners said they wouldn't have enough time to do their jobs and American's planes would become flying garbage cans. Salespeople worried that they couldn't sell enough tickets to fill all those extra flights. The list of potential problems went on and on.

"I can remember one meeting over at D/FW where I was trying to coordinate the scheduling people with the operations people there in early 1981," Carty said. "Hans Mirka, now our international vice president who then was running D/FW for us, said he could tell those sons of bitches from scheduling definitively that you cannot put sixteen planes on the ground at D/FW. It cannot be done. We had sixteen gates, but it was going to be chaos. You wouldn't be able to move the bags. You wouldn't be able to move the passengers between planes. It was just going to be a mess.

"It's funny now, with forty-five gates at D/FW, looking back to when we thought of sixteen gates being a problem."

Olsen remembers the same meeting. "They said you couldn't put sixteen planes on the ground because they didn't have enough tractors and other equipment to handle them. I said 'I know that. But I also know you *can* do it. We'll just buy more tractors or whatever. Just tell me how much it'll cost.'

"But this really was not a hard fight. We showed them the slides [charts]. I'd say people saw the light very quickly. The only question was the feasibility of doing it. And by December of 1980, we pretty much had determined that it could be done. In fact, when I ran into pockets of resistance, Crandall himself ran the interference for me," Olsen said.

Kaldahl said convincing the people in American's operations departments, who actually would be the ones to make the new system work, was "simply a matter of letting a new, creative idea that's a tremendous challenge grow on you.

"We'd tell people about it and it would shock them. They would go home and sleep on it, and dream and think about it, then one day would wake up and say 'Damn! We can do it!'

"Their first reaction always was 'We can't do it. It can't be done.' Two weeks later they were saying 'Maybe we can get close to it.' A week after that they were saying 'Yeah, maybe we can.' And in another week they were saying 'Yes, we can get it done.' It just takes people time to adjust to new ideas, and as managers we had to give them that time to adjust. We couldn't force them to do it against their will. We needed everybody on board with the idea emotionally, intellectually, and physically. If they weren't, the whole thing would have failed. We had to have full cooperation from every bag handler and mechanic, from every gate agent and flight attendant, from every pilot and from all the SABRE people and all the administrative people," Kaldahl said.

AMERICAN'S GRADUAL buildup of service into what became its loose hub at D/FW after 1977 almost immediately began to have an impact on Braniff International Airways. Braniff had been the local heavyweight at Dallas's old Love Field for more than three decades, and it was the largest carrier at D/FW. Even after American beefed up its service at D/FW in 1977 Braniff continued to retain its lead over American in terms of its share of passengers. But American slowly was closing the gap. Delta, too, had been slowly adding flights and picking up market share at D/FW, largely at Braniff's expense.

Braniff actually was an easy target. Like its hometown, the often uppity Dallas, Braniff desperately wanted to be considered a major leaguer. Though most of its flying was done up and down the country's unglamorous midsection, it took great pride in its long history of international service, even though most of that was to Mexico and Latin America—hardly premier international markets in terms of either prestige or profits. In the late 1970s, in part as a response to the growth at D/FW of the sophisticated, smooth-running American, Braniff rolled out several marketing gimmicks that redefined pretentiousness. Its planes were repainted in several "designer colors" instead of all the same color. Renowned artist Alexander Calder painted one Braniff 727 white with long, curly dashes of red paint that looked like a bundle of flying snakes. The airline's flight attendants were issued silky, flowing new uniforms designed by Halston. The corporate pretension of Braniff even extended to the airline's new headquarters complex built in the late 1970s on the west side of D/FW, inside the city limits of suburban Grapevine, Texas. The complex, which collectively was known as "Braniff Place," included a hotel known as "Braniff House" for overnighting flight crews and other employees in town on business and administrative offices known as "Braniff World Headquarters." The building also had a huge penthouse apartment for Braniff chairman Harding Lawrence that included an indoor/outdoor swimming pool and millions of dollars' worth of rare artworks purchased by the company.

Lawrence, a seasoned industry veteran who learned the business under longtime Continental Airlines chief Bob Six, had been opposed to deregulation because he correctly recognized that only two types of airlines would survive, large ones with pockets deep enough to carry them through several years of tumultuous, expensive transition and small, low-cost, low-fare niche carriers. And Lawrence knew that Braniff fit neither category. It didn't have the abundant resources of an American, Delta, or United. Yet Braniff wasn't at all like the maverick Southwest, a Dallas-based start-up carrier, because it was encumbered by the same high labor and capital cost structures that made even the biggest airlines vulnerable under deregulation.

When the Airline Deregulation Act was passed, Lawrence determined the only way Braniff could survive would be to expand rapidly into many new markets. That would give Braniff the size he believed it needed to survive, or at least to make it an attractive bride in a merger. On October 25, 1978, the first day when airlines could apply for the right to fly any one of the nearly 1,300 routes opened up by deregulation, Braniff applied for 626 of them. Other carriers typically applied for 20 or 30 new routes. In any case, Braniff was granted just 67 new routes, barely a tenth of the number it had requested. Still, no one believed little Braniff could launch service on that many new routes within the forty-five-day time limit that came with those new route rights.

Until then, Braniff had operated what amounted to a natural hub at D/FW and, earlier, at Love Field. Braniff's hub wasn't timed nearly as tightly as even American's loose hub of the late 1970s, but it did give passengers the opportunity to make connecting flights on one airline. To serve the routes it got after deregulation, however, Braniff literally broke apart its natural hub at D/FW. As a result, its aircraft utilization tumbled in some cases by more than 50 percent, meaning Braniff's planes, which cost on average more than $15 million each, were in the air earning money fewer than six hours a day. Worse, when they were in the air, they flew more than half empty. Because the airline had so little time to begin serving those new routes, it had been unable to develop an effective marketing program.

Meanwhile, when Braniff reduced service on its old routes to go serve the new ones, usually American, and to a lesser extent Delta, moved in. With fewer connecting opportunities at Braniff's D/FW terminal, passengers were forced to take American or Delta flights. Passengers used to Braniff's uneven, often just plain bad service were easily impressed and won over by American's highly professional or

Delta's extremely gracious service. Thus Braniff's loads dropped on its old route, too.

Before long, Braniff was relying almost exclusively on passengers who hailed from the Dallas-Fort Worth area, its stronghold. That meant revenue projections almost never were met. And that was critical because Braniff had gone heavily into debt to acquire new aircraft, including a stable full of Boeing 747s and 747SP long-range variants that cost more than $50 million apiece. It didn't take long for Braniff to go from a profitable little regional airline that served Texas and the Great Plains area to a money-losing carrier that had allowed its ambitions to overtake good business judgment.

About the time Olsen was explaining his "big hub" theory to Crandall and Plaskett over at American, Braniff already was deeply in arrears on its debts and its creditors were pushing for Lawrence's ouster. The colorful Braniff chairman bowed to that pressure and retired on December 31, 1980. Despite widespread media speculation that Braniff might go bankrupt, Lawrence publicly expressed confidence the company would make it. But there's plenty of evidence to suggest that he really didn't believe what he said. Perhaps Lawrence's biggest failing was that his overbearing ways had prevented him from developing a strong management team. Too often talented staff members moved to other airlines or out of the industry rather than put up with Lawrence's petty abuses of them and the constant turmoil in senior management. Thus Lawrence himself was painfully aware that the staff he left behind at Braniff almost certainly was not up to the task of saving the carrier. Indeed, even Lawrence had not been able to control the panic within Braniff that built up in 1979 and 1980.

Braniff actually hung on for sixteen months after Lawrence's retirement, until May 1982, when it filed a Chapter 11 bankruptcy petition and became the first airline to cease operations after passage of the Airline Deregulation Act. Many charges were hurled, mostly by Braniff employees and its loyal Dallas passengers, against American. American was accused of various dirty tricks, such as manipulating its SABRE computer reservations system to show no seats available on Braniff flights that competed directly with American flights when, in fact, plenty of seats were available. Another frequent charge was that American captains regularly cut in front of Braniff planes to get ahead in the line of aircraft on D/FW's taxiways awaiting takeoff. However, no one ever produced hard evidence of those or other allegations. To be sure, American, under the leadership of Crandall, did everything in its power to run Braniff out of business and, in fact, probably hastened the airline's final day of reckoning. But Braniff's fate was sealed six months before American ever threw the switch to turn on its massive D/FW hub.

Braniff committed suicide. American just buried the body.

A LOT of people thought that Al Casey, Bob Crandall, and the rest of American's management had fried their brains in the hot North Texas sun in the year since they'd moved the airline's headquarters out of New York City. What they were proposing to do just didn't make any sense at all.

In November 1980, without any advance warning, Casey announced that American would take a $57 million charge against its fourth quarter and ground its fleet of Boeing 707s. The nine oldest and least efficient of the sixty-seven planes in American's 707 fleet were decked immediately. By year's end, Casey said, twenty-four more would be taken out of service. All sixty-seven, including nine 707 freighters, would be gone by October 1981. The $57 million write-off was to cover the shortfall American expected from its sale of the aircraft at prices below their listed book values.

At the beginning of 1980, the 707s had represented 21.1 percent of American's total capacity. Twenty-one months later they were to be gone, victims of their advanced age, smallish seating capacity, antiquated first-generation jet engine technology, gross fuel inefficiency, and skyrocketing fuel prices.

The commercial aviation world was shocked. Everyone knew the recession-affected 1980 was going to be a bad year for the industry, but few people had been willing to believe—let alone speak publicly about—how bad the situation really was getting. Besides, people wondered, how could any carrier with rising fuel, labor, and capital costs afford to ground 21 percent of its capacity? Even if it could make up for some of that with better scheduling or withdrawing from a few unprofitable markets, there seemed to be no way it could generate anywhere close to as much revenue as it had the previous year.

Indeed, that concerned American's management too.

"It was a very hard decision to make," said Carty, who participated in the analysis that led to the grounding.

"We kept studying that and concluding that if we grounded them the company was going to shrink dramatically, and we couldn't find enough overhead costs to get rid of to offset the revenue we were going to lose. But what we finally convinced ourselves of, after we had worked it and worked it and worked it and worked it, was that our studies didn't tell us all. We just sort of reasoned that by getting rid of an entire fleet of inefficient planes, and by making a truly fundamental decision and getting it behind us, we could improve the profitability of the company, if we squeezed hard. So we did. That's one reason why we did the layoffs in the second half of '80," Carty said.

Kaldahl, who as the airline's chief strategist was at the eye of this particular storm, said the grounding of the 707s proved the value of having experienced airline pros who also were well trained in financial and business analysis. The decision required huge doses of both sophisticated analytical skills and intuitive understanding of the business. Had American's management been made up entirely of old-style, seat-of-the-pants airline managers, the question of whether the 707s should be grounded probably never would have been asked. And, had management been populated by business school grads who had little personal understanding of the industry, their detailed analysis would have left them unable to make the decision that American did make.

"Anybody who is real analytical also knows that there's eventually an end to the numbers. You can't prove everything with the numbers. If you can, then something's wrong," Kaldahl said.

The 707 decision was almost a leap of faith. Luckily for American, in Casey and Crandall it had not one but two leaders who, once convinced of something, do not hesitate to act no matter how unconventional or shocking those actions might be.

Carty said the final decision came down to management's more or less intuitive recognition that the 707 fleet was coloring all of the airline's other critical decisions regarding repositioning itself to compete in the deregulated environment.

"Those airplanes could be used only on certain routes. They didn't fit other routes. They were okay on the transcon routes. But they had four engines and fewer than 150 seats. You couldn't afford to operate them on short-haul flying, which we did a lot of in the Northeast and which we knew we would be doing more of as we moved toward a big hub-and-spoke operation at D/FW," he said.

"In a sense, the 707s inhibited us from doing other structural things that needed to change in a route sense. So we just forced the decision on ourselves, plowed through it, and made it profitable by brute force."

Everyone in management knew American had to change its route structure. Its traditional stronghold, the transcontinental routes, had been invaded, and it was unable to defend its position on those routes. At one point in 1980 eleven carriers flew nonstop between New York and California. Fares dove all the day down to $99 one way. American could fill every seat on its 707s with passengers flying at that price and lose money. And it, like every other airline, lacked any reliable way of limiting its exposure to such ridiculously unprofitable pricing schemes cooked up by the competition.

Meanwhile, the change in route structure being discussed also seemed to dictate a change in the mix of planes in American's fleet. But the company lacked the financial resources it needed to go out and order a large number of new aircraft.

"Grounding the 707s was really an important part of Al's drive to build up our cash position. Since they were producing direct operating losses, grounding them saved cash. And the [$57 million] write-off was an accounting thing. It didn't reduce our cash," Kaldahl said.

American ended 1980 with just $292.4 million in cash and short-term investments on its balance sheet. A year later that figure had risen to $459.9 million, which enabled the airline to begin placing relatively modest orders for new aircraft.

Also, while the grounding of the 707s got a lot of attention, it was only part of American's plan to revamp its fleet without spending a lot of money. Originally, American had expected to start replacing its 707s in 1982 with new Boeing 767 mini-widebodies already on order. But with the dramatic acceleration of the 707s' retirement schedule, the airline moved quickly to acquire fifteen relatively new Boeing 727s from Braniff, which needed the cash. Another ten brand-new 727s had been delivered to American in 1980, with twelve more scheduled for delivery in 1982. In addition, American embarked on an aircraft modernization program that included installing new, overhead carry-on luggage compartments that reduced the need for onboard closet space and new, trim-line seats that reduced the aircraft's weight. American also began packing more seats into its aircraft, taking its 727-200 fleet from 129 to 144 seats (150 seats today), its shorter 727-100 fleet from 102 to 108 seats, its 747s from 366 to 396 seats, its standard McDonnell Douglas DC-10s from 264 to 269 seats, and its DC-10s used to serve Caribbean vacation destinations from 264 to 294 seats.

American claimed the trim-line seats made it possible to add those extra seats without compromising passenger comfort. No one, of course, believed that for a moment. But American officials didn't really care if anybody bought that lame argument. The financial leverage those extra seats created was dramatic. For example, adding 15 seats to its 125 727-200s added 1,875 seats to the fleet. That was roughly equal to adding thirteen new 727-200s to the fleet without having to pay for them, the fuel they burned, the pilots who flew them, or any other related labor costs. Even assuming only a 13.2 percent occupancy rate for those 15 extra seats on each plane, the airline expected to see an extra $26 million in revenue over a year.

Obviously Casey, Crandall, and company weren't quite as crazy as their grandstanding announcement concerning the 707s made them appear. To be sure, the decision was daring and bold. It was not simply a show. But by making the announcement appear an even more dramatic move than it actually was, they sent several messages.

First, American's employees could not look at the decision to ground 21 percent of the airline's capacity without wondering whether their jobs—and their handsome incomes—were actually as secure as they had thought them to be. Management hoped that would have an impact on labor's approach to the next round of contract negotiations. Second, the rest of the airline industry had to wonder what else American had up its sleeve. American had always been looked on as the industry's leader. The move to ground the 707s indicated that a dramatic shift already had begun in the way American—and by extension, the rest of the industry—operated. What really worried the other carriers was that they didn't know exactly where American was leading them.

Funny thing is, the people at American, Casey and Crandall included, weren't quite sure exactly where they were headed either. They just figured it had to be better than where they had been.

12

Advantage American

INTELLECTUALLY, EVERYONE from low-level managers all the way up to Al Casey himself knew that American would have to change many things about the way it did business if it was to survive deregulation. Still, few if any of them really understood—more on the emotional or "gut feeling" level—what or how much would be required of them if American was to make it.

The immensity of the task didn't begin to register, even on American's senior management, until the disastrous last half of 1979 and first half of 1980. Not until then did everyone seem to wake up and realize that new marketing programs, new cost controls, new types of aircraft, new routes, and new executives alone weren't going to save American. Rather, everyone began to realize that what was needed was drastic, fundamental change, even if that change was painful in the short run.

American entered the 1980s with a long list of negatives on the tally sheet. At the top of that list were the airline's incredibly high labor costs. Labor gobbled up 38 percent of the airline's revenues in 1980. Because airlines always had been able to pass along labor costs to passengers in the form of higher fares, the airlines rarely if ever showed any real toughness in dealing with the powerful unions in the industry. American was no different. It regularly capitulated to union demands for more pay and more work rules that stifled productivity. The reason airline managements gave in so easily and so often to labor is that airline managers fear strikes more than anything else. While they have little or no ability to collect revenue during strikes, airlines, which are extremely capital intensive, must continue to make their monthly payments for airplanes and facilities. An airline can run out of cash in a matter of a few weeks if it is shut down by a strike.

Second, American had one of the oldest fleets in the industry. In 1980, its planes' average age approached eighteen years. That was bad for three reasons. The old planes were inefficient gas guzzlers. Because they were first-generation jets, most also were too small for the demand on the routes they served. And the older planes were beginning to put American at a marketing disadvantage versus competitors that were starting to bring newer, more comfortable, quieter jets on line. Grounding the Boeing 707s was American's first step in addressing that problem. But that decision didn't completely solve the airline's big problem with its fleet.

That's because American's third big negative going into 1980 was its lack of capital resources. American had enough cash on hand and available credit to buy a few planes, but not enough to fully replace the grounded 707s, let alone to expand into the new markets to which deregulation gave it access.

Fourth, American's route network was all wrong for deregulation. The airline was heavily deployed in two markets, the transcontinental routes and the densely populated northeastern states. The transcon routes acted like a magnet for every major wannabe airline in the nation. With all that competition forcing fares ridiculously low, American was exposed to huge potential losses.

Meanwhile, the airline regularly lost money on its network of short- and medium-haul routes in the Northeast. It had served many of those routes since the 1930s, even though some weren't very profitable even in the best of times.

The process of finding some sort of overarching operating strategy that would create the fundamental change American needed began in earnest in 1979, after the headquarters move was completed, and picked up steam steadily throughout 1980. In varying amounts, management gave serious attention to three possible strategic plans, all of which carried a lot of downside risk and little upside benefit.

One solution to American's problems would have been to shrink the company. By selling aircraft, withdrawing service from all but the best routes, furloughing thousands of employees, or even selling off part or all of the airline, the company's stockholders would benefit from having their investment turned to cash, presumably at a nice profit. But many, and maybe even all, of American's employees would be hurt. And there was no evidence to suggest that American could save enough by downsizing to overcome the corresponding drop in revenue. Still, at one point, Bob Crandall and others at American began muttering in public that if the airline's unions didn't accept the contract terms offered and tried to force the airline to raise its offer, he would recommend that the airline be sold. The company's primary business then would be the SABRE computer reservations system.

A second possible solution that was discussed was to bully the airline's workers into agreeing to wage and work rule concessions against the threat of selling or shrinking the airline.

A third possible solution was to re-form American as a nonunion, low-cost carrier. That would require the dissolution of the existing company and the sale of its assets to the new, nonunion company.

But none of those three solutions was acceptable to either Crandall or Casey. Besides its negative impact on American's employees, the idea of shrinking the company seemed like the easy way out. By doing so, management would abdicate its responsibility to find ways to make the company profitable. And giving up like that would have been anathema to the never-say-die Crandall.

Both of the other two possibilities were guaranteed to thoroughly tick off American's workers. Many of them may have been overpaid relative to what they'd earn with the same sets of skills in some other business, but Crandall feared the negative impact a dissatisfied and angry work force could have on American's remaining business. No airline, he reasoned, could afford to be at war with its employees. The airline business is a service business; customers' perception of the quality of service they receive is most directly affected by the efficiency and friendliness of the workers they encounter. A frustrated employee who is angry at headquarters is far more likely to provide slow or poor service; that, compounded by large numbers of other employees doing the same thing, could run off passengers over time.

History proved Crandall right on that score. Every airline that in the early and mid-1980s sought and won give-backs, even temporary ones, from its employees eventually filed for reorganization under Chapter 11 of the U.S. bankruptcy law or failed outright. The give-backs weren't the root causes of all those bankruptcies, but they were significant contributing factors.

Crandall determined that some other solution to American's fundamental problems had to be found.

MEL OLSEN'S hub idea wasn't going to solve American's labor cost problem. But if it worked, it promised to do a lot to help the airline's revenue problem. By December 1980 Wes Kaldahl, Olsen, and their team in planning and scheduling had identified the markets into which American should expand and tie to the new hub. They also had decided from which markets, all in the Northeast and Ohio Valley regions, they would withdraw in order to get the planes needed to expand the hub-and-spoke network.

More important, by the beginning of 1981, American had determined that the massive Dallas/Fort Worth Airport, its new "home" airport, would be the site of its first big hub. With 18,000 acres of flat prairie surrounding four long runways and very little bad weather each year, D/FW was a flight operations manager's dream. And since American's new headquarters building was then going up on the southern edge of the sprawling airport grounds, management could closely monitor the hub's development.

"We also looked at doing it at Chicago, where we were a pretty big player, and at St. Louis, which geographically seemed appealing because it's smack dab in the middle of the country," Kaldahl said. "But at D/FW we had a facility that was much bigger than anything we had or could have in Chicago, and that was when we had just the 3E Terminal at D/FW, before we acquired the rights to Terminal 2E as well. More important, D/FW was not a slot-controlled airport."

Indeed, the use of slot controls at Chicago's O'Hare International Airport was a major concern to Kaldahl and his cohorts at American. Formally known as the high-density airport rules, the Federal Aviation Administration began imposing the so-called slot controls on certain heavily congested airports in the late 1960s as a way of limiting the number of arriving and departing airplanes during any hour-long period of time to a number that the agency's overwhelmed air traffic controllers could manage safely with the antiquated computer and radar systems they had to use. Originally implemented at about twenty airports as a temporary solution to the nation's shortage of adequate runways and taxiways, slot controls continue to exist at three of the most congested airports in the nation, O'Hare, New

York's LaGuardia Airport and Washington's crackerbox-like National Airport. To serve slot-controlled airports, an airline must have two slots—essentially time-specific landing and takeoff rights—to operate one flight. Each plane landing uses one of the slots allocated to that airline at that airport. When that same plane takes off, it uses a second slot. Thus a carrier that owns 200 slots, in theory, can operate 100 flights.

Kaldahl explained: "We were unclear at the time what the slot-control situation at Chicago would be over time and were concerned that it would limit our ability to grow there. And the ability to grow was critical if we were going to follow the big hub theory all the way to its logical conclusion, which would be one humongous connecting operation.

"Plus, we wanted to be able to test the idea under ideal conditions, somewhere where we knew wouldn't have a lot of operational factors confusing the issue. D/FW was a wide-open airport that gave us that ability. And we were going to be right there on top of it to watch it up close as it unfolded. But, really, I guess the biggest thing that made us go to D/FW instead of Chicago first was the weather. Texas has a lot of great flying weather. Chicago has horrible winters, and that can cost an airline millions of dollars," Kaldahl said.

American announced its plan to beef up its D/FW hub on February 21, 1981. The company dispatched officers to each of the eleven cities that were to get new American service tied to D/FW to deliver the news in simultaneous news conferences. The people of Shreveport, Louisiana, for example, were so overjoyed with the news that they would be able to fly to D/FW and make easier connections for service to points beyond the hub that they took only minor offense when American sent a relatively junior officer to make the local announcement in their city. Little did they know that the junior officer they got was the instigator of the whole thing, Mel Olsen.

On June 11, 1981, American threw the switch on a new era in the U.S. airline industry. The modern hub was born. Eleven new cities never before served by American—Amarillo, Austin, Corpus Christi, Midland/Odessa, and Lubbock in Texas; Baton Rouge and Shreveport, Louisiana; Jackson, Mississippi; Birmingham, Alabama; Orlando, Florida; and Portland, Oregon—were added to the D/FW hub-and-spoke network simultaneously.

"When we brought up the [connecting] complex the first time at D/FW, we went from about 100 departures a day to 200 departures a day at one cutover," Carty recalled. "The operating people at

D/FW were frightened out of their minds. Some of us in management had never been to all of the communities in Texas that we were about to put into the complex. We didn't even know the places where we were flying while we were cutting services in the Northeast that we'd flown for forty-five years.

"So these were not trivial decisions we were making. They were really very significant things. So the decisions were tough in one sense because of our concern about implementation and the risks we knew were associated with them. But, in another sense, they were easy decisions because we all knew we had to do big, dramatic things or we were going to be out of business pretty soon," he said.

Three months later, in September 1981, American added service from D/FW to seven new international destinations in the Caribbean and Mexico and to half a dozen more U.S. cities the airline either had never served or had not served from D/FW. In a span of four months, American went from offering a little more than 100 flights a day at D/FW to more than 300 flights a day.

Two months into the new hub operations, however, the whole thing almost fell apart. PATCO, the Professional Air Traffic Controllers Organization, went out on strike despite the federal government's warnings that members would be fired for participating in an illegal strike of essential public employees. Sure enough, when the controllers took a walk in August 1981, President Ronald Reagan fired them. Suddenly the government was unable to monitor the biggest air traffic control system in the world. The Federal Aviation Administration quickly slapped slot control restrictions on flights from twenty-two major airports around the nation.

The FAA also required the airlines to send representatives to Washington to negotiate flight schedule reductions. The airlines had little choice. If they didn't attend, the FAA had promised to implement further restrictions that would have amounted to mandatory imposition of flight restrictions.

American sent its top scheduler, Mel Olsen.

"They wanted us to pull down our schedules based on what our spring schedules had been," Olsen said. "I said we can't do that! We can't go back to where we were in the spring because we had just gone through a major schedule revision to get the hub at D/FW up and running. We'd pulled out of a dozen or so cities in the Northeast. We couldn't go back in there. And we'd just started service to eleven cities. We couldn't pull out of there. They wanted me to pull down 35 percent of our April 17 schedule base, but we just couldn't do that. So I worked and worked and worked to get them to let us work off our June 17 base schedule, which had all the changes associated with the D/FW hub in it."

How big an impact did launching the big hub at D/FW have on American?

Despite the huge disruption caused by the PATCO strike, despite the lingering effects of the national recession during the first half of the year, despite the shrinkage of the airline's fleet and a 1.3 percent decline in revenue passenger miles flown compared with 1980 because of the grounding of the 707s, and despite the expensive escalation of a fare war with Braniff in the last four months of the year, American reported a $47.4 million profit in 1981. A year earlier it had lost $75.8 million. American's revenues also rose to $4.1 billion, up from $3.8 billion the preceding year despite the decline in passenger miles flown and the fare wars.

What made the difference?

The hub.

ROLFE SHELLENBERGER remembers thinking "We've got a winner here." As manager of marketing planning at American Airlines in 1980, he had been charged by his superiors "to come up with a way for someone who was a very heavy traveler to win a free trip to Hawaii."

Within six months of receiving his charge, Shellenberger and three associates—American staffers Nick Babounakis and Frank DeNuzzo, and Dallas-based direct mail expert Hal Brierly, who was hired as a project consultant—had put together something called the AAdvantage Travel Awards Program. But even the members of the small group that gave birth to the first frequent flyer program didn't fully understand the implications of what they unleashed on the world on May 1, 1981.

"I don't remember exactly what the number was, but our expectations for memberships [in AAdvantage] were low, something very achievable," said Shellenberger, who left American in 1982 and who now is a senior consultant with Runzheimer International, a major travel research, management, and consulting firm.

"I think we said we expected to have about 50,000 members that first year," he said.

They weren't even close.

More than a million people joined AAdvantage before the end of that year. And nearly a million more people joined the frequent flyer programs that quickly sprouted up in 1981 at most of the nation's other carriers in response to AAdvantage.

Ten years later, 28.2 million people were card-carrying members of at least one frequent flyer program. On average those people held memberships in 3.5 such programs at once, meaning that altogether, the nation's airlines had issued a total of 98.3 million memberships to their programs through the end of 1991. American's AAdvantage still signs up an average of between 150,000 and 200,000 new members each month. AAdvantage membership totals flew past the 19.1 million mark in 1992 and are growing now at a rate of nearly 2 million new members a year. United's Mileage Plus program is the second largest frequent flyer program, with more than 17.6 million members.

Randy Peterson, editor and publisher of *Inside Flyer* magazine, based in Colorado Springs, points out that such programs have become so enormously popular that they have transcended the business world to become a part of pop culture.

"Frequent flyer programs really have become a part of Americana. Whether it's Johnny Carson mentioning them in his monologues or the Monday Night Football announcers joking that such-and-such a player has been traded so many times he's got more frequent flyer points than he can ever use, they've become a part of everyday life," Peterson said.

"And other businesses are now imitating them. AMC Theaters has a frequent moviegoer program. CBS is thinking about starting a frequent viewers' program. Amoco, 7-Eleven, Diamond Shamrock, and other gas stations and convenience stores have frequent filler programs. Radio Shack has come out with a frequent customers' program. Grocery stores are coming out now with frequent shopper programs. Even fast food outlets are doing it. Beefsteak Charlies, a chain in the New York–New Jersey area, now has a frequent eaters' program," Peterson said.

"Simply put, they are the most effective marketing programs the airlines have ever created," said Joe Brancatelli, editor of *Frequent Flyer* magazine, a New York–based publication.

According to Brancatelli, American has been able to cut back its advertising and save hundreds of millions of dollars because of AAdvantage.

"For example, my magazine reaches 1.5 million of the most frequent flyers, who on average take thirty trips a year. But American didn't buy advertising on its [1991 London] Heathrow [Airport] service start-up from us because they feel like they can reach their market better through their own direct mail list."

Tony Bacci, who now oversees the AAdvantage program, said: "When you advertise in the newspaper you are talking to everybody, when in fact you really want to reach just a certain select group of customers. With AAdvantage we can do that by using our mailing list, and we can individualize the message. The AAdvantage customer on the West Coast may be targeted for a somewhat different message than the one in Chicago or here in Dallas-Fort Worth, depending on our needs and the market conditions.

"As a result, while in many industries they are paying millions to attract the same customers over and over, we've got tremendous brand loyalty while spending relatively much less to attract those customers," he said.

Offering such programs—which, in effect, further discount the price of a product that already is sold at a discount to nearly 90 percent of the people who buy it—is expensive. Peterson said that in 1990 American redeemed 975,000 free travel awards and carried the cost of doing so on its books at about $155 million.

Still, that "is not a big expense for an almost $12 billion company (in 1991). If they feel that the cost of administering their program coupled with the liability on their books is less than the amount of additional travel generated by the program, then they came out ahead. And believe me, they feel that way," he said.

Of course, no one associated with the creation of the AAdvantage program back in 1981 ever considered that they might be working on perhaps the most effective marketing program ever created—in any industry. All they knew they were doing was looking for a solution to what had been a long-standing, unsolvable problem within the airline industry. How does an airline build customer loyalty?

"Doyle Dane Bernbach was American's ad agency at the time," Shellenberger recalled. "They suggested to Crandall that American ought to come up with a loyalty fare of some sort. This concept was passed to American's tariff department, probably sometime in 1979, right about the time we moved down to Texas.

"About that time I moved from sales back into marketing planning, where I had worked years earlier, and I gotta admit, I kinda pooh-poohed the whole idea of a loyalty fare. I said 'You'll never attract anyone's loyalty with a fare cut because nine times out of ten they're not paying for it, their company is.' I said that you would need to give something personal to the traveler, something that means something to him personally."

The loyalty fare notion languished in American's tariff department, where the staff tended to view it simply as a fare discount that would reduce American's yield (the average amount of revenue received for flying a passenger one mile). So Tom Plaskett, the airline's new senior VP of marketing moved the project over to the marketing planning department, directed by Babounakis, to see what it could come up with.

"Nick then gave me responsibility for putting the project together. I don't remember whether he said it, or if it came out of Plaskett's office, but my responsibility was defined as being to come up with a way for someone who is a very heavy traveler to win a free trip to Hawaii. Hawaii was never *the* goal, it was just a token, emblematic of what it was we wanted to do. It was a very popular vacation destination, and we wanted businesspeople to do all of their business flying on us so they could earn a free vacation trip to some exotic locale like Hawaii. We always figured that if they won one free trip, they'd end up buying a ticket for their husband or wife or friend.

"At the same time, Plaskett brought in a consultant who was a very bright guy and an expert on direct mail. Hal Brierly taught us all the things you have to do when you're putting a program together and you want to communicate it by mail.

"I designed the rules, and with Nick Babounakis's help put together the economic justification," Shellenberger said.

The fourth member of the team, DeNuzzo, had spent years at American working on direct mail marketing projects. He had worked on American's first significant customer loyalty program, called An American Traveler, in which American representatives called on customers whose phone numbers appeared regularly on reservations forms and offered them special gifts, such as a free dinner at a nice restaurant, for being a loyal American traveler. DeNuzzo also had worked on ways to improve that program and other customer loyalty programs based on using the passenger record data picked up by SABRE.

"Frank was responsible for the data base part of AAdvantage. He showed us how to set up the information traps and how to glean the information we wanted out of SABRE. That gave us the data base we needed, the kind of in-depth market information we needed, and the tools we needed to come up with and manage something like AAdvantage," Shellenberger said.

"Really, AAdvantage was the product of four guys, Hal Brierly, Nick Babounakis, Frank DeNuzzo, and me. Plaskett had a lot of imput. Crandall wasn't directly involved. I never attended a meeting at which AAdvantage was discussed and Crandall was present. But that's not to say he didn't know about it or wasn't informed. Plaskett kept him briefed and I suppose some of what Tom told us came from Bob. But, despite what some people think, Crandall is good at delegating responsibility. He gave the job to Tom and let him run it. And Tom, in turn, gave it to us to do the development work. Now, the Super Saver program, which was introduced in 1977, that was pure Crandall, a solo home run if there ever was one. But by 1980 he was so busy running the show as president that he delegated the creation of AAdvantage, gave us what we needed to the job and then got out of the way and let us do our jobs."

Still, after six months in development, introducing AAdvantage wasn't a sure thing. Mike Gunn, who in 1981 was vice president and general sales manager, was opposed to it and worked to gather enough support throughout the higher levels of the marketing department to torpedo the program. Gunn's opposition stemmed from his concern that AAdvantage, which was to be aimed primarily at business travelers, quickly would lead to corporate discounting: that corporations would use those free mileage points earned by their employees traveling on business to bargain for reduced corporate fares now instead of free trips for the employee later.

"Just goes to show I'm not a genius," Gunn said years later. "My concern was alleviated when companies began to see those mileage points and free trips and free upgrades to first class as a way of giving their corporate travelers a benefit that the companies didn't have to pay for. Air fare prices in those early days of AAdvantage were so low that companies weren't focusing on trying to cut travel costs by negotiating discounts. So it worked, and it's been a huge success."

Just in case, however, American had prepared a corporate version of AAdvantage, which would have rewarded businesses, not individuals, for their loyalty. Luckily for all those millions of members of frequent flier programs, American never felt compelled actually to introduce Corporate AAdvantage.

WHEN AMERICAN introduced AAdvantage, it also tipped its hand regarding another innovation it was developing, one that would have a far bigger impact on the company's bottom line, and on the industry, than even AAdvantage.

American had held off on introducing AAdvantage for several months primarily so that the folks running SABRE could develop the software applications and procedures that would be needed to track the miles flown by AAdvantage members. Members could have been required to keep track of their own miles and turn in the last page of all their ticket coupons as proofs of travel when claiming a free trip or service upgrade, but by waiting for SABRE to get ready, American ensured that AAdvantage was as user friendly and as hassle-free as possible.

But when data processing experts at competing airlines learned how American planned to keep track of all its AAdvantage members' miles, they knew immediately that American already had or soon would have an effective yield management system.

The idea of yield management actually began at American in the late 1950s, when the airline introduced overbooking as a standard operating procedure. Quite by accident, American had discovered that in most cases flights that were overbooked—that is, had more reservations than available seats—still departed with a few empty seats because of no-shows. By doing careful flight close-outs—checking off the names of passengers who no-showed and adding the names of people who got on without reservations—and keeping those close-out records, American was able to predict with reasonable accuracy how many no-shows there would be for any given flight on any given day. With years of experience and data, the airline was able to refine its ability to compensate for seasonal differences in demand, holiday date movements, conventions going on in certain cities, and a host of other factors. Then, based on its predictions concerning the likely number of no-shows, American could safely overbook flights. Occasionally more people would show up for a flight than there were available seats, and the airline would have to compensate the passengers left behind with a voucher for a free trip later, a free dinner or a free night in a hotel room if the displaced passengers had to spend the night before catching the next flight. As long as overbooking was approached conservatively, the extra revenue produced by making sure the maximum number of seats were filled before a flight departed far outweighed the minimal costs incurred when passengers with reservations got bumped off overbooked flights.

American, United, Eastern, and TWA—the owners of the four

competing computer reservations systems in the market in the late 1970s—all worked hard to refine that form of yield management. But when fares tumbled to ridiculously low levels after deregulation, all the overbooking in the world couldn't help the airlines. Except for their first-class seats, all seats on their planes were available at those low prices. Typically, at $99 a seat or some similarly low fare, a plane can take off with a paying passenger in every seat and lose money.

Obviously, some way had to be found to reduce the airlines' exposure to that kind of rampant, self-destructive discounting.

Enter Bob Crandall and SABRE. Though he himself was not a computer genius, Crandall had recognized very early in his career how powerful computers could be as information management tools if properly programmed. The problem always was giving the computer enough of the proper data to enable it to perform a reliable statistical analysis. If that could be done, then a human could make an objective or even a subjective decision based on that analysis. With the rapid advance of technology, by 1981 it was possible to program computers to make certain decisions automatically based on the results of their statistical analyses.

In the mid-1960s, that's just what Crandall had learned to do while working in data processing at Hallmark. He had participated in Hallmark's development of one of the first effective computerized inventory management systems in U.S. business history. By computerizing and speeding up the processes of tracking which cards sold the most and which stores sold the most cards, Hallmark was better able to determine what type of cards it needed more or less of, what kind of messages sold best, and where the best locations for its franchisees' shops were. It also was able to speed up and refine the restocking process, which in turn cut overhead costs for both the company and its franchisees and reduced manufacturing waste and other costs.

Crandall believed the same principles that allowed computers to track demand for various types of greeting cards at various times of the year could be translated to the airline business. He believed it was possible to predict with reasonable accuracy what the demand for full-price seats on any given flight on any given day would be. And, if that could be done, Crandall figured computers could also help the airline determine what the demand for seats would be at various discount prices.

"An airplane seat is not unlike a gallon of milk on the shelf at the grocery store," Crandall said. "Once that gallon of milk goes beyond the expiration date without selling, it can never be sold. Just so, once a plane leaves the gate, any empty seats on that plane cannot be sold. They are useless. Now, if we determine that 35 percent of the seats on a given flight will be sold at full coach prices, but we need to sell 50 percent of the seats at those prices in order to break even on that flight, it behooves us to find some way to sell as many of those remaining, unsold seats at whatever price we can get for them. Otherwise we will get nothing for them.

"And if by reducing the price of those seats we can stimulate enough people to fill up that plane, we make money. If we induce some people to fly at discount prices, but not enough to fill up the plane, we certainly narrow our losses on that flight and maybe even break even or make a little money. That's because it doesn't cost us any more to fly the plane full than it does to fly it almost empty. You might use 1 percent more fuel, and you might need to staff that flight with an extra flight attendant. But once you've bought the airplane and all the equipment and facilities you need to handle it, and you've trained the people who fly it and take care of it and serve the food on it, the incremental costs of carrying an extra passenger are negligible."

But until the late 1970s, American had no effective way of offering just a portion of its coach seats at discount prices. All coach seats were the same price, with only a few exceptions. That made offering discounts senseless. If 100 people were willing to pay $100 each for a flight, cutting the fare to $75 would force the airline to attract 34 additional people—for a total of 134 passengers—before its revenues for that flight would exceed what they would have been had the fare remained $100. And because airlines nearly always match their competitors' lowest fares, the odds of generating a 34-percent increase in demand with only a 25-percent price cut are incalculably high.

American solved part of that problem in 1977 when it first offered Super Savers, discount fares priced 60 percent below the full coach fare. Super Saver fares had a number of restrictions that effectively prevented high-yielding business travelers from using them. They also had rigid capacity controls, meaning only a certain percentage of seats on each flight would be sold at the Super Saver fare prices. All other seats were sold at the coach fare price.

Still, the problem for American and other airlines was figuring exactly how many seats should be and could be sold at full fare prices, how deep discounts had to be to stimulate demand, and what the proper mix of fare prices should be to assure maximum revenue per planeload. The very fluid nature of airline reservations complicated the problem. Based on history, an airline might determine that it could sell 25 percent of the seats on a given flight at full fare. So it would discount the price on the remaining 75 percent of the seats. Tickets at those prices would be bought in advance, in accordance with the rules governing discounted fares. But what if, as the date of departure moved inside the twenty-one-day advance purchase window, there was a sudden surge in demand for that flight? People willing to pay full-fare prices would have to be turned away because bargain hunters had already snapped up all the remaining seats. Or what if demand for full-fare travel was weaker than expected and the airline couldn't sell 25 percent of the seats on that flight at those prices? Could some of those seats have been sold at a discount price, providing at least some revenue?

The introduction of AAdvantage indicated that American was closing in on a solution to that problem. Since SABRE would be able to track the miles flown by individual AAdvantage members, it also could track the miles flown by any passenger in any seat, traveling at any fare price. Thus American would gain a lot of knowledge about travelers' habits. It would be able to learn how far in advance business travelers typically booked their travel. It would also learn how sensitive business travelers actually were to price changes. From there, the next logical step would be to introduce multiple fare levels. And, indeed, that's what happened.

Instead of offering first-class, coach, and one level of discount fares, American began offering several layers of discounts. The bigger the savings off full-fare prices, the more restrictions the tickets had. The more modest the savings, the fewer restrictions. So fourteen-day and seven-day advance purchase discount fares cost more than twenty-one-day fares, but they were less restricted. Because of this sliding scale of discounts, American could juggle the percentage of seats on any airplane allocated to one fare type or another. If, for example, demand for full coach tickets was weaker than expected, the airline could expand the number of seats it would sell at the seven-day advance purchase fare price. By the late 1980s American would be able to, and often did, juggle the mix of fares right up until the moment of departure.

This enhanced yield management capability, which did not arrive full blown but rather evolved over a period of years—and continues to evolve even today—gave American a huge competitive advantage over other airlines. It could respond to competitors' deep price cuts by lowering its own discount fare prices or by increasing the number of seats available at the lowest prices. But it didn't have to cut the price on all of its seats. It could still hold some seats for late-booking full-fare business travelers who appreciated American's quality of service.

THE FIRST airline to feel serious pain from American's three big innovations in 1981—the D/FW hub expansion, AAdvantage's introduction, and the implementation of the new yield management technology—was Braniff. Already on the ropes thanks to Harding Lawrence's ill-conceived post-deregulation expansion plan and its own notoriously second-rate service, Braniff was a sitting duck.

But that put Al Casey in the unenviable position of being his brother's tormentor. John Casey, the man whom so many people at American at first thought American's board must have meant when they announced in 1974 that "Al" Casey would be American's new chairman, had succeeded Lawrence as Braniff's chairman in 1980. A solid airline operations manager, John Casey had been given the chairmanship at Braniff almost by default. He was the best of the senior Braniff executives, all of whom had noticeable deficiencies in their résumés. John Casey's biggest shortcoming was that, unlike his little brother Al, he had no great love or feel for things financial. He also was prone to impulsive decision-making. Unfortunately, Braniff needed a leader who was capable of solving its huge debt problem and who could create a long-term strategy for the company and stick with it.

By September, Al Casey's American had so damaged John Casey's Braniff that Braniff's board forced John Casey to hire a new president. Howard Putnam, a United-trained marketing executive who had served three years as president at Dallas-based Southwest Airlines, was brought in as president and chief operating officer. Though Casey continued as chairman and CEO, Putnam had been quietly assured by senior Braniff board members that he, not John Casey, had the real authority and backing of the board.

Why did Putnam take the job, especially when there already were very strong indications that Braniff could not survive? One reason might have been that Putnam realized he was not popular at Southwest, a carrier whose loosey-goosey corporate culture could not accommodate the bureaucratic style he had learned in his twenty-three years at United, and that Southwest chairman Herb Kelleher was not inclined to renew his contract. A second possibility is that he jumped for the money. Braniff offered Putnam $250,00 a year, a car, a country club membership, a $750,000 insurance policy, and options on 300,000 shares of Braniff's stock that, if a turnaround was achieved, would make him very wealthy. A third possible reason why Putnam took the Braniff job was ego. If he succeeded in turning Braniff around he'd be a hero and a highly sought-after CEO. And if he failed, no one would hold it against him since it must have been too far gone when he arrived.

Whatever his reason for taking the job, it is clear in retrospect that Braniff was beyond saving by the time Putnam arrived. Indeed, Putnam now says that had he known the company's real condition he never would have accepted the job. But, he said, he was deceived by Braniff's board and by Casey into believing the airline had more resources than it actually had.

"When I walked in the door I found out that we only had ten days of cash. That's not quite the way the directors painted things for me before I went in," he said.

Still, based on his prior job performance, there's no reason to believe Putnam had either the ability or the moxie to save Braniff, whatever its condition. In fact, his first and only significant strategic decision at Braniff probably hastened its demise.

As Lawrence had correctly guessed going into deregulation, Braniff was being squeezed on the high end of the business by American and Delta, two much larger, better-financed organizations with something approaching national flight networks. On the other end of the scale, low-cost, low-fare Southwest was stealing lots of business travelers away from Braniff's flights in the Southwest. Before Putnam arrived, Braniff had stripped out the first-class seats in several of its planes and begun copying Southwest's service style: all one class, no meals, low fares.

That approach didn't heal Braniff, but it caused the revenues-to-costs equation to move in the right direction. So Putnam's first major act as president was to introduce Braniff's Texas Class service.

"I only saw one thing we could do, and that was to go to a transcontinental, Southwest-like service," Putnam said. "We kept the pitch [distance between seats] in seating the way it was before because these were going to be longer flights than Southwest flew. And we simplified the meal service. It wasn't just peanuts, like on Southwest, but it wasn't full meal service either. And then we lowered our fares and simplified the fare structure."

It was, to be kind, a serious miscalculation. The change in service pushed Braniff onto the critical list.

"The goal was to get a yield of 12.5 cents per passenger mile flown. We did all the simulations we could in a short period, but we missed it. We ended up at 11.5 cents, or something like that. Had we stayed in business long enough, I believe we would have raised the yield to an acceptable level," Putnam said.

But that's debatable. American responded to Braniff's Texas Class simply by cutting its fares. It did not change its service. In other words, passengers could fly on Braniff and get a snack, or fly on American—or for that matter, on Delta—and get a full meal, for the same price. And American and Delta both had much better reputations for quality of service and on-time performance. American also used its yield management system—though simplistic compared to today's system—to limit its exposure to Texas Class–level fares. Still, American also lost millions of dollars in the eight months that Putnam was at Braniff's helm.

"One of American's complaints was that we had put in a pricing system that we couldn't make any money on," Putnam said. "That was true in the first sixty to ninety days. But we got our costs down from 8.5 cents per available seat mile to 7.22 cents six months later. And if we had stayed in business long enough we could have got it down under 7 cents. At 6.8 cents, with the 12.5 yield we were striving for, you would have been looking at a very profitable company."

Of course, while Putnam tries to paint a picture of a Braniff that just barely missed its cost and yield projections, Braniff in fact missed its cost projections by 6.1 percent and its yield projections by 8 percent. In any industry, those are remarkably wide misses. And in a business where margins are so slim that changes in costs or yields of 1 percent can cause multimillion-dollar swings in profitability, Braniff's failures on both scores were gargantuan.

But that doesn't explain why in early 1982 Braniff announced a two-for-one ticket sale lasting six hours that allowed passengers in the Fort Worth–Dallas area to buy a full-fare ticket and receive a second identical ticket for $1. The second ticket could be used by a companion or by the same person on a later trip. The purpose was strictly to raise cash needed to make payroll, and everyone, including the travelers, knew it. Despite Putnam's claims to the contrary, it was clear to everyone that Texas Class would never work because American was determined to match Braniff fare for fare all the way down to zero if need be.

The only ones, it seemed, who failed to understand that Braniff was playing with a shorter deck than American were Putnam and his top aides. Matching Braniff hurt American very much. Matching Braniff was costing American as much as $12 million a month in lost revenues. Putnam should have recognized that he could have at least slowed the bleeding at his own airline by raising prices. American, clearly, would have been willing to go along with a fare hike. And the reduced losses might have given him more time to reach his cost-reduction goals.

By November 1981 the fare war with Braniff and the industry's rapidly deteriorating fare structure had American's management so worried about their airline's dwindling cash reserves and its ability to meet its financial commitments and to pay for new airplanes that the company asked its workers for a temporary pay freeze, to commence on January 1, 1982, and for a 5 percent pay cut during the first quarter of 1982 only. While American's nonunion workers approved the idea, the unions did not. So management withdrew the proposal rather than get into a fight over it.

But as weak as American was financially, it was the rock of Gibraltar compared to Braniff. That's why Crandall directed American to lay siege to Braniff's cash-poor balance sheet.

"The strategic plan was to do everything you can to put maximum pressure on Braniff," Plaskett said. "Even though that hurt American too, we knew that if we didn't match [Braniff's fares] we would lose even more. It was the old 'Who runs out of cash last?' deal. We knew we would win that one, and the sooner we did, the quicker we could return to a normal, sane pricing system and maybe start making some money again."

Calling the competition between Braniff and American in late 1981 and early 1982 intense is like saying the Dallas Cowboys and Washington Redskins had a nice little rivalry going in the late 1970s and early 1980s when George Allen was the 'Skins coach and had a special knack for getting under the skin of the Cowboys' players and coaches. Charges of unethical and even illegal conduct were regularly thrown at American by Braniff or its supporters. Civic leaders took sides. Government officials, corporate leaders who traveled a lot outside the Southwest region, and businesses that were part of the circle dominated by the Republic Bank of Dallas, American's lead bank, tended to back American. Dyed-in-the-wool Texans, small business people and entrepreneurs interested in keeping fares as low as possible, and First International Bancorporation, parent of the First National Bank of Dallas and Braniff's biggest lender, supported Braniff.

Tom Landry, the legendary coach of the Dallas Cowboys, a Texan's

Texan and an icon in the eyes of most Metroplex residents, donated his time to make a commercial on behalf of Braniff. Landry looked square in the camera and asked viewers to help save "Dallas's airline" by choosing Braniff over the competition next time they flew.

Casey and Crandall—especially Crandall—were enraged by such pleas to civic pride and duty. After all, American had only recently relocated its headquarters from New York to the Metroplex. It had been the subject of the biggest corporate recruiting campaign in North Texas history only two and a half years earlier. Yet American and its employees believed they were being treated like carpetbaggers and were not being given the respect and consideration they deserved as vital contributors to the area economy.

Day after day, the three major newspapers in the market, plus the *Wall Street Journal* and *The New York Times*, carried stories about the latest round of fighting in the Braniff-American war. Crandall in particular believed that most of that reporting was unfair and biased in Braniff's favor. He became more frustrated and angry about the war with Braniff each passing day. His famous fits of rage came closer and closer together and, if possible, grew more vitriolic with each new round of charges that American was playing dirty. He was like a volcano with a huge pressure dome already formed, primed for some critical event to trigger an eruption.

"It made going into the office in the morning and reading the newspaper and facing Bob's angst and anger at what was happening almost unbearable at times," Plaskett said. "That was a very difficult time for all of us.

"What really made Bob mad, and all of us mad, was that all these allegations against us for dirty tricks, none of that was true. We didn't do anything that any prudent business wouldn't have done to protect itself from a competitor that was dying and bent on bringing the whole industry down with it. But the media went with those stories painting us as the bad guys, Yankee carpetbaggers, and a lot of people down here in Texas believed them. It didn't make any sense. What were we supposed to do, let Braniff take business away from us and go broke ourselves?"

Crandall finally had had enough on February 1, 1982.

He'd just come in from his morning run through his North Dallas neighborhood and had joined his high school sweetheart and wife, Jan, at the breakfast table. Rummaging through the *Dallas Morning News*, Crandall happened upon what became known around American's headquarters as simply "The Braniff Ad."

In its ad, Braniff claimed to have a better on-time record than American. It was the first real comparative ad Braniff had run.

By the time he got to the office, Crandall was livid. Putnam had gone too far this time, and Crandall was going to put a stop to it. After discussing the ad—more accurately, ranting about it—with Plaskett, Crandall put in a call to Howard Putnam. But the Braniff president was not immediately available.

Crandall's intention, Plaskett said, was to say "Listen, Howard, if you want to play the game that way this can get pretty ugly, and it does not make very much sense to continue to fight our way through the newspapers like this. It doesn't do anybody any good. It doesn't help the industry's image. It creates a lot of ugliness and dissension. And it's not very effective advertising."

But that's not how the conversation went once Putnam called back. Plaskett had left Crandall's office, so it was just the two of them, Crandall and Putnam on the phone, or so Crandall thought. He was unaware that Putnam, on the advice of his attorney, was recording their conversation.

Putnam barely had time to say hello and identify himself before the American president jumped him like an angry father hammering his daughter's date for bringing the girl home late.

"Don't you know we've always had an agreement that we wouldn't run that type of ad against each other?" Crandall said.

"No, Bob, I never heard of such an agreement. Besides, that sort of agreement would be illegal," replied Putnam.

Crandall was already into his rapid-fire, accusatory and arrogant I'm-smarter-than-you-so-you-should-do-what-I-say-and-we'll-both-be-better-off routine. Without giving Putnam much chance to respond, he quickly turned from that morning's Braniff ad to the general subject of Braniff's deep-discount fare strategy, the real source of his anger and frustration.

"I think it's dumb as hell, for Christ's sake, all right, to sit here and pound the shit out of each other and neither one of us making a fucking dime," Crandall growled, selecting several choice words from his well-stocked arsenal of profanity.

"I mean . . . you know . . . goddamn! What the fuck is the point of it?"

The Braniff president tried to defend himself. "Nobody asked American to serve Harlingen," he replied. "Nobody asked American to serve Kansas City, and there were low fares in there, you know, before so—"

"You better believe it, Howard," Crandall interrupted. "But you . . . you . . . you know, the [hub] complex is here! Ain't gonna change a goddamn thing, all right! We can . . . we can both live here and there ain't no room for Delta. But there's, ah, no reason that I can see, all right, to put both companies out of business!"

"But if you're going to overlay every route of American's on top of . . . over . . . on top of every route that Braniff has, I can't just sit here and allow you to bury us without giving our best effort," Putnam said.

"Oh, sure, but Eastern and Delta do the same thing in Atlanta and have for years," Crandall countered.

By this time, Crandall was revved up like a '57 chevy on a Saturday night. All Putnam needed to do was lure his angry adversary into taking one more verbal step in the direction that he clearly was headed and the trap would be sprung.

"Do you have a suggestion for me?" he asked, playing up to Crandall's ego.

"Yes. I have a suggestion for you," Crandall snapped, taking the bait. "Raise your goddamn fares 20 percent! I'll raise mine the next morning!"

"Robert! We—"

"You'll make more money and I will too!"

"We can't talk about pricing."

"Oh, bullshit, Howard! We can talk about any goddamn thing we want to talk about!"

THREE AND A HALF months later, on May 12, 1982, Braniff ceased operations. Putnam filed a Chapter 11 bankruptcy petition with U.S. Bankruptcy Judge John Flowers at Flowers's home in Fort Worth minutes after midnight on May 13.

The war was over.

13

People and Planes

WHEN AMERICAN established its big hub at Dallas/Forth Worth airport and trimmed its unprofitable service in the Northeast, it went a long way toward solving one of the four big problems it faced going into the era of deregulation. The airline's old route network had been all wrong for deregulation. But the changes American made in association with the opening of the big hub at D/FW created perhaps the best domestic route network in the industry. The fare war with Braniff prevented the hub from having the huge, sudden impact on the bottom line that it might otherwise have had. But Braniff died just ten months after the hub was turned on. So while it was a particularly trying period for American, mercifully it was a short one.

As 1982 began, the airline also went to work on the second of its four major problems: its balance sheet. Al Casey had been able to stabilize American's financial condition in the mid- and late 1970s. By the dawn of deregulation, American ranked in the top half of U.S. airlines in terms of financial health. But weak profits—American did not achieve Casey's goal of a 5 percent annual operating profit margin until his tenth year as chairman—and the big $75.8 million net loss (and $151.6 million operating loss) in 1980 had kept the airline from building up the kind of financial strength Casey liked and knew he would need if Crandall and his young turks could pull off some of the radical maneuvers they were planning.

So, with Braniff still alive and playing havoc with American's revenue generating ability, American slammed the brakes on its capital spending. Casey and Crandall went hats in hand to Seattle to cancel American's order for fifteen new Boeing 757s and to stretch out the airline's order for thirty Boeing 767s. It cost American $5.1 million in cancellation penalties, but that was small change compared with what it would have cost the airline had it bought the planes. The 185-seat 757s were to have replaced the 707s American had abruptly grounded that winter. But at more than $30 million each, American determined it could not afford them.

American also chose to use lease financing for all its major acquisitions in 1982, including three Boeing 767s. That allowed it to conserve its cash. Indeed, though the company eventually lost $19.6 million in 1982, largely because of the fare war with Braniff, its cash and short-term investments position rose slightly, from $459.9 million to $465.9 million. By adhering to this same policy in 1983, the airline's cash and short-term investments position more than doubled, to $1.1 billion.

American also added $112 million in equity to its balance sheet in 1982 by converting two different bond issues on favorable terms. Then it sold 4 million shares of common stock, to add another $473 million in equity. It ended the year with $836.2 million in equity and just $751.8 million in long-term debt.

Obviously, American was filling up its war chest. But for what?

With its route network problem more or less solved with the establishment of the D/FW hub and its balance sheet problem being addressed, American still had two major problems that needed to be dealt with. The grounding of the 707s had helped, but American still needed to rationalize and modernize its fleet of aircraft. And the airline's labor costs still were way too high in comparison with the low-cost new entrant carriers that were driving air fare prices through the floor.

The $1.4 billion American paid in labor costs in 1981 was equal to 36.5 percent of its revenues. That figure was higher than the industry average and, on a revenue-per-employee basis, higher than United's labor costs.

But Casey and Crandall had something up their sleeves that they thought would address both American's labor and its fleet problems.

Based on a study done in 1980 by Don Carty during his short run as vice president of profit improvement, Crandall and his team were developing a radical strategy that, if it worked, would propel the airline to the top of the industry in terms of size and revenues while drastically reducing its unit costs. The basics of the plan called for American to double the number of planes in its fleet over about five years. This growth would be financed in large measure by savings on labor expenses. American would pay the thousands of new employees it would need to handle growth salaries comparable to that paid by the new entrant carriers. By adding lots of lower-paid new employees—without cutting the pay of existing employees—American could bring its *average* unit costs down dramatically. Thus, the faster American grew, the faster and farther its unit costs would fall. At least that was the theory.

Thus, while the airline could address its route network and balance sheet problems relatively independently from other issues, its labor and fleet problems were joined at the hip.

"I think it was becoming clear to us, or at least to some number of us in management, that the solution for the company was growth," said Don Carty, who in 1982 was promoted to senior VP and controller. "If we could grow fast enough and cheaply enough that we could bring our average unit costs down, we'd make ourselves more competitive with the new entrant carriers that were giving us fits. And with our size and the strength of our hubs, we thought we could move a significant amount of market share in our direction. We wouldn't have to get our labor costs all the way to the level of the People Expresses that were cropping up everywhere. With our strong route network and our marketing capabilities, we knew we could pull lots more market share than those guys, but only if we could get our costs down closer to theirs. That would give us the ability to selectively match their discount fares without losing too much money.

"So we had started to think about the growth plan, but we were not prepared to go ahead with the growth plan unless our employees wanted to participate in the growth plan. We weren't prepared to buy any airplanes until our employees came to the party."

In short, American could not afford to buy planes unless it got the labor deals it wanted. On the other hand, there was no way the airline's unions—the Transport Workers Union, representing mechanics, bag handlers, and other ground workers; the Allied Pilots Association, and the Association of Professional Flight Attendants— were going to go for the kind of cost-saving contracts American wanted without assurances that management would plow the savings into new airplanes, which in turn would create more jobs and more opportunities for rapid advancement up the pay ladder.

EVERYONE IN the industry knew American was looking for a new plane in the 130- to 150-seat class to fly feeder routes to its new hub at D/FW and the big hub it planned to launch at Chicago. The plane American was looking for had to be super–fuel efficient. It had to be quiet to meet all the new regulations. It had to have only a two-pilot cockpit to save on crew costs. And, most important, it had to be cheap.

Yet American's management was determined not to buy any airplanes until it had obtained the favorable new labor deals it wanted.

Jim Worsham had other ideas.

The executive vice president of McDonnell Douglas Corporation's commercial aircraft division had been watching his company wither away. The division, still known as the Douglas Aircraft Company even though it had been acquired in 1967 by St. Louis–based Mc-Donnell Aircraft Corporation, had seen hard times before. Founder Donald Douglas often was hailed as an aeronautical engineering genius. But he was no threat to land on anyone's list of all-star businessmen. Indeed, though it politely was called a merger, the fact is that Douglas's heirs had sold the old man's company to McDonnell Aircraft—forming the McDonnell Douglas Corp.—because it was too weak financially to compete against the giant Boeing Company. Had Douglas Aircraft remained on its own, it almost surely would have failed under the weight of its own high costs, big debt, meager product line, and slow sales.

But by 1982 the Douglas division was in trouble again. Its DC-9 twin-jet production line had been closed for several years. The DC-10 widebody line was winding down, and the revenue stream it produced had slowed to a trickle. That would have been okay had sales for the MD-80, a more technologically advanced, elongated derivative of the DC-9 design, met expectations. But they had not. No major U.S. airline had bought the plane in its two years on the market, and only a handful of planes had been ordered by small carriers from elsewhere around the world. With its cash dwindling, Douglas was desperate for revenue.

Worsham needed a major U.S carrier to buy the MD-80. Many

smaller carriers, both in the U.S. and elsewhere, lacked the analytical skills and staff to do the kind of in-depth analyses that the big U.S. carriers—American, United, or Delta—did before selecting airplanes. As a result, the big U.S. lines often had a profound influence on the aircraft purchasing decisions of airlines worldwide. In fact, Worsham was so desperate for a big sale to one or more of the really big carriers that he was willing to sell them MD-80s at cost or below. He figured such a sale would spawn additional sales; then McDonnell Douglas could make money by charging subsequent buyers higher prices and by bringing its unit costs of production down as it increased productivity.

But McDonnell Douglas had a problem. United Airlines already had the biggest fleet in the industry and did not utilize its planes as efficiently as most of its competitors. On top of that, United had a bunch of Boeing 737s, the plane most directly competitive with the MD-80.

Delta Air Lines could afford to buy airplanes, and it could use MD-80s on feeder routes tied to its hub at Atlanta. But Delta already had 737s too, and besides, Delta rarely acquired airplanes until other carriers moved first.

Eastern could use some MD-80s too, but its balance sheet made Douglas's look good. TWA was interested in buying a few MD-80s, but the internationally oriented TWA hardly qualified under Worsham's definition of "major U.S. carrier."

Northwest was loading up on Boeing 747s for its transpacific routes. USAir was buying 737s for its short hops around the Northeast, and Pan Am was looking to sell—not buy—assets to stay afloat. Meanwhile, the rest of the nation's carriers either were too poor, too small, or both to be potential MD-80 buyers.

That left one realistic potential customer for the MD-80 among major U.S. carriers: American.

Worsham knew that American didn't want to buy airplanes until it got its labor situation cleared up, but he needed a sale. So immediately after Braniff's demise, he approached American—which previously had looked at the MD-80 and rejected it.

Worsham met privately with Bob Crandall to see what it would take to get American off its no-new-planes-right-now position. Their meeting produced perhaps the most unusual and risky aircraft deal in industry history. The unusual aspect was that all of the risk—every bit of it—was carried by McDonnell Douglas, not the airline.

American agreed to lease twenty MD-80s—which for some silly reason it renamed the "Super 80"—for five years. After five years, American could return the planes, no questions asked, no money owed. Also, at any time during the five-year period, American could return one or more of the planes on thirty days' notice with only a very small penalty. American and McDonnell Douglas officials steadfastly refused to say what American's lease rates on those planes were—though it is widely believed to have worked out to the equivalent of a purchase price between $17 million and $18 million. The sticker price on an MD-80 in those days was about $22 million, depending on how it was equipped.

Not surprisingly, Wall Street airline analysts loved the deal. Analysts who followed aircraft manufacturers hated it. But both generally agreed that American had just about raped McDonnell Douglas.

"No! No way did we rape Douglas. You can't rape a willing soul," Don Carty said. "We all made our own decisions. We told Douglas when they approached us that we didn't want any airplanes and they should go away. But they wouldn't go away. So we told them what we wanted, and they said okay."

"Worsham and Crandall came up with that deal together. We didn't force them into it," added Wes Kaldahl, who as senior vice president for airline planning was deeply involved in the decision to take the MD-80s. "Bob knew he had a guy in Worsham who was really trying hard to get a deal done. And Bob didn't want to kill McDonnell Douglas with this deal. He wanted to save them so we wouldn't get down to just one manufacturer left in the United States.

"I wasn't at the McDonnell Douglas board meeting where Worsham took the deal to the directors, but I understand it was a real hard sell. But Worsham was a hell of a salesman and got the deal approved. At the price they gave us on that first batch of planes, they were betting on the come, of course. But they never had any idea we'd eventually own 250 of them. They were probably thinking more like 75 or 100."

The deal was announced in September. While all the employees took the planes' acquisition to be a sign that good times were ahead, the Allied Pilots were particularly pleased. Several hundred of their members had been on the streets for nearly a year as a result of layoffs in the last half of 1981 and the grounding of the 707s.

Management made sure the unions did not take the acquisition of twenty MD-80s on incredibly favorable terms to mean it was wavering in its determination not to grow the airline until it had gotten what it wanted from labor.

"When McDonnell Douglas came along and said 'Look, we really want you to have some of these MD-80s, so we'll tell ya what we're gonna do. Here's the keys. Try it. You'll like it. And if you don't, just bring 'em back,' " Carty said, "we said 'We can't beat that.'

"But we knew if we took 'em and started to grow the airline, our employees would never agree to the kind of labor pacts management wanted. So we told our pilots, in particular, 'Guys, we've decided to take some airplanes to show you that we're serious about the future of the company. On the other hand, we're not serious about growth unless we can grow competitively with the new start-ups eating our lunch. So unless we can make this deal with you guys, we're going to retire old airplanes. As we take new ones, we're going to have to get rid of the oldest planes.' But for whatever reason, the leadership of our pilot group did not believe that's what we planned to do. They sort of took the position that if we took new airplanes, we were growing the company."

To prove management's point, when the first MD-80 joined the fleet in May 1983, American retired one of its oldest Boeing 727-100s. And each subsequent MD-80 going into the American fleet that summer crossed paths with an old 727 coming out of it. To the pilots, that was particularly bad news because the 727 is a three-pilot airplane and the MD-80 needs only two people in the cockpit.

THE FIRST union to come to the plate was the Transport Workers Union, representing more than 10,500 American employees, mostly mechanics and fleet service clerks (bag handlers, airplane cleaners, and a host of other types of ramp workers). While not the most highly paid workers, TWU members represented a big chunk of American's labor bill simply because of their numbers. And, in many cases, management believed they were the most overpaid of the airline's 41,000 employees given what they could have earned in jobs outside the airline industry.

American had no quarrel with its fully licensed and experienced A&P (airframe and powerplant) mechanics. Their special skills were considered to be very valuable; therefore, those mechanics were worth the money they were getting. Those same job skills used outside the airline industry would have commanded similar pay.

But Crandall and company were very concerned about what they were paying fleet service clerks, who essentially were unskilled laborers who had been trained to perform a variety of tasks that required few special skills. Management also was concerned about the starting pay rates of apprentice mechanics and what they believed was a too-short pay ladder in nearly every work classification covered by the TWU.

"We had to get lower starting pay rates and more cross-utilization," said Charlie Pasciuto, the sad-eyed, gravel-voiced veteran airline labor negotiator who spent twenty-two years in American's employee relations department, nearly all of it as VP and chief negotiator. "Labor was costing us more than 35 cents out of every dollar of revenue we got. Continental eventually got its [labor] costs down to less than 25 cents. We had to close that gap, maybe not all the way, but we had to get our costs more in line with the competition's.

"We had a hell of a lot of fleet service people all over the system. In the hubs at D/FW and Chicago, they stayed pretty busy all day long. But elsewhere, we had more TWU fleet service people than other airlines had per flight. We had guys who were productive only maybe 25 percent of the time, and the rest of the time, because of the long times between flights at the outlying stations, they were sitting on their hands. So we needed the ability to use TWU workers part time, especially at the stations, to eliminate a lot of that spending," Pasciuto said.

"And we had to have cross-utilization. Bag handlers were certainly capable of policing the ramp area and could help clean the airplanes. And there were a whole host of other jobs that could be done while there wasn't any flight activity. But the way our contract had evolved over decades of regulation, where you just passed your costs through to the passenger, you had to have one worker to handle bags, one to pick up the trash, one to clean the planes, and so on. A bag handler could be disciplined for picking up trash or straightening up his work area. It was ridiculous.

"We also wanted fleet service people to push back the airplanes. We had mechanics doing that. And we had mechanics working as wing walkers on pushouts. All they were doing was making sure the guy pushing them out didn't hit something. That didn't require a mechanic's skills. We could train fleet service people to do that and use that mechanic somewhere where his skills were needed. That would have reduced the number of mechanics we needed per plane, but the mechanics would have been happy about it because they didn't like being wing walkers any more than we liked them doing it. They wanted to work on airplanes, and that's what we wanted them to do," Pasciuto said.

American also wanted to stretch the pay ladder. At the time, a newly hired mechanic would reach the top of the pay scale in two years. For a fleet service clerk it was two and a half years. That wasn't really a problem for American in the 1970s and early 1980s because it wasn't growing. Relatively few people were being hired. But such a short pay progression ladder would have been very expensive for a company trying to grow rapidly. And it would have defeated the purpose of seeking lower entry-level pay rates.

Pasciuto canvassed the industry and discovered that Piedmont Airlines, a puddle-jumping outfit that had grown up into a regional jet carrier in the East and Southeast that consistently got high marks for customer service, had the lowest entry-level wage for fleet service clerks among all established carriers: $8 an hour. That became the baseline on American's proposal to established new, lower entry-level wages.

"I told Crandall that if Piedmont was having no trouble hiring people at $8 an hour, we sure as hell could do the same thing," he said.

After months of negotiation with the TWU's leadership, which was very recluctant to take such a contract offer to their members, American began communicating directly with the members. The union leadership complained that American had violated the Railway Labor Act by going around the union's official negotiating committee. American argued that it did not communicate anything to the rank-and-file that it hadn't already submitted to the negotiating committee, and, therefore, it had the right to communicate directly with employees and to bypass the union's information filter.

American also began signing contingency contracts with a number of third-party maintenance providers. If the TWU went out on strike, American wanted to have its necessary maintenance work covered so it could continue operating most or all of its scheduled flights. Of course, word of this got back to the TWU, just as management had expected and hoped it would.

The TWU's master executive council issued a do-not-pass recommendation but allowed the members to vote on the contract. Management remained confident that logic would win out. But it was almost too confident. Members ratified the new contract, but only narrowly.

"The big selling point for us was that in return for lower starting rates, cross-utilization, et cetera, we gave them lifetime job security," Pasciuto said. "That meant a lot to those guys in the TWU. They were just average people, working hard to make a living and to provide for their families. They weren't the kind of guys who could set back a lot of money for the future every year the way pilots or senior executives could. These guys had house payments and car payments and boat payments to make, and kids to put through college and dentist bills. They were just average working stiffs. And lifetime job security really meant a lot to them. It gave them peace of mind, especially as they looked around and saw what other airline managements were doing to their workers."

Next up were the pilots, who agreed to American's request to enter negotiations early on a contract that didn't expire until 1984. Initially they didn't believe management would hold off on adding planes until it got the deal it wanted, but when management retired one 727 for every new MD-80 coming in, they started to get the picture.

The deal Pasciuto offered the pilots contained all the same principles established in the TWU contract: cross-utilization, increased productivity, and more flexible work scheduling in exchange for growth. But the offer to the pilots differed from the deal with the TWU in two distinct ways.

First, American asked the pilots for the right to establish an entirely separate pay scale for newly hired pilots. Those already on board with the airline would continue to work on the existing pay scale. Those hired after contract ratification would work on a new, lower scale. Not only would their starting wages be lower than the old starting wages, the top pay on the new scale would be lower than the top pay on the old scale.

And second, American put a written guarantee into the proposal, promising to grow the fleet from 230 planes to at least 454 aircraft by a given date down the road. By doing that, the airline's need for captains would more than double in a short time. And the time it would take for a pilot to move from rookie flight officer to captain would be reduced from about eighteen years to six or seven years. Management, of course, knew that the goal of every airline pilot is to be promoted to captain, because captains typically make between 75 percent to 125 percent more money than the pilot in the right seat.

This guarantee, American said, would make up for the fact that newly hired pilots would never make as much per hour as those already working for the airline. Because they would be promoted to captain so early in their careers, their longer terms in the higher-paying left-hand seat would net them more money over their lifetimes than they would get by waiting eighteen years before being promoted to captain.

"We also promised the pilots that if we didn't do what we said we'd do, the guys who would have been promoted to captain but weren't because we didn't live up to our end of the deal would be paid as if they were captains. We put that language into the contract to show them we were serious about growing the airline if we got what we wanted," Pasciuto said.

"But, at the same time, we told them that if we didn't get the deal we wanted, not only would we not grow the airline, we'd shrink it. I told them that they would never see this management team walk up the bankruptcy court's steps the way Braniff's management had. That's just not part of this management's principles. Before we'd do that, we'd shrink and use our assets elsewhere. And Crandall said many times, in many places, privately and publicly, that if forced to do it, he'd sell the airline and keep the computer [SABRE]. He was committed either to grow the airline or to do something else more productive."

Somewhere between the $19.6 million loss in 1982 and the retirement of old 727s to offset the acquisition of new MD-80s, management persuaded the Allied Pilots' board of directors, who had the authority to ratify the agreement without a vote of the membership.

The 1983 deal between the Allied Pilots and American established the first true two-tier labor contract in U.S. business. Literally hundreds of other companies, including most successful airlines, were to copy all or some of that plan over the next few years.

"I don't know how exactly we did it, but we finally convinced our two larger unions that we meant what we said," Pasciuto said.

"And it was very important to Bob, and to all of us, that we lived up to our end of the bargain. I remember that while the APA board met to ratify the agreement before the signing ceremony, Crandall and I were talking. I said it would be important to follow up quickly with a positive note by recalling furloughed pilots. He said, 'Why don't we announce it tonight?' Just he and I talking led to that spur-of-the-moment announcement.

"Later there was a management meeting after the TWU and the pilots' contracts were done, where Bob told all the managers that

'We've got some good contracts and I don't want you to sharpshoot it. We've made some promises and I don't want you to screw it up. We're going to live up to our end of the agreement. If you start thumping your chests and saying that we've got one up on them, that's bullshit. We gave them some pay raises and job security and made some pretty ambitious promises. And if any of you guys screw it up for us, you're outta here.' And he meant every word of it," Pasciuto said.

The nearly 6,000-member Association of Professional Flight Attendants (APFA) was the last of the three unions to agree to a new deal with American in 1983. Flight attendants historically have had little leverage against airlines. While pilots and mechanics have special skills, licenses, and training that make them absolutely vital, anyone in decent health can be trained in the safety and evacuation procedures that the Federal Aviation Administration requires flight attendants to know. Now, using flight attendants certified after taking crash courses in aircraft safety won't help an airline's marketing image. Spilling hot coffee on the passenger in 26C and serving the pork chop dinner to the Orthodox Jew in 18D who had special-ordered a kosher meal are the kinds of problems an airline could expect if it actually tried to replace striking flight attendants with hastily trained replacements. But at least it would be able to continue flying.

That's what American was prepared to do if the APFA voted to reject American's two-tier contract offer. When the union leadership initially rejected American's proposal and threatened a strike, the airline sped up flight attendant training in order to have trained replacements ready to go. Also, hundreds of nonunion employees, including virtually every secretary and a lot of middle managers at the airline's headquarters, volunteered as emergency replacement flight attendants. But those volunteers weren't needed. Having backed themselves into a corner by threatening a strike that they knew at least half of their members would not support out of fear that they would be replaced permanently, the APFA's leadership could do little but sign on the dotted line.

So, in relatively short order American completed its mission and gained significant labor cost reductions from its unions without a fight. Had it been necessary, the airline's war chest could have been tapped to help it ride out a strike. But doing that would have made it more difficult and expensive for the airline to launch its growth plan once things settled down.

In a sense, American is lucky that its employees were represented by two in-house unions and the least strident of all the AFL-CIO-affiliated unions with a presence in the airline industry, the TWU. Had the Air Line Pilots Association, the International Association of Machinists, and the Teamsters been American's negotiating partners, the outcome of those 1983 contract negotiations might have been very different.

That's not to say American's workers would have gotten a better deal if their unions had refused to go along with what American wanted. Management did live up to its end of the bargain and began to grow the airline rapidly. Today American operates a fleet of more than 670 aircraft. It has about 10,000 pilots, nearly 20,000 flight attendants, and almost 30,000 TWU members. Pilots who would never have been hired by American had the 1983 contract not been signed already have been promoted to captain and are making more than $100,000 a year. Flight attendants who were in high school in 1983 today are making about $30,000, in many cases without benefit of a college degree. Mechanics who otherwise would be tinkering with single-engine general aviation airplanes and holding down a second job to pay off their school debts today are making nearly $35,000 and working on 40,000 pound thrust jet engines.

LIKE MOST of American's innovations over the past two decades, Bob Crandall did not dictate the specific details of the two-tier wage scale plan. In fact, not even the germ of the idea originated with him. But he rightfully should be credited with the creation of the two-tier system—and dozens of major innovations—because he created the electrically charged atmosphere within American's management ranks that gave rise to such ideas, then nurtured those ideas into full-blown, coherent, detailed, and effective strategies.

That was the case with the two-tier labor contracts. The idea grew out of management's never-ending discussion of how to achieve the kind of low-cost growth Carty had suggested in his 1980 study. One obvious answer was to seek employee concessions. Some in American's management preferred this way. But Crandall, with a strong second from Pasciuto, the man who had to sell the deal to the unions, didn't like that answer.

"Bob always preached that every contract with labor had to be win-win," Pasciuto said. "If it's lopsided, it's not a good contract.

"The downside of a contract that favors the unions is obvious.

That's what we had going into the three sets of negotiations in 1983. No matter what else we did with the airline to increase revenues, our labor costs were too high. You do that for very long and you're out of business.

"But the downside of a pro-management contract is that you won't get a motivated work force. That's really a bad thing if your product is, like ours, a service. The difference between getting a plane off on time and fifteen minutes late is a couple of guys not doing their jobs well enough or fast enough, or not caring enough to do it right the first time and having to do it over. Even one person who's not motivated or who is ticked off at management all the time over pay or something or other can screw up a service organization just by the way they treat the customers.

"Look at the incumbent carriers that struggled in the early and mid-1980s. They were the ones that asked their people for concessions. Those of us that are doing a little bit better today, us, United, and Delta, we're the ones who didn't ask our people to give us concessions," he said.

"Bob told me on many occasions that he wanted to do everything possible to avoid having to take money back from incumbent employees. He wanted to protect the incumbents. He didn't want to lower their standards of living. He wanted to protect the people who by their work had made American great. It wasn't their fault that the world had changed and we had to find a way to save money on labor. He really, honestly believed that we had made a moral contract with them when we hired them about what they could expect their pay to be, and reducing those numbers would be breaking that moral contract. That's how we ended up coming up with the idea of two-tier. If you want to protect the paychecks of the people you've already got, but you need to get your unit costs down, the only way to do it is by hiring lots of new people on a lower pay scale," Pasciuto said.

Ironically, Crandall, who has been called "the father of the two-tier pay scale," almost didn't survive long enough to see it implemented. On February 23, 1983, twelve days after negotiations with the TWU reached an impasse and the union's leadership decided to put the matter to a vote of its members, with a do-not-pass recommendation, the ghost of Howard Putnam came back to haunt him.

The U.S. Department of Justice antitrust division filed a civil suit against both American and Crandall, alleging that the airline and its president had conspired to violate the Sherman Antitrust Act by attempting to monopolize airline passenger services at Dallas/Fort Worth Airport. Specifically, the Justice Department pointed to Crandall's intemperate phone call to Putnam in which he had told the Braniff chairman, "Raise your goddamn fares 20 percent! I'll raise mine the next morning!"

Obviously, Crandall and Putnam never reached an agreement to fix prices. In fact, neither man said anything else about fares during their now-famous telephone call.

Curiously, shortly after it announced the civil suit seeking Crandall's ouster, the government said a federal grand jury—impaneled a year earlier in Fort Worth to investigate American's alleged dirty tricks against Braniff—would be disbanded without any indictments being issued.

Also, the grand jury's inaction and the Justice Department's decision to file a civil rather than a criminal suit was a clear admission that government attorneys knew their case wasn't strong enough to meet a criminal case's stronger-burden-of-proof requirement. Still, Justice claimed Crandall had attempted to enter into a conspiracy to fix prices and therefore should be barred from any management role at American or any other airline for two years.

The immediate reaction around the industry was one of absolute shock. Crandall's pit-bull competitiveness, his penchant for speaking his mind freely, and his perceived arrogance had earned him no love in the industry. But no one was respected more, both for the results he got and for his raw honesty.

Indeed, some of Crandall's competitors in the industry quietly worked behind the scenes on his behalf. They spoke to members of Congress, suggesting that they intervene with the Justice Department because Putnam, not Crandall, was the one who had behaved dishonestly by taping the phone call without Crandall's knowledge.

Tom Plaskett, Crandall's heir apparent as president at the time, had a professional falling out with Crandall and left American in 1986 to become president of Continental Airlines and then chairman of Pan Am. Still, Plaskett defends his former boss's integrity.

"I know just about everything there is to know about that phone call. I was in Bob's office when he placed the initial call to Howard, though I was not there when Howard returned the call. But that phone call is totally in character with Bob Crandall, not because he was conspiring to fix prices but because he is so focused in his intensity on an issue or on a problem, on what is right economically and from a business perspective, that it sometimes just comes out. I mean, sometimes something inside of him just explodes and it all spills out. But he wasn't trying to conspire to fix prices. He was trying to teach Howard airline economics 101. It was unfortunate that it happened, but there was never any intent or attempt to fix prices."

Still, on the surface, once the Justice Department filed its suit, it looked as if Crandall was a goner. Responding to the news, one industry executive who requested anonymity told the *Fort Worth Star-Telegram*, that "It's been a long time since the Justice Department had someone so cold." Another anonymous source who was familiar with the case filed by Justice told the same newspaper that "Crandall is in big trouble."

For a few minutes, that was more true than anyone knew.

Al Casey pretty much had turned the day-to-day operation of the airline over to Crandall upon his elevation to the presidency in 1980. Casey, meanwhile, focused most of his attention on building up the airline's balance sheet, his pet plan to diversify into the oil business as a hedge against the sometimes violent cycles of the airline industry, and government affairs. Though they clashed regularly and did not socialize together much, he and Crandall were quite close. He would have trusted his fellow New Englander to hold his wallet in a Las Vegas casino.

But he did not know about the phone conversation with Putnam until shortly before the Justice Department announced that it had filed suit.

"I was in the dark on it till then," Casey said. "I guess Bob thought that he was doing me a favor to do it that way. And I guess in retrospect he was right, but at the time I could have throttled him.

"I knew I didn't have much time to make a decision because the media would be calling in a few minutes for a reaction. I sat down and said to myself 'What's the best thing to do from a corporate standpoint?' And I determined from what I knew of the case they had against him—which our lawyers said later was pretty weak when you started looking at what the law said and what their evidence was—it was clear that what was best was to defend Bob and stay with him. He's the best there is. And I believed in him. Besides, what do you do? Suspend the guy and somebody has to run the airline, then you bring him back? Everything goes into a state of suspension with him if you do that. The only other thing you could do would be to fire him."

Did Casey actually consider that most drastic of options?

"I thought it through, that's all I can say. I didn't have much time, but I thought it through very carefully," he said.

IN ONE sense, that was the last major decision Al Casey made as chairman of American Airlines. He retired in March 1985 and turned the reins over to Crandall, though he stayed on as a member of AMR Corp.'s board of directors.

Before he left, Casey saw the airline fully establish its second hub at Chicago's O'Hare International Airport. He also presided over the company as it reported back-to-back record net profits of $227.9 million and $233.9 million in 1983 and 1984 respectively. In each of those years American exceeded its goal of a 5 percent operating margin, an achievement that made it possible for Crandall to launch the aggressive, rapid growth plan that promised to propel American to the top of the industry.

Casey, a financier first and foremost, also took immense pride in the fact that the $5.4 billion company he left had a solid—even strong—balance sheet with $1.35 billion in cash and short-term investments, a $1 million line of credit, and $1.6 billion total equity. Its long-term debt of $775 million and its capital lease obligations of $767 million were easily under control. The company was ready, willing, and able to finance what would be the biggest, boldest capital spending and expansion plan in industry history.

But even if Casey had done none of those things, he still should be regarded as the man who saved American Airlines. History undoubtedly will place his tenure as chairman as third in importance behind those of C.R. Smith and Bob Crandall. But it is fair to say that without Casey, neither Crandall nor Smith would be regarded quite so favorably.

For all his successes in nearly forty years at American's helm, Smith failed at his most important task. He did not provide the company with an adequate successor. As a result, his airline was perhaps only a year or two away from financial disaster when Casey was recruited. Without Casey's drastic steps to improve the airline's balance sheet—and its morale—American might not have survived the initial turmoil of deregulation.

And for all of Crandall's heralded achievements, both in the years he worked for Casey and in the years since he succeeded Casey as chairman, those achievements might never have happened had it not been for the Boston Irishman who didn't know the first thing about airlines when he became chairman of one. Because Casey was not an airline man, he had no choice but to seek the advice and wisdom of others. He was fortunate that the best young mind in the industry already was on his staff the day he took office. But a veteran airline executive in Casey's shoes might have been far less willing to listen to the maverick, opinionated Crandall and may well have felt threatened by his intellect, intensity, and ambition.

Indeed, though it is impossible to know for certain, it probably is fair to say that had there been no Al Casey at American Airlines, there would be no Bob Crandall there today. That he selected and groomed as his successor the man who arguably is the most important character in industry history should be enough to qualify Casey for corporate and industry sainthood.

IN JULY 1985, four months after Casey retired, American and the Justice Department reached a settlement in the price-fixing case against the airline and Crandall. The defendants admitted no guilt, but Crandall was required for two years to make and keep written notes of every conversation he had with any senior executives of competing carriers.

The settlement amounted to a very embarrassing and somewhat annoying slap on the wrist. Privately, Crandall seethed over the Justice Department's efforts to kick him out of the industry on the basis of such questionable "evidence" as the taped phone conversation with Putnam.

Publicly, the outspoken Crandall, who in other cases might have used his knack for self-deprecating humor to deflect the criticism and suspicion that resulted from the case, adopted a very uncharacteristic stoicism. More accurately, he stonewalled the entire subject. For several years American's public relations staff regularly warned reporters preparing to interview Crandall that only one subject was off limits. "Ask any question you want," reporters were told. "But mention the phone conversation with Putnam and the interview is over."

Al Becker, American's longtime, highly professional managing director of corporate communications and the company's principal media spokesman, once explained to a reporter that "Mr. Crandall was very embarrassed by the whole incident. He just felt that as unfair as those charges were, he'd somehow brought shame upon American and upon himself. One time he told several of us, 'That'll be in my obituary.' And you know what? He's right. It will be in his obituary. And it's not fair. He didn't do anything wrong. And he's done so many other good things for this company and its people, and for the industry, and even for the traveling public. But people are never gonna let him forget the Braniff thing."

14

Misunderstandings

THERE'S AN old Chinese curse that says "May you live in interesting times." Bob Crandall must have made a lot of Chinese people mad sometime in his life.

"The day after it was announced that I would become chairman, we announced a new package of fares, and our stock didn't open for three hours," Crandall said.

It was on that day, January 17, 1985, that American introduced its Ultimate Super Saver fare program, a valiant but futile effort to bring some degree of rationality back to an airfare price structure gone mad. Crandall, who happened that morning to be en route to New York to speak at a luncheon meeting of the prestigious Wings Club of New York, was certain that the Ultimate Super Saver plan was the right thing to do. American hoped to raise the average fare price actually paid by travelers by introducing a sane, easy-to-understand, and more controllable discount fare structure. The airline, however, heavily promoted Ultimate Super Savers as discounts.

And in a classic misunderstanding, that advertising focus on the deep discounts is what caught the financial markets' attention. Stock traders were so flooded with sell orders that they could not immediately find enough buyers to take all the dumped AMR stock. It took three hours to straighten out the order imbalance and open the stock for normal trading.

Crandall, of course, knew nothing about the stock's trading imbalance until he got off the plane at New York's LaGuardia Airport. Company officials there rushed up to meet him and delivered the troublesome news.

"I thought, 'Great! What a way to start off as the company's new chairman.' Things like that will make you kind of nervous," he joked.

But that's pretty much typical of Crandall's tenure as chairman. Despite his many efforts to communicate his views—and no airline industry executive ever has done more to communicate with his employees, investors, government officials, and the general public than Crandall—he remains one of the most misunderstood executives in the United States.

In truth, Crandall is a very good communicator. Like a master professor at an elite university whose enthralling lectures make his or her classes the hardest on campus to get into, Crandall has a natural ability to break down complicated issues into bite-size pieces that average people can easily understand. In addition to his natural ability to communicate, Crandall has worked to improve his communication skills. He has sought professional help to sharpen his public speaking and writing skills. In 1985 he hired Russell Mack, a former speechwriter in the Reagan White House, to add polish and pizzazz to the many speeches he gives each year. And when Mack left American in 1988 to head up United Airlines' public relations office, Crandall recruited Reggi Ann Dubin, a former airline industry reporter for *Business Week* magazine. Yet Crandall continues to be widely misunderstood.

One reason is that he has much to say about many things. People are shocked to learn that on a personal level, Bob Crandall is kind of shy, covets his privacy, and is very reluctant to share any details about his personal life—which by all accounts is boringly traditional. (He is happily married to his high school sweetheart, has three grown kids, shuns the night life, has a limited social life, and likes to jog.) Yet the professional Bob Crandall is anything but shy.

It seems as if he has thought a lot about every subject that can possibly affect his airline and has a strong opinion on them all. A noted detail monger, Crandall can give you ten minutes on why airplane passenger seats made by one company are superior to those made by a competitor or on how the hydraulics system on a DC-10 works. And he can give you two hours on international trade policy and how nations stupidly use their airlines to project national economic power abroad instead of to generate more economic activity through more and better travel opportunities and lower fares for both businesspeople and leisure travelers.

Another reason Crandall is so commonly misunderstood is that he often appears to contradict himself. In some cases, he actually does contradict himself. For example, in AMR's 1989 annual report to shareholders, which he uses as a forum for his and the company's positions, the company (that is, Crandall) argued that those who opposed American's proposed purchase of rights to serve Central and South America from Eastern Airlines and its acquisition of TWA's Chicago–London route authority were wrong when they claimed that such route authorities belong to the government and not to the carriers that held those routes and wanted to sell them to American. But American and Crandall had made exactly the opposite argument in 1986 when it asked the government to strip the Chicago–London route from TWA and give it to American. TWA, American claimed, was underutilizing a national asset that American could put to better use on behalf of the national economy and U.S. travelers.

In other cases, Crandall only appears to be contradicting himself. Like any good leader, he tries to avoid painting himself in a corner. So he often uses "out" clauses and provisos in his speeches and even in his ordinary conversations.

But the biggest reason Crandall is so regularly misunderstood is that, unlike most of us, who tend to think in one or two dimensions, Crandall thinks multidimensionally. While most of the rest of us intellectually are playing checkers, he's playing three-dimensional chess. Thus, when he says he favors cabotage—the right of foreign airlines to pick up U.S. passengers in one city, say, New York, and fly them to another U.S. city, say, Chicago, in competition with domestic carriers—organized labor blasts him for trying to give U.S. pilots', mechanics', and other airline workers' jobs to lower-paid foreign workers. But organized labor misunderstands him on that point. Crandall supports cabotage because he wants to use it as a trading weapon to gain access to other nations' domestic air travel markets. He knows full well that only the most foolhardy of foreign carriers would actually attempt to compete head-to-head on U.S. domestic routes against the strongest U.S. carriers. To compete profitably in the domestic U.S. market, a foreign carrier would have to duplicate its U.S. rivals' entrenched, well-financed hub-and-spoke networks overnight, which because of the cost and logistics involved would be impossible. Thus, in Crandall's view, cabotage does not threaten U.S.

airline workers' jobs at all. In fact, if anything, there would be increased demand for workers in the airline industry if Crandall had his way on the cabotage issue.

SOMETIMES THERE'S a price to be paid for being misunderstood.

For Crandall and American, that price was $1.5 million and a ton of embarrassment in 1985.

In the spring of that year, the Federal Aviation Administration, under pressure from Congress and safety watchdog groups, launched what it called its "White Glove" safety inspection program. Over about a two-year period, every airline in the nation would be paid a visit by a special team of FAA safety inspectors. In essence, these inspectors would audit the airline's maintenance records and procedures to make certain it was doing everything it was supposed to be doing in terms of both repair work and preventive maintenance. The White Glove program grew out of increasing concern about the unusually high safety-related incidents and the rapidly rising average age of the aircraft in the nation's commercial aircraft.

American happened to be first in line on the White Glove inspection team's list. But no one at headquarters in Fort Worth was very alarmed. Believing their own rhetoric, they assumed American had the best maintenance program in the industry. That may or may not have been true. But it wasn't good enough to meet the FAA's standards.

The FAA found hundreds of violations, some of which were particularly disturbing. In one instance, a mechanic in Chicago working on a wing slat—a movable control surface on the wing's leading edge that extends forward and down during takeoff to increase lift—on a DC-10 jumbo jet determined that a small spring in the linkage that moved the slat back and forth had to be replaced. The mechanic could not find that particular part in stock at American's Chicago hub. Yet, he admitted later, he felt intense pressure from his superiors to get the plane ready to make its next flight in a couple of hours. So he got in his car and drove to a nearby auto parts house and bought a similar-size spring, then returned to the airport and installed it on the DC-10. The spring, which was made of slightly smaller gauge and inferior metal, held up for several flights before failing. Luckily, no in-flight incident resulted because of the mechanic's "creative" response to the pressure he felt to get the airplane back in the air pronto.

In several other instances, mechanics reported being ordered to "sign off" in aircraft log books that they had completed inspections and/or repairs of problem items reported by pilots when, in fact, they either had not done so or had made an inspection but not a repair they felt was necessary.

The biggest problem the FAA found with American's maintenance operations was that the airline allowed many, even most, of its planes to fly with a very long list of "open" maintenance problems on its "Minimum Equipment List." In the sometimes backward-sounding vocabulary of the FAA—which is, after all, a highly bureaucratic governmental agency—every commercial jet has a Minimum Equipment List, or MEL (a list of items on the plane that don't work). But, because they are not essential to the safe operation of the plane, the plane can continue to fly with passengers aboard with those items "open," or not fixed. Typically, all the airline has to do is place a placard—often a piece of tape with something scribbled in ink on it—over the broken device to inform cockpit or cabin crew members.

However, it is one thing for a plane to operate with one of its on-board coffee makers on the fritz. But it is an entirely different matter if a dozen switches in the cockpit don't work or if the entire cabin PA system is plagued by an intermittent short. A properly operating PA system is important, because if it is broken, issuing important safety instructions in an emergency becomes much more difficult. No one of those items alone will automatically cause a problem. But taken together, if enough items on a plane don't work, crew members may suffer critical delays in finding solutions to in-flight problems or emergencies. Safety experts say that the snowballing effect of multiple mechanical failures, even on relatively insignificant items, can reduce human performance below minimum tolerance levels.

The FAA found that American was allowing the number of open items on its MELs to skyrocket and that some items remained on the MELs for weeks before being fixed.

All told, the agency discovered enough violations to propose a fine of more than $3 million. American's lawyers challenged the accuracy of the FAA's findings and the wisdom of making an example out of American, arguing that doing so could result in a serious decline in passenger traffic and, therefore, in revenues that the airline would need to address the FAA's legitimate concerns.

Rocco J. "Rocky" Masiello, American's senior vice president of operations, took the blame. The FAA announced in September of 1985 that American had agreed to settle the claims for $1.5 million.

By the end of the year, Masiello was gone, via the early retirement route.

No one who worked with Crandall could miss his zeal for cost cutting. But not everyone who worked for him fully understood what Crandall meant when he stressed the importance of keeping costs down and reducing them where possible. Masiello is a sterling example of that. A one-time aircraft mechanic who had worked his way to the top, Masiello could discuss classical literature and philosophy as easily as he could the inner workings of a Pratt & Whitney JT8D engine. But for whatever reason, he could not, or would not, stand up to Crandall and some of his closest aides when the pressures to cut costs and maximize revenues threatened the integrity of the airline's aircraft maintenance program. Crandall never meant that American should cut corners on safety or quality-of-service items. But the way Masiello interpreted Crandall's emphasis on cost cutting led directly to compromising the carrier's maintenance and safety programs.

Under pressure from Wes Kaldahl, the head of planning, and Mel Olsen, American's chief flight scheduler, the maintenance department had begun adjusting aircraft maintenance schedules so the planes spent less time in line hangars around the system or in Tulsa during their overhaul visits and more time in revenue passenger service.

"Rocky tried too hard to be a nice guy," said one American executive. "He would bend over backward to do whatever Bob wanted, or whatever Kaldahl and Olsen wanted to do with the airplanes. But he bent over too far. He stretched our [periodic] maintenance times on airplanes too far. He didn't do anything illegal, but it was too much. When it all happened, he tried to blame Kaldahl and Olsen for pushing maintenance too far with their schedules, but it was actually Bob who was the one doing the pushing. Kaldahl and Olsen were just doing their jobs. Rocky should have done his and said, 'Okay, we can do this, this and this, but no more. Any more than that and we're compromising the maintenance of those aircraft and we're compromising the margins of safety.'

"In hindsight, American had been too conservative on its maintenance schedules. So it could afford to stretch out the times on its planes some. So Kaldahl and his people pushed, and maybe they pushed too far. But no one ever said stop. That was Rocky's job. But he didn't do it, or, if he tried, he failed to get Bob's attention, which is also his responsibility. You've got to be strong to be in that position, and he wasn't strong enough."

WORD OF the FAA's investigation and preliminary findings leaked out in July 1985. The airline and the government were still haggling and rattling legal swords at one another, and neither side would comment publicly. So two of the three newspapers in the Dallas-Fort Worth area, the *Dallas Times Herald* and the *Fort Worth Star-Telegram*, launched their own investigations. The *Star-Telegram* contacted the Aircraft Owners and Pilots Association (AOPA), which maintains an office in Oklahoma City, near the FAA's central computer operations, in order to process title and maintenance history searches for parties interested in buying airplanes. The newspaper paid the AOPA to run a check on the incident history of every plane in American's fleet. That check produced a voluminous computer printout on every incident reported by American pilots or mechanics involving one of the airline's planes with passengers aboard over about an eighteen-month period.

It took several weeks to distill all of that information, but the paper was able to document a series of problems that, while not endemic to every plane in American's fleet, tended to indicate that certain specific aircraft had recurring problems that the airline could not seem to fix.

The *Star-Telegram* took that information to American for its response. But American, which usually is very cooperative and forthcoming with reporters—especially beat reporters at major national newspapers, such as *The New York Times* and the *Wall Street Journal* and at the three local papers—went to its rarely used four-corners delay offense. Normally, one of the airline's several top-notch public relations representatives would have handled the interview requests. But this time Lowell Duncan, American's vice president of corporate communications and a former television newsman at KXAS, the NBC affiliate in Fort Worth, handled the issue personally. First he instructed the *Star-Telegram* to put its interview request in writing, with plenty of background on what kinds of questions would be asked, what the results of the paper's own investigation were, and why the reporters and editors there felt the matter was worth reporting. Sensing that it had hit a very raw nerve, the *Star-Telegram* responded immediately.

Duncan, though, threw the paper a curve. After waiting nearly a week to respond to the newspaper's letter, he laid down an unprecedented set of ground rules. The paper was instructed to submit its questions in written form. The company then would respond in writing to any of the questions it chose. After that, he said, a reporter would be allowed a one-hour interview with Masiello.

Star-Telegram reporters and editors debated whether to simply print the results of the paper's investigation of American's maintenance operations. The paper could have issued that threat to American in hopes of sparking a quicker answer to its questions, or it could have run its report with an accompanying explanation about American's delaying tactics. However, the decision was made to play it American's way, for two reasons. First and foremost, the newspaper wanted to make it very clear that it was not out to get American and was willing to give the airline every reasonable opportunity to state its position. And, second, there was some concern among the newsroom management about starting a feud with one of the country's largest employers, the largest company headquartered in Fort Worth, and one of the newspaper's largest advertisers. However, had the newspaper's evidence shown a clear-cut case of willful abuse of FAA safety standards or of incidents where serious personal injuries or death resulted from American's mistakes, these secondary concerns almost certainly would have disappeared and the story would have been rushed into the paper.

Duncan assigned staffer John Hotard, a former state editor with the Associated Press in Dallas and the airline's PR specialist on maintenance and safety issues, to the job of getting the answers to the *Star-Telegram*'s questions. Hotard devoted most of his time to the project, but it still took more than two weeks for him to get American's technical staff to supply precisely worded answers to the questions and to get those answers approved by the airline's legal department and senior management.

After the paper received American's answers, it was made to wait nearly a week more for the promised interview with Masiello. That interview was set up for a Thursday afternoon. Whether the timing was coincidental or purposeful is uncertain, but by scheduling it so late in the week, American effectively prevented the newspaper from running its story in the Sunday paper. Masiello, who unbeknownst to the *Star-Telegram* had already been stripped of any real responsibilities and was being allowed to stay on until his retirement at the

end of the year, was accompanied at the interview by Duncan and
Dick Lempert, American's senior vice president and general counsel.

By this time it was late September, and the newspaper had prepared
four stories to run as a package in its Sunday editions, ten days after
the Masiello interview. But on the Friday before the report's scheduled publication, the FAA announced that it and American had
reached an agreement to conclude the FAA's White Glove inspection
of the carrier's maintenance operation. American and the FAA both
said most of the problems uncovered in the inspection were a matter
of poor or sloppy record keeping. The FAA did, however, release a
summary of some of the more serious problems it had uncovered.
However, the FAA refused to release its full report. Eventually the
FAA's report was made available in response to several news organizations' formal requests under the Freedom of Information Act.

American agreed to pay a $1.5 million settlement, which the air-
line's public relations staff stressed was *not* a fine. The company also
defended its maintenance operations by quoting a phrase in the settlement agreement—a watered-down version of the FAA's preliminary findings—that said the FAA's inspection had "confirmed the
integrity of the company's maintenance and airworthiness functions."

The *Star-Telegram* hastily scrapped its four-story Sunday package
on American's maintenance problems. Instead it came out on Saturday with three stories, one carrying the news of the $1.5 million
fine/settlement. The other two stories reported on the paper's own
investigation's findings and American's response.

The *Dallas Times Herald* produced a similarly large, tough-minded,
and damaging package of stories about American that day. However,
The Dallas Morning News, the largest of the three papers and easily
the softest when it comes to examining the uglier sides of businesses
with headquarters or substantial operations in the area, produced
only one story, albeit a lengthy one, about American's $1.5 million
settlement of FAA fines.

Nearly two months later, the *Star-Telegram*'s president and publisher Phil Meek, now president of the publishing division of the
Star-Telegram's parent company Capital Cities/ABC, met with senior
American officials. Meek wanted to discuss why American had not
been running ads in the *Star-Telegram* and the *Times Herald* when it
had been advertising regularly in the *Morning News*. Meek was told
that because it was fall, typically a slow period for airlines, American

had reduced its advertising all over and the decision to advertise in just one of the three local papers was part of its normal ad buying schedule. That soon would change, though, he was told.

Meek graciously accepted that explanation. But it was obvious that American had conducted a brief, unannounced advertising boycott of the two local papers that had been most aggressive in covering its maintenance problems. A few years later, as the now-defunct *Times Herald* was losing marketshare and money, it might have made sense to buy ads in only the larger *Morning News* and in the *Star-Telegram*, which dominates newspaper circulation statistics in the western half of the Metroplex, where about 35 percent of the region's population lives. But in 1985 it simply did not make sense to advertise in just one of the three papers that served the area. Shortly after Meek's meeting with Crandall, American resumed advertising in both the *Star-Telegram* and the *Times Herald*.

Still, American officials would not discuss the airline's maintenance operations for more than a year. Nor would it allow reporters to visit its primary maintenance base at Tulsa, Oklahoma. In fact, the first reporter—incidentally, from the *Star-Telegram*—to visit the base after the FAA's inspection did not do so until October of 1986.

Meanwhile, several months after the settlement was announced, Crandall, in one of his frequent messages to the airline's employees, vowed that American never again would be so "embarrassed."

Crandall quickly replaced Masiello with his top troubleshooter, Robert Baker. Crandall had come to like and trust Baker in the mid-1970s when he had served as assistant VP of marketing administration. In that job Baker had shown both a solid understanding of the financial aspects of the company and great managerial skill and toughness. From there, Baker had gone on to be vice president of the airline's southern division, where he managed the development of American's loose hub at D/FW and acted as front man for the company in its dealings with Dallas and Fort Worth and the big airport in relation to its possible headquarters relocation. In early 1979, when Crandall detected a management problem in American's cargo operations, he recalled Baker's early career background in cargo and sent him in to clean up that problem.

Eight months later, just as the company was relocating its headquarters to Texas, Randy Malin left to become senior VP of marketing at USAir, and Baker was moved into Malin's old slot as VP of passenger sales and advertising, reporting to senior marketing VP Plaskett. One aspect of Baker's job included supervision of marketing automation—the selling of SABRE computer reservations system hookups to travel agents. But, thanks to fare wars and all of the attendant advertising and marketing efforts, and thanks to the explosion in travel agents' use of SABRE, Baker's job became too big for one person to handle. Baker decided to stay with the SABRE part of the job. Mike Gunn, senior VP of marketing at American today, moved up from his post as general sales manager to take the passenger sales and advertising part of Baker's old job.

Shortly thereafter, Max Hopper, who had moved up to run American's data processing operations in 1980 when Jim O'Neill moved over to manage the airline's Sky Chefs in-flight catering division, left to become executive VP of operations for Bank of America. Crandall then gave Baker responsibility over both the marketing and operations sides of SABRE and made him VP of marketing automation systems. In that job, Baker managed SABRE through the period of its most explosive growth, which was complicated by the court-ordered breakup of AT&T. Instead of dealing with one set of national standards for installing the dedicated dataphone lines needed to connect travel agents' offices to SABRE, American had to deal with all the different Baby Bell companies that took over local phone service in various regions of the country. Technical standards, scheduling processes, and even paperwork requirements varied widely among the Baby Bells, and even among different city offices of the same local telephone company. Meanwhile, SABRE's own operations were expanding rapidly to meet the increased demand. In effect, Baker in short order had to install an entire new management system for a division that was closing in on $1 billion in annual revenues.

For Baker, the promotion in 1985 to senior VP of operations was a dream come true. He had asked Crandall for the job in 1981, when Don Lloyd-Jones left to become chairman of Air Florida. But Crandall had handed that job to Masiello instead and put Baker in charge of SABRE.

"I thought that was *the* job in this business that I was best suited for with my experience," Baker said. "But Bob declined to give me the job because I was neither a pilot nor a mechanic. He felt that would be too much structural shock on the company, and particularly on the pilots. I accepted that and that was fine with me because I was having plenty of fun with the computers, and learning a lot. But I was rather disappointed.

"But when the Feds laid that $1.5 million fine on us, that set the world on fire around here. It really lit the employees off. If there's anything that employees get upset about, it's when their confidence in the airplanes and the pilots and our maintenance and our management somehow gets shattered. That's what really happened when George Spater got nailed for making those illegal contributions to the Nixon campaign in '72. Then it happened again in '85 with the maintenance thing.

"It got a lot of attention in the media. And we perceived it as a huge problem externally for us. Obviously, it was a problem with our board, which we frankly had disappointed. And I think it's fair to say that Bob was disappointed that he hadn't seen this coming. And it was at that point that Bob was able to talk Max Hopper into coming back to the airline from the Bank of America to take my place so I could move over to the ops department. And maintenance wasn't the only thing wrong in ops department. We had kinda screwed up the crew scheduling function a bit and had run ourselves out of crews a couple of times. So Bob was generally unhappy with operations, and then this maintenance thing kind of lit the final rocket," Baker said.

Baker's down-to-earth, low-key personality, his reputation for fairness as a boss, and his skill as a people manager have combined to make him perhaps the most popular member of senior management among the troops since C. R. Smith. Nevertheless, Baker cleaned house, both at the Tulsa heavy maintenance base and throughout the line maintenance network, which sees to the fleet's day-to-day and overnight maintenance needs. He wiped out nearly the entire top layer of management in the maintenance department. All but one of their replacements came from within American's own maintenance department, and they were instructed not to make the same basic mistake their predecessors did.

Their mistake, Baker said, was in failing to tell senior management—and especially Crandall—what was really going on.

"Everyone's style is kind of different in interfacing with Bob. My own style is one of complete candor," Baker said. "I will always tell him as much bad news as good news. But some people just can't stand to tell him the bad news. But it's best to do it that way because when Bob finds out there's bad news from another way, and he will find out, then he gets very uptight, and he should be. I manage my own people that way. I expect them to tell me the good and the bad.

"I'm sure that some people try to tell Bob what they think he wants to hear because Bob, being a very aggressive guy who seeks perfection in everything we do, naturally gets quite excited when something isn't going right. Now, some people worry themselves to death every time Bob raises his voice or is critical. But you can't survive around here very long that way because Bob is never satisfied. That's one reason why American is what it is today. You always have to take what he says seriously. But you can't let it destroy you. You've got to learn to put that into perspective so that you can do your job as a manager effectively. That's what went wrong previously that led to the fine," Baker said.

In addition to changing upper management in the maintenance department, Baker conducted an industrywide search for "the right man" to head up the maintenance organization under him. Baker found Dave Kruse, buried in middle management of TWA's maintenance department. Though he obviously was one of the brightest young engineers and best managers in the airline maintenance world, Kruse had been lost in the constant managerial shuffle at TWA.

"Dave was sort of a middle manager at TWA. He was not a vice president, so he got a big, big boost going from middle management of the maintenance department at TWA, to vice president of maintenance and engineering at American," Baker said. "But he was the right guy for the job. We needed a new leader who was much more in tune with the people, much more in tune with making changes. And Dave was a very bright guy who knew how things should be done. So we told him to go in and forget the way things were done in the past and do 'em the way they should be done."

Baker also brought in Dixon Speas, a former American executive and industry consultant "who is something of a legend around the industry," Baker said, to conduct a thorough review of the airline's entire maintenance operation. Using the FAA's findings as a starting point, Speas and his team of consultants spent eighteen months analyzing American's maintenance operations to find the specific problems. One major result was a total overhaul of the system American used for handling and distributing replacement parts. The use of that spring bought at an auto parts house on a DC-10's wing slats was a prime example of the problem with the parts system. Had the right part been available as it should have been, the incident never would have occurred.

"In retrospect," Baker said, "it was probably good" that the FAA found problems with American's maintenance operations. Had American not been forced to rebuild its maintenance management, the explosive growth of its fleet from 260 aircraft in 1985 to about 670 today almost certainly would have overwhelmed the department.

"It got us ready to expand. We kind of rebuilt the place and expanded simultaneously," he said. "But because of all that happened, when we expanded we expanded the right way. I'd hate to have to go fix that sucker today as big as it is now."

OF COURSE, the sword of misunderstanding cuts two ways. While Crandall and his airline often are misunderstood, they too sometimes misunderstand.

Take, for instance, American management's profound fear that the FAA's investigation of the airline's maintenance operations and the $1.5 million settlement that it paid would have a chilling effect on passenger demand. If travelers were so affected, there is no statistical evidence to prove it. AMR Corp. reported a record $345.8 million net profit in 1985, up 47.8 percent from the preceding year, on only a 14.5 percent increase in revenues to $6.1 billion.

Granted, part of the reason for the big jump in profits was a 7 percent drop in unit costs thanks to slight moderation in fuel prices, close attention to cost controls, and the impact of hiring many new employees under the two-tier labor contracts. A robust economy in 1985 and the introduction of the Ultimate Super Saver fares also helped fuel that profit growth. In addition, AMR earned a record $173.9 million net profit in the second quarter alone thanks to United Airlines' pilots, who went out on a twenty-eight-day strike to show the strength of their commitment against accepting a two-tier contract similiar to the one American's pilots had agreed to. (The United pilots eventually signed a two-tier deal to end the strike.)

Another example of how American misunderstood what was going on around it was its fierce opposition to efforts by the Civil Aeronautics Board, in one of its last actions before going out of existence, to force airlines to remove the so-called bias from the computer reservations systems used by travel agents. Before 1984, when a travel agent using American's SABRE system asked for a flight between Kansas City and Washington, D.C., chances are the first flight listed was on American even though competing carriers may have offered better service—better times or a nonstop flight versus a connecting one—than American. Similarly, an agent using United's APOLLO system who asked for a display of service on that same route probably would have seen a United flight listed first on the computer screen.

No deception was involved. Everyone in the industry, airlines and travel agents alike, knew the systems were biased in favor of the airline that owned them or in favor of co-hosts, airlines that paid to have preferential listing of their flights. However, smaller carriers that believed computer system owners were using them to gain greater shares of the travel market than they would have had otherwise convinced the CAB to investigate. American argued that because it had spent millions of dollars to develop SABRE, and did so only after its efforts to get other carriers to join it in a single industrywide system failed, it had the right to give its own flights preferential treatment. American officials grew quite angry and exasperated as it became apparent that the CAB was going to ban bias from the computer systems.

Obviously the folks at American failed to understand what the real impact of the CAB's decision would be.

"But that's the best thing that ever happened to us," said one American executive. "We thought banning bias on agents' terminal displays would really hurt us. But the government compensated us by allowing us to charge $1.75 per flight segment booked through SABRE. So every time a passenger books a flight on some other carrier through SABRE, the other carrier involved pays us $1.75 per segment booked. Now we have to pay $1.75 per segment booked on American through APOLLO or SystemOne or PARS, but since SABRE is substantially bigger than all of those, we make a lot of money off that. That's why I say it's the best thing that ever happened, getting rid of bias."

THERE WAS one thing, however, about which there was absolutely no mistake: American's growth plan worked like a charm in the mid- and late-1980s.

"Within about six months after all the labor agreements were signed in '83, there was a working plan of what the fleet would be. My recollection was that it was in the high 400s," said Wes Kaldahl, who retired in 1988. "But at that time we did not have nearly the kind of ambitions that American has today in the international arena."

The airline began to grow almost immediately after the two-tier deals were signed. The first really big order for MD-80s—beyond the first two groups of twenty and thirteen, respectively, that were brought in on the McDonnell Douglas test-drive program—came down in February 1984, two and a half months after the flight attendants joined the ground workers and pilots in accepting two-tier contracts. American ordered sixty-seven more MD-80s, to take the fleet up to an even 100. It also took out options on one hundred more for deliveries scheduled through 1990. Ultimately, American placed orders and options on 300 MD-80s and ultimately bought 260 of them before the decision was made that that would be enough.

Of course American had to find someplace to put those aircraft where they could make money. Initially the airline wanted to establish a hub at Denver, but congestion at old Stapleton International Airport, Denver's inability to commit to building a new airport in a short time frame, and the presence of two hubs there run by United and Continental forced American to look elsewhere. Kaldahl came up with a new wrinkle in hub-and-spoke operations when he proposed building two small hubs instead of one big hub east of the Mississippi River. The first one, at Nashville, was designed to serve a big X pattern of connecting traffic. One of the legs of that X connected the Mid South on one side of the hub to the Northeast on the other side. The other leg of the X connected the Midwest with the Southeast and Florida. To some degree, the Nashville hub was supposed to shift some of the more illogically routed traffic away from American's D/FW and Chicago hubs and away from competing carriers' hubs located in the middle of the country. For example, the passenger traveling between Jackson, Mississippi, and New York previously had to backtrack through D/FW, go the long way through Chicago on American, or go east to Atlanta to connect to a New York flight on Delta. Later that same passenger would have the choice of going over Northwest's hub at Memphis, Delta's Cincinnati hub, or American's Nashville hub.

Meanwhile, American's second hub east of the Mississippi River was established at the Raleigh/Durham Airport in North Carolina. It was designed mainly to serve connecting passengers in the heavily traveled East Coast corridor. In some ways it competed against Delta's Atlanta hub and against both Eastern and Pan Am, which continued to do a lot of flying in that corridor until 1991.

A third new hub, the fifth overall in American's network, was established at San Juan, Puerto Rico, in late 1986. It helped solidify American's dominance of the Caribbean market, where Eastern was fading. Eastern eventually withdrew from its San Juan hub in 1989 after it filed a Chapter 11 bankruptcy petition.

A sixth hub was added to American's network in 1987, at San Jose, California. It was the result of American's surprise $225 million acquisition of AirCal, a regional jet airline that served the heavily traveled West Coast corridor. The deal, which was announced in the fall of 1986 and consummated the following spring, was put together over a weekend primarily by Crandall. It is the only notable exception to the central principle of American's growth plan, which was to reduce average operating costs by growing the airline from within. But Crandall had become concerned about American's lack of presence in the north–south markets on the West Coast and how that allowed United to carry a disproportionate share of transcontinental traffic originating on the West Coast.

American targeted Los Angeles–based Western Airlines, a major player in the West Coast markets, as a possible merger partner, and initiated discussions. But Delta beat American to the punch and announced that it had agreed to buy Western in the fall of 1986. Then American got word that Frank Lorenzo, chairman of Texas Air, the parent of Continental and Eastern Airlines and at the time the nation's largest airline company, was trying to buy AirCal. Crandall moved quickly to prevent that.

In early 1987 American announced a major transaction with both the Boeing Company and Airbus Industrie that turned the aviation finance world on its ear. American placed orders for fifteen Boeing 767-300ERs for use on transatlantic routes and twenty-five Airbus A300-600Rs for use primarily on Caribbean routes. American had intended to buy only twenty-five planes. However, the two manufacturers were so desperate to sell what had been their slow-moving "mini–wide-body" jets—and to prevent each other from selling planes to American—that they offered low-ball prices and leasing terms similar to American's original rent-a-plane deal with McDonnell Douglas on MD-80s. The airline got the right to return any of the 767s or A300s on short notice with virtually no penalty, and American executives calmed worried securities analysts by saying that if things got really bad, American would exercise those rights. Of course, it never intended to do any such thing. First, American executives believed demand was so strong and growing that there was little chance of things going badly. And even if market conditions did change, the airline would be very reluctant to get rid of the 767s and A300s because they are the most efficient planes in the fleet. The airline would have grounded all of its 727s first.

The acquisition of the 767-300ERs also pointed to American's growing interest in serving Europe. For decades, nearly all transatlantic service had focused on John F. Kennedy Airport in New York, where American had only a small presence despite its dominance of domestic service in the New York market with its large presence at La Gaurdia and Newark airports. But Pan Am and TWA, the two dominant U.S carriers in the transatlantic market, were both in severe financial distress and losing market share rapidly to such foreign behemoths as British Airways. American realized that it could generate enough passenger traffic from its two big hubs at D/FW and Chicago—and the spokes tied to those hubs—to fill up DC-10s on flights to London and Paris. American started serving the D/FW–London route in 1982, shortly after bankrupt Braniff gave it up. It was the airline's first transatlantic service since the early 1950s.

Gradually, American's brain trust realized that if they could fill DC-10–size aircraft on flights from the hubs to major European cities, they could probably fill long-range versions of the 767 on flights between the hubs and secondary European cities, such as Zurich and Dusseldorf. Additionally, because American had dominated the New York domestic air travel market for decades and had a large number of loyal fliers and AAdvantage program members there, management figured it could steal Pan Am's and TWA's market share by flying 767s from Kennedy Airport to London, Paris, and Frankfurt. The idea worked. In fact, American flew the 767—with 215 seats—full almost year round on those routes, while Pan Am's 400-seat 747s flew relatively full during the peak summer season and more than half empty in the winter.

AMR Corp. earned a record $233.9 million in net profits in 1984, the first full year in which the two-tier contracts and the growth plan were in effect. In 1985 that figure jumped to $345.8 million, thanks in part to the monthlong pilots' strike at United. Profits dropped in 1986 to $279.1 million and to $198.4 million in 1987, primarily because of increased discounting throughout the industry sparked by Frank Lorenzo's Texas Air Corp. and its two operating carriers, Continental and Eastern. But through its dramatic route and schedule expansion and its masterful use of computerized yield management techniques, American was able to maximize its revenues vis-à-vis those of the Texas Air twins. While American suffered declining profits because it was forced to selectively match Texas Air's discounts, both Continental and Eastern failed to generate either profits or sufficient cash flow to properly service the company's massive debt load. As a result, as American grew bigger and stronger, Eastern and Continental grew weaker and had to shrink and sell assets to stay alive. Texas Air reported a 1988 net loss of $718.6 million, an industry record at the time.

The growth plan hit a crescendo in 1988, when AMR earned a record $476.8 million net profit and a $806.5 million operating profit, the largest operating profit in industry history. The airline took delivery of 64 new aircraft and ended the year with 468 planes in the fleet. Capacity grew by 15 percent, but revenues grew by 22 percent. Employment grew by 12,000 workers to 61,700, but unit costs grew by just 1.2 percent. As a result, most of those 61,700 employees were able to split the $122 million that went into the company's profit-sharing plan that year.

Finally, in November 1988, American moved past United to become the nation's largest carrier in terms of revenue passenger miles flown. United has regained that position on a monthly basis a handful of times since then. But, annually, American continues to be the largest airline in the nation. And, thanks to the collapse of the Soviet Union in 1991 and the effective dissolution of its pseudoairline, Aeroflot, now American also can lay claim to being the world's largest airline.

"It was never our intent to be the biggest airline in the world, or in the country, or even in Texas," Crandall said in 1991. "What our intent was, way back in the early '80s when we created a partnership with our employees and promised them that we would grow the airline if they gave us the kind of flexibility we needed to make money, was to be the most profitable airline in the world."

In 1988 Crandall and American not only achieved that goal, they seemed to be in position to reign forever over the high-flying industry that they had grown to dominate. It seemed as if they had created an American juggernaut that nothing could stop.

15

Big Deals

THE YEAR 1989 wasn't a month old when word began to leak out
that Bob Crandall and Ron Allen were talking about a deal. Allen,
chairman of Delta Air Lines, personally had led a group of senior
Delta executives who met with Crandall and other American executives in Texas in early January. Concerned that Allen and company's
appearance at its headquarters would create a stir and a news leak,
American set up a safe house of sorts in a nondescript one-story
office park in Arlington, a couple of miles south of its Fort Worth
headquarters.

Still, the word got out that American and Delta were talking about
some major deal. But what kind of deal? There was no way the federal
government would allow the largest and third-largest U.S. airlines
to merge. So what were the two carriers' chairmen discussing?

Computers. Or, more accurately, computer reservations systems.

In 1988 United Airlines had announced that it would sell a 49
percent stake in its Covia subsidiary, which operated the APOLLO
computer reservations system, for about $500 million to a group that
included USAir, British Airways, and several other European airlines.
At the time, someone asked Crandall if he'd be willing to sell up to
half of SABRE if the buyer put up enough cash. He said he'd consider
doing that, but also indicated buying half of SABRE would cost as
much as $750 million, based on American's belief that it was worth
$1.5 billion.

Allen took the hint. During the fall of 1988 Delta approached American and began a careful courtship that the people at Delta headquarters in Atlanta hoped would solve their carrier's biggest problem. In the mid- and late 1970s, while American, United, and others spent millions of dollars developing their computer reservations systems, tradition-bound Delta, which purposely tries not to be an innovator because of the huge costs that often are associated with innovation, dismissed the rush to marketing technology as an expensive luxury that was likely to be replaced by a single system owned and operated by all airlines together. By the time Delta's management realized that wasn't going to happen, SABRE and APOLLO were generating hundreds of millions of dollars in revenue for their respective airlines. Delta launched its DATAS II system in 1982, but it was vastly inferior technologically to SABRE and APOLLO. And though Delta was able to improve the system's performance dramatically by 1986, it was too late to make up the ground it had lost to the competition. DATAS II's market share of travel agents using computer reservations systems never reached double digits while SABRE's and APOLLO's combined market share soared above 70 percent.

The news broke on January 27 in the *Fort Worth Star-Telegram* and in *Travel Weekly*, one of the largest magazines aimed at travel agents. Initially Delta and American officials were silent. Then they jointly issued a terse statement acknowledging that they were discussing a possible computer reservations systems alliance. The airlines warned that a deal might not be reached and said they would have nothing to say until there was either an agreement or an end to their discussions.

Nine days later, on Sunday, February 5, Crandall and Allen met with SABRE workers at the system's operations center at Tulsa to break the news to them. They then boarded a rented private jet for D/FW, where they met with more SABRE employees before flying on to Atlanta for a similar meeting with DATAS II employees. A detailed news release was issued jointly on Sunday morning, and a joint news conference was scheduled in Atlanta for eight-thirty the following morning.

Delta agreed to pay American $650 million for a 50 percent stake in a joint venture company that would operate the combined SABRE/DATAS II system under the SABRE name. The companies also said they planned to sell equity positions in the company to other carriers, though Delta and American both were pledged to maintaining no less than 25 percent stakes in the partnership.

At the news conference, held in a meeting room on Delta's corporate campus adjacent to Hartsfield Atlanta International Airport, Allen said: "It was clear that DATAS II had very little chance to ever be a major player in the market. Now we are a partner in the biggest, and, we believe, the best system in the industry."

Crandall said the decision to sell half of SABRE stemmed mainly from American's growing fear that Congress would force it to divest SABRE.

He knew, but didn't say, that if the government forced American to sell part or all of SABRE it would have a hard time getting anything close to the kind of sweet deal it got with Delta. True, Delta was paying only $650 million for half of SABRE, $100 million less than Crandall had implied it was worth six months earlier. But Delta was also contributing its own system and travel agent subscriber base. The kicker was that Delta wasn't really buying half of what was commonly understood to be SABRE. Delta was buying into the SABRE Travel Information Network, or STIN, the marketing arm of American's vaunted data processing operations that previously had been known as American's marketing automation department. In 1987 STIN, which was charged with selling the SABRE service to travel agencies, had been formally separated from the hardware and technology side of SABRE, known as SABRE Computer Services, or SCS. Not only was American retaining full ownership of SCS, the group that actually built and operated the world's largest privately owned, real-time computer network, but the Delta/American partnership was going to pay SCS about $200 million a year for five years for its services. Thus American could expect an extra $100 million a year in revenue from its SCS unit—Delta's half of the $200 million service fee—for services American previously had considered part of its own overhead costs.

Don Carty, American's senior VP for finance and planning, admitted a few days after the deal was announced that American got a much better deal than it appeared at first glance.

"We didn't make Delta sign the deal. They felt the access to the biggest and best CRS in the industry was worth the big price. And, yes, there was a markup in that price. It was agreed to by Delta as part of the basic deal," Carty said. "You'll have to ask them, but I think they saw this as the price they had to pay to play in the big leagues of the CRS business, especially since they had made the original decision ten or fifteen years ago not to invest in developing their own CRS.

"We think we worked the deal right. Last year, when United sold half of its Covia/APOLLO system to USAir and a consortium of European airlines, it sold everything. The agency contracts. The hardware. The communications equipment. The software development aspects.

"We didn't. We just sold 50 percent interest in the agency terminals and printers, the agency contracts and our expertise. We kept the hardware, the communications system and software development. United is having to pay Covia for all those things. We'll be getting paid by the SABRE partnership for those things," Carty said.

In other words, it was a typical American deal, one which Crandall likes to refer to as a win-win deal. Of course, in the American Airlines lexicon of business terms, a win-win deal is one in which the other party receives some modest benefits while American rakes in significant rewards.

The day after Crandall appeared with Allen at the SABRE/DATAS II news conference in Atlanta, he, Carty, and several other senior American officials hosted a news conference at New York's Grand Hyatt Hotel. The subject was another poorly kept secret. For three weeks the news media had been carrying reports that American was about to place a $7.5 million order for McDonnell Douglas's new MD-11 widebody jet and more MD-80s. American announced just that, and added that the deal included a unique agreement with General Electric, which would supply the jet engines associated with the MD-11.

American placed firm orders for eight of McDonnell Douglas's brand-new MD-11, long-range aircraft that essentially was a longer, technologically advanced derivative of the DC-10. In addition, American said it had taken out purchase options on another 42 MD-11s. Such options actually amount to price-protected, guaranteed spots in the delivery line. But the airline placing an option doesn't have to make a down payment as it does on firm orders. And if it decides later not to exercise its options the airline does not have to pay a cancellation penalty. American said it wanted the MD-11 for its planned expansion in the transpacific markets and, to a lesser degree, for use on some transatlantic and long-range domestic routes.

The airline also put another 100 MD-80s on option, with deliveries scheduled to begin in 1992. Since the airline already had 149 MD-80s in its fleet at the time of the announcement and another 101 already on order, obviously American saw a potential need for as many as 350 MD-80s in its fleet.

The most intriguing part of the announcement was the curious deal with General Electric. American agreed to buy up to 200 GE-made CF6-80C2 engines, one of the largest turbofan engines available at the time. Unlike most aircraft-and-engine deals, American was not limited to mounting its new CF6-80C2s on just the MD-11. It also had the right to mount those engines on any airplane not already in its fleet. Not coincidentally, American's Boeing 767-300ERs and Airbus A300-600Rs used the very same engines. The airline could put the GE engines ordered that day on any A300s or 767s it took delivery of thereafter.

Everyone assumed that American was taking the concept of parts interchangeability to a new level. But a careful examination of what American officials said about the MD-11 and GE engines deals showed there was more to the deal than just increasing the degree of engine commonality in the fleet. Under the terms of its deal with GE, American was required to buy 200 engines by a specified date in the early 1990s. If it didn't, the price on the ones it did buy would go up and American would owe GE more money. But the MD-11 order was set up so that the airline would receive only 25 MD-11s from McDonnell Douglas by 1995. In short, American's deal with GE on engines meant that it had another major aircraft order in the works but was not yet ready to announce it.

Indeed, Carty hinted as much at the news conference. He said that the MD-11 probably was too big an airplane for all but a handful of the transatlantic routes into which American planned to expand.

"If you think the [transatlantic] market will fragment, as we do, then you're probably talking about higher frequencies [or, several departures each day on each route] and smaller planes than the [Boeing] 747. You're talking about something like the 767-300ER. We think that may be the plane of the future in Europe," he said.

Crandall, also, all but admitted that American was preparing to order even more planes. The airline's fleet plan as of the day of the MD-11 announcement called for 591 aircraft by the end of 1991. But Crandall said: "If you assume just a modest 2 percent growth rate from 1991 through 1995, American would need something like an additional 48 aircraft," beyond the 591 aircraft then called for in the publicly disseminated fleet plan.

Carty threw in that American also was studying the need for planes smaller than the 142-seat MD-80, the smallest plane in the fleet except for 25 old Boeing 737s it had inherited from AirCal and that already were scheduled to be phased out by the end of 1991. Carty said the candidate airplanes were the 737-500, a quieter, more fuel-efficient version of the 737 that still was in development at the time; the Fokker 100; and the MD-87, the little brother of the MD-80.

Thirty-five days later, the same group of senior American officials who had been present at the Grand Hyatt Hotel assembled at New York's Plaza Hotel for the announcement of another not-so-well-kept secret. American announced two separate aircraft deals. The first one was with the Dutch aircraft maker Fokker B.V. for 150 Fokker 100s. American placed firm orders for 75 of the 98-seat aircraft and put the other 75 on option.

The second deal was a complicated one with Boeing for additional 767s and 757s, slightly smaller narrow-body aircraft that are so similar to the 767 technologically that a pilot trained to fly one needs no additional training or certification to fly the other. First American said it was exercising 25 of its existing options for 757s. Those options had been a part of an order/option package deal on 100 757s announced by American in May 1988.

In addition to exercising those options, American said it was converting ten more of its existing 757 options to firm orders for 767s. And, finally, American took out another 70 so-called convertible options, which it could convert to firm orders for either 757s or 767s.

Industry analysts estimated the Fokker and Boeing deals to be worth between $7 billion and $8 billion; the higher number would apply if American exercised all 70 of those options as firm orders for the slightly more expensive 767.

The Boeing and Fokker deals, along with the earlier deals with McDonnell Douglas and General Electric, were estimated to be worth at least $15.5 billion, a figure that easily qualified American's 1989 first-quarter aircraft orders as the biggest shopping spree ever by an airline.

But American was not finished. It also ordered 150 commuter aircraft from Saab, the Swedish aircraft maker. Those planes, which were worth about $1 billion, were to be used by American's sister companies in the American Eagle commuter airlines network. Then, in June, another 100 commuter aircraft worth about $450 million were bought for the American Eagle network from British Aerospace.

That same month American announced it would build a second major maintenance base at Fort Worth's new Alliance Airport at a cost of about $485 million. American needed the facility up and running by 1992, when it expected its fleet to total more than 600 aircraft. Even though the Tulsa maintenance base was scheduled to undergo a $400 million expansion and improvement program, a second was needed to handle the full load.

Located about fifteen miles due north of downtown Fort Worth and about fifteen miles west of D/FW, the airfield at Alliance was owned by the city, but all the land surrounding it was owned and being developed by the Perot Group of Dallas, headed by Ross Perot, Jr., son of the legendary founder of Electronic Data Systems, H. Ross Perot. Young Perot's dream was to create the world's first industrial airport: one designed solely to serve the needs of aircraft maintenance organizations, corporate aviation, aircraft manufacturers, and manufacturers in other industries seeking to reduce their costs through the use of just-in-time parts delivery and rapid product distribution systems.

The selection of Alliance ended a politically charged, three-month bidding war between Fort Worth and Oklahoma City, which desperately wanted American to build its second maintenance base at its wide-open, underused Will Rogers World Airport. The tug-of-war over the American base included a well-publicized recruiting raid on American's headquarters by Oklahoma Governor Henry Bellmon and intense behind-the-scenes political maneuverings by Texas Governor Bill Clements and Texas legislators to get several state tax laws changed so that the Alliance site could compete against the inducements offered by Oklahoma.

Also, in the first quarter American began construction on a 750,000-square-foot office building across the highway from its Fort Worth headquarters. Company officials did not say so for nearly a year, but the new building was to be the airline's new headquarters. American already was outgrowing the $80 million headquarters building it had occupied in January 1983. The old 550,000-square-foot building, of which only about 350,000 square feet were usable as office space, was to become headquarters for the SABRE Travel Information Network.

Altogether, in 112 days American placed orders or took out options on 620 airplanes valued at about $16.75 billion. Counting the 100 757s ordered or put on option in May 1988, the airline had signed up for 720 aircraft worth $20.75 billion in less than fourteen months. If we include the March 1987 deal for 25 Airbus A300-600Rs and 15 767-300ERs, American had signed up to buy 760 airplanes worth a combined $23.15 billion. And, counting all the spending on new ground facilities, American had committed to spending $24.6 billion since March 1987.

The unprecedented aircraft buying binge virtually assured American that it would be able to grow bigger and faster than any of its competitors well into the 1990s. By ordering so many planes in such a short time, for delivery mostly in a four-year window from 1990 through 1993, American locked up much of three aircraft manufacturers' production capacity. "If any other airline wants to buy planes now, they're going to have to take a number and wait in line behind American," one Wall Street analyst said after the news conference.

Robert Joedicke, a senior advisory director at Shearson Lehman Brothers in New York and the dean of Wall Street's airline analysts, said: "If United, Northwest, or anybody else except Delta and USAir, which also have large orders on the books already, wants planes now, they're going to have to talk to International Lease Finance Corp., GPA Group, or one of the other big leasing firms. Or maybe they can buy some Airbuses in Europe, but they've got a pretty deep production backlog too."

Paul Turk, an analyst with Avmark, Inc., an aviation consulting firm in Washington, said of the deals: "American, in effect, is dictating to other airlines what planes they're going to fly."

But the analysts also noted that American wasn't signing up to buy all those airplanes just to confound its competitors.

"No, they're not spoilers, in that sense, though that is the effect," Edward Starkman, airline analyst with the PaineWebber Group, said immediately after the Boeing and Fokker deals were announced. "They're doing this because it's in their best long-term interests."

As mentioned, not all of the 760 aircraft American had on order or option were scheduled for short-term delivery. And in their more candid moments American officials quietly allowed that there was a pretty good chance that the company might not exercise every option it had taken out on additional airplanes. But they steadfastly maintained that they were irrevocably committed to very rapid growth and that the carrier was contractually bound to take all of the planes for which it had firm orders. Their intention, the American officials said, was to grow the fleet to between 650 and 800 aircraft by the mid-1990s, not counting commuter airplanes. They also said that they had mapped out a $14 billion, seven-year capital spending plan to pay for all those airplanes plus all the related equipment and ground facilities that would be needed. Management added that the capital spending plan probably would have to be increased if they saw opportunities to make strategic acquisitions of assets by financially weak carriers put up for sale.

It sounded like very bold talk for a company that eight years earlier had been forced to cancel its orders for a piddling 15 Boeing 757s and to stretch out the delivery schedule on 30 Boeing 767s because it simply couldn't afford them. Was American's management getting too daring, too adventuresome, too full of itself?

Nope. At least not according to those in management. The big spending on airplanes and related equipment and facilities, management said, was all a natural product of American's bargain with its employees to establish the two-tier labor contracts back in 1983. To reap the benefits of those labor pacts, American had to grow to reduce its average unit costs. And the more it grew, the more it could afford to grow. All that changed in the first half of 1989, management contended, was that the growth plan had just been pushed into high gear.

"We're a $9 billion-a-year company," Robert Baker said during the spring of 1989. "In an absolute sense [$14 billion] is a huge number. But with our balance sheet and our ability to generate cash, we should be able to take on that large of a capital commitment without too much difficulty."

Interestingly, Crandall said that the airline's growth plan, which that $14 billion capital spending plan was intended to support, included an economic forecast that did not foresee a national recession occurring in the next five years.

"We see no reason, and very little likelihood, for there being a recession in the next five years, except bad governmental policy. And we're hoping we don't have bad governmental policy," Crandall said.

Yet by the time American placed the last in its string of orders for new aircraft, the $450 million deal with British Aerospace for commuter airplanes announced on June 8, management already was starting to reassess that economic forecast.

IT ONLY seemed as if everything American touched in the first half of 1989 turned to gold.

One of its big projects turned to rust instead.

Two months after American and Delta announced their plans to merge their computer reservations systems in one to be sold under the SABRE name, Ron Allen and Bob Crandall made another announcement. Like carnival sideshow barkers dropping the price of admission a couple of minutes before showtime, Crandall and Allen said they had just cut the price of joining the CRS consortium they were building around SABRE from $20 million to $15 million for each percentage point of ownership acquired.

The announcement showed that something was beginning to go wrong with their deal. The problem was that opposition to the SABRE/DATAS II merger was growing in Washington, where two groups were actively building support to block it. One group was comprised of monopoliaphobics, people in Congress and the Justice Department who break out in a rash every time the chief executives of two large companies in the same industry have coffee together. The other group consisted of members of Congress whose constituents included other airlines that feared the market power of an even larger SABRE owned by the No. 1 and No. 3 airlines in the nation—which, as it so happened, also were the best-financed airlines in the nation.

By cutting the price of joining the SABRE consortium by 25 percent, Allen and Crandall hoped to make it easier for smaller U.S. airlines, or even international airlines, to join. But the price cut betrayed their fear that if the consortium didn't get additional partners signed up soon, the Justice Department might oppose the merger on antitrust grounds.

Crandall said: "We want to bring others into the venture as quickly as possible. We have formed this partnership in good faith, and we are serious about building the partnership into a worldwide computer reservations system. The more partners we have, the more attractive and viable the system becomes to potential customers around the world."

Allen added: "We are actively recruiting the participation of domestic and international carriers, and there have been a number of discussions with these entities. We are also interested in the participation of non–airline-related firms such as hotel and car rental companies."

But, for whatever reason, there were no takers. And sure enough, without additional partners, the Justice Department would not support the SABRE/DATAS II merger. In June the department said that if the carriers tried to go through with their deal, it would file a civil antitrust suit to block it. U.S. Attorney General Dick Thornburg made the announcement personally at a news conference on June 22. He said the combined SABRE/DATAS II would have controlled nearly half of the CRS business in the nation and would violate Section 7 of the Sherman Antitrust Act.

"The likely result of this transaction would be higher fares and poorer service for airline passengers," Thornburgh said.

Whether his statement reflected his and his agency's total ignorance of economics and of how the airline and CRS businesses operate, or whether it was simply an excuse to cover the political machinations that led to the decision to oppose the merger, it made no sense. The merger might have been anticompetitive. And it might have violated the spirit, if not the letter, of the nation's antitrust laws. (If that's true, why doesn't the federal government force the breakup of General Motors or other companies that dominate their industries more than the SABRE/DATAS II partnership would have dominated the business of selling airline tickets?)

But there was no way the merger of American's and Delta's computer reservations systems would have led to either of the evils Thornburgh said would be the result. Poorer service? Come on! American and Delta are widely regarded as the two best carriers in the nation in terms of their quality of service. Both had hundreds of aircraft on order, meaning they were going to expand their service. And expanded service meant offering more frequent flights in cities they already served and new flights in cities they did not yet serve or where they did provide much service.

As for the claim that the SABRE/DATAS II merger would result in higher fares, there's no credible evidence that suggests that control of computer reservations systems gives an airline or group of airlines the ability to raise fares. Fare prices are a function of two things: competition between carriers that serve any city-pair market and the consumer's willingness to pay. If only one carrier offers same-airline service with a reasonable schedule from Des Moines, Iowa, to Birmingham, Alabama, the fare will tend to be very high relative to the fare for travel in city-pair markets where there is a lot of competition. But if three carriers serve both Des Moines and Birmingham, the fare for that trip likely will be lower, even if the carriers provide that service via connections at three different hubs. It's that simple. That's one illustration of how deregulation has worked to the consumer's benefit. While no airline would fly the Des Moines–Birmingham route nonstop, several carriers undoubtedly serve that route through their respective hubs. As a result, people who travel that route have more options, albeit via connecting flights, than they did before deregulation.

And even if only one carrier offered same-airline service between Des Moines and Birmingham on a reasonable schedule, the fare would only be as high as the market would bear. Since the industry was deregulated, there have been hundreds of illustrations of how consumer resistance to fare increases have led airlines either to cut their prices outright or to offer more and easier-to-obtain discount fares. Whether an airline owns or does not own all or part of a computer reservations system has nothing to do with the price of fares.

Still, despite the very shaky legal and theoretical ground on which the Justice Department stood in making its decision to oppose the SABRE/DATAS II merger, American and Delta agreed not to contest the decision. They could have done so simply by consummating the merger and waiting for the government to file suit. But both airlines said the legal battle would be too long and expensive and that even if they prevailed, the benefits of the merger would be lost by the time the case was concluded.

Six months later Delta announced a similar deal to merge DATAS II with the PARS system. PARS, which was originally developed by TWA—with some significant contributions from a young data processing and financial executive named Bob Crandall—in the late 1960s and early 1970s was owned by a partnership that included TWA and Northwest Airlines. The government blessed the combination of the fourth-largest (PARS) and fifth-largest (DATAS II) systems in the industry. Combined, the renamed Worldspan system now ranks as the third largest of four systems in the industry, ahead of SystemOne, originally developed by Eastern and now owned by Continental, but well behind both SABRE and APOLLO.

IN THE 1989 AMR Corp. annual report, Bob Crandall wrote: "The year 1989 should establish once and for all that the airline business is, and is likely to remain, highly cyclical. During the first six months, earnings were strong, continuing the pattern of 1988. Unhappily, the second half demonstrated how quickly good times for airlines can turn bad."

Understatement is not one of the clubs Crandall usually carries in his bag. But this time, if anything, he soft-pedaled the negative turn-around in the second half of 1989.

American earned $177.9 million in net profits in the second quarter of 1989. It was the best quarter in company history, slightly exceeding the previous record quarter profit of $173 million in the second quarter of 1985, when a pilots' strike virtually shut down United for a month.

But by the fourth quarter of 1989, earnings had fallen to $38.9 million, $20.3 million of which was the result of the sale of old airplanes. That huge drop in earnings over nine months clearly told the story of how demand for air travel, especially for domestic air travel, fell off during the last half of the year. The only thing that kept American's second-half figures from being worse was its rapid growth in international markets and the huge surge in revenues from that growth.

American, like the rest of the industry, had been caught pretty much by surprise. After earning a $476.8 million net profit—and an incredible $806.5 million operating profit—in 1988, after earning a record first-quarter net profit of $101 million to begin 1989, and after placing orders for 620 airplanes worth $16.75 billion in less than four months, the nation's largest airline had been on a very heady roll. But American and other carriers found themselves stumbling to the finish in 1989. Still, on the basis of the strong first half, AMR reported net profits of $454.8 million, down just 4.6 percent from the record year of 1988.

Disappointing finish or no, by any measure 1989 was a tremendous year for American.

IF THERE ever was an industry that should have been safe from attack by the financial barracudas known as corporate raiders, it was the U.S. airline industry. Because they are both capital and labor intensive, and because they are very sensitive to changes in consumer spending, airlines are inherently volatile and highly cyclical enterprises. Even in the very best of times, their high costs of operation and ownership prevent their operating margins from rising much above the Standard & Poor's 500 average. And, in bad times, airlines can consume incredible amounts of cash in the blink of an eye.

But that didn't keep the takeover artists at bay in 1989. Financiers Alfred Checchi and Gary Wilson, with the financial backing of KLM Royal Dutch Airlines and the Elders Group of Australia, outbid oil-man Marvin Davis and paid $3.65 million to acquire Northwest Airlines. In mid-September a group including United Airlines' employees and management and British Airways PLC outbid Davis again by agreeing to pay $300 a share, or about $6.75 billion, to take over UAL Corp., United's parent.

Then, on October 4, high-profile New York real estate developer Donald Trump, who had been rumored for nearly two months to be accumulating AMR Corp. stock in expectation of making a takeover bid, faxed his short letter to Crandall. But why? Did he really want to own American's parent? Was it going to be his biggest trophy yet? Or did he have some hidden agenda?

In several public forums, including an interview with ABC television reporter Barbara Walters on her 20/20 program, Trump contended that though AMR was well run, it really hadn't done enough for its shareholders. He also claimed that he really did want to own and run American and wasn't interested in just making money on a stock play.

But a close examination of what was going on in Trump's financial empire—which already was beginning to crumble, though it would be more than a year before most people saw the evidence of that— and of the way Trump pursued AMR suggests that he had some other motivation.

First off, Trump had a checkered history of publicly disclosing that he had taken a small stake in various publicly owned companies and was studying whether to make a buyout offer. Often such a revelation triggered a quick jump in the stock's price, and Trump would undersell the market at a nice profit. He earned $122 million that way in deals involving Allegis (the parent of United Airlines that later changed its corporate name back to UAL Corp.), Bally, and Holiday Corp.

Second, the team of American executives and outside financial advisors, investigators, and lawyers hired to discover and analyze the motives and possible moves of any would-be buyers quickly learned that Trump never made any effort to arrange financing for his proposed takeover of AMR, either before or after making his offer. They also concluded that Trump was beginning to run short of cash.

In the year or so leading up to his bid for American, Trump had bought the Plaza Hotel in New York for $400 million, the Eastern Shuttle for $365 million, and the Taj Mahal Hotel and Casino still under construction in Atlantic City for $363 million (including a cash infusion necessary to complete construction). In the two years before that, he had plowed more than $100 million into smaller real estate deals, mostly in New York, and had spent $90 million improving the Trump Castle, his hotel and casino at Atlantic City Marina. All or nearly all of that was done with money borrowed at relatively high interest rates.

But by the late summer of 1989 there were clear and growing signs that the national economy was slowing down and might be headed for recession. Unfortunately for Trump, he was heavily exposed in two industries that are very sensitive to cyclical downturns, real estate and travel and tourism.

Then there was the matter of the Taj Mahal. Trump paid $288 million for it in 1988 but had to put $75 million into it to finish construction. He structured the deal as a limited partnership, with him as the only partner. The limited partnership then issued $675 million in junk bonds carrying a $94 million annual interest payment. He made the 1989 payment, but documents filed with the Securities and Exchange Commission (SEC) showed that he had raised enough money to buy and complete the huge hotel and casino and to cover the 1989 interest payment, but not enough to make more than half of the $47 million installment on his interest payment due in May 1990. When he sold the junk bonds, Trump had expected the Taj Mahal to open in December of 1990 and to generate the other half of the $47 million payment due the following May. But construction was running behind schedule. It was clear the hotel and casino weren't going to be open before spring, and he was going to have to come up with the cash for that interest payment on his own.

As a private business, the Trump Organization's financial situation supposedly was cloaked in secrecy. But because Trump had used financial instruments such as junk bonds, which carry some requirements to report financial data to the SEC, and because he had succeeded in attracting enough media coverage, the Trump Organization's finances were a half-open book. It didn't take a genius to figure out that Trump was looking at the possibility of running out of cash before the Taj Mahal opened.

Now why would a man in that situation go out and buy 3 million shares of AMR stock at a cost of more than $200 million, make a buyout offer, and then never try to make any effort to line up the financing he would need to takeover AMR?

Several theories about Trump's real motivation were developed.

One suggestion was that Trump wanted to put AMR into play in hopes that someone else would outbid him, thereby allowing him to sell his shares at a huge profit. Several analysts had placed AMR's ultimate takeover value at between $140 and $150 a share. Trump may have gone into his bid thinking he had left room for someone else to come in and top his $120-a-share offer.

A second theory is that Trump hoped AMR's stock price would move up close to his $120 bid price. If that happened, he would have the option of quietly selling his stock into the advancing market. Such a plan would have to be carefully executed, however, to avoid breaking securities laws against manipulating stock prices.

A third theory is that Trump was banking on Crandall's strong desire to stay in control of his airline. If Crandall and his management team really wanted to stay in place, perhaps they would be willing to negotiate to buy Trump's stock at a premium price. Or maybe Crandall would pay all shareholders a dividend or execute a recapitalization in order to make a special payout to them.

The least likely theory was the one that said Trump really did want to own American Airlines. This theory assumed that Trump planned to sell some American assets to help pay for the acquisition of the company and to pay himself. Perhaps SABRE could be sold to raise cash. Or, with American's large fleet and huge number of planes on order, there would be ample opportunity to do sale-leaseback deals on those aircraft. That would create a lot of cash that could be used to retire the debt incurred in a junk bond–financed buyout, to cover Trump's other debts, or to finance future deals in other industries. Of course, doing that also would have put a ton of pressure on the carrier's balance sheet and compromised the growth plan. But in such deals, the corporate raider often sells the company back to the public and is gone before the balance sheet problem has to be dealt with.

The most likely scenario is that Trump was holding all these cards in his hand, and had not decided which one to play, when the world changed on Friday, October 13. That's the day UAL Corp. announced that several major Japanese and U.S. banks—including Citibank—had refused to participate in the financing of its employee-led takeover. The banks had become concerned that both the price of the takeover and the risk involved were too great. The banks' decision sparked a sharp selloff of UAL and other airline stocks, including that of AMR. And that, in short order, triggered the second biggest one-day fall in the Dow Jones Industrial Average in history. The Dow lost 190.58 points that day.

In effect, that put an end to the era of the leveraged buyout in the U.S. airline industry. The following Monday, October 16, Trump announced that he was withdrawing his offer to buy AMR. He said he would consider submitting another bid later, but no one at American ever heard from him again. Three months later, in mid-January, there were widespread reports that Trump, who immediately after withdrawing his offer to acquire AMR had pledged to warn the market before he dumped his stock, did just that without warning. Since he never owned 5 percent of AMR's stock, he never had to reveal how much of it he did own. In any case, sources close to Trump said he sold out at a price near $55 a share, after having bought most of his stock at prices of more than $80 a share. Estimates of his losses ranged from $30 million to $80 million, depending on how many shares of AMR's stock he actually owned.

Trump's withdrawal probably was a good thing for American and for its employees. Even if the airline had won the fight and forced Trump to go away, it almost certainly would have suffered some damage. And American's employees would have been caught in the crossfire. But ending the battle for control of American Airlines before it ever really got started left a lot of intriguing questions unanswered. Principal among them: What would American have done to defend itself?

Sources familiar with American's plans said the airline had a particularly nasty surprise cooked up for Trump. Had he not withdrawn, American was prepared to file a civil RICO suit against him in a friendly federal court in Fort Worth.

The criminal provisions of the Racketeer-Influenced and Corrupt Organization Act are common causes in action in federal felony cases against drug runners, members of organized crime, or even businesses accused of paying off government officials. But few cases have ever come up under the civil provisions of the RICO Act, in large part because of the difficulty and cost involved in proving a conspiracy charge. The cost of such a case can easily run into the tens of millions of dollars. But American was willing and able to pay any legal bills if it had to.

If nothing else, a civil RICO suit against Trump would have been an effective delaying tactic. No one offering to buy a publicly traded company could afford to wait a year or two until such a case came to trial. And American certainly would not have agreed to any settlement before a trial if it left Trump capable of pursuing his takeover bid.

And, had the mere filing of a RICO suit not scared away Trump, the thought of subjecting his financial records to the legal discovery process or having his New Jersey gaming licenses suspended because of a RICO case against him might have done the trick.

Finally, in the extremely unlikely event that such a case ever would have come to trial, American would not have to win the case in court to achieve the desired results. All American would have to do would be to convict Trump in the court of public opinion. He would have been damaged goods in the eyes of public relations–conscious bankers, and his ability to continue wheeling and dealing would have been sharply reduced.

BOB CRANDALL and his team had been lucky. They might have won a tough fight with Donald Trump. But luck saved them the trouble, the expense, and the very real financial pain that they might have had to inflict upon themselves to save the company. Thanks to the collapse of the employee-led takeover of UAL, American didn't have to throw a punch. And, more important, that painless, almost effortless victory over the wheeler-dealer Trump left Crandall and company in even better position to do some wheeling and dealing of their own.

The national economy was showing some early signs of weakening during the summer of 1989. American's earnings were tailing off. And the company already had a very full plate of growth and capital spending set before it. But Crandall also recognized that if those conditions were beginning to pinch American a bit, they had to be putting a real squeeze on the weak sisters of the industry. A new and perhaps final round of consolidation within the airline industry was beginning, and, like any good investor with deep pockets, Crandall wanted to be ready to scoop up prime assets shed by financially distressed competitors trying to raise cash to stay alive.

But he wasn't looking for just any assets. Crandall knew exactly what pieces he wanted to add to the American system. The shopping list was short: increased route authority to serve Japan and other Asian nations; increased route authority to serve Europe; and either Pan Am's or Eastern's Latin American route authorities. American's management had always figured that eventually both of those bumbling airlines would sell their Latin divisions to raise cash to stay alive. So American adopted what was called the "Windows of Opportunity" plan. If any assets deemed to be strategically important became available, American was determined to do anything and everything necessary to acquire them, even if doing so meant delaying implementation of or scuttling altogether other aspects of the previously sacrosanct growth plan.

As things turned out, Eastern, which had little transatlantic service and no service to Asia, was the first of the two carriers serving Latin America to go into bankruptcy proceedings.

On March 4, 1989, the moment Crandall had been waiting for arrived. The International Association of Machinists, representing Eastern's mechanics and other ground workers, walked out on strike, just as they had threatened to do for months. Many of them knew it probably would cost them their jobs. But they no longer cared. That's how angry they were at Texas Air's Frank Lorenzo and how fed up they were with working for Eastern. After years of inept management and horrendous management-labor relations, Eastern had been sold to Texas Air in 1986. At first, its heavily unionized employees thought the acquisition might be good for Eastern, even if Texas Air did own Continental Airlines, which had used its Chapter 11 bankruptcy in 1982 to bust its unions and slash pay by 50 percent. But that optimism quickly faded as Texas Air began slowly shifting Eastern's best assets, such as its SystemOne computer reservations system and its best Airbus aircraft, to either Texas Air or Continental. Eastern's management also steadfastly refused its employees' pay demands.

So, to the surprise of no one—with the possible exception of Frank Lorenzo—the labor relations powder keg at Eastern blew up on March 4. The airline was virtually shut down and filed a Chapter 11 bankruptcy petition in New York on March 9. Still, with management personnel, union members who crossed the picket lines, and hired scabs manning the planes, ramps, and ticket counters, Eastern was able to gradually rebuild much of its old flight schedule.

As Eastern tried to come back from the strike and its subsequent bankruptcy filing, it had to fight not only its own striking employees, but American too. As soon as Eastern filed for bankruptcy, American filed petitions with the Department of Transportation for emergency exemption rights and permanent rights to fly from Miami to Colombia, Costa Rica, and the Cayman Islands. It already had received rights to fly from Miami to Guatemala and several other Central American nations and was operating a New York–to–Caracas, Venezuela, route via its San Juan, Puerto Rico, hub.

American was certain it would be taking over those Miami–to–Latin America routes; in fact by March 15, eleven days after the Eastern shutdown, American's pilots picking up their April bid sheets—used to determine who flies what schedule in the coming month—found they could bid to fly some of those routes.

Then, on April 6, thirty-three days after the Machinists walked out at Eastern and twenty-eight days after Eastern's bankruptcy filing, American executive VP for operations Bob Baker held a news conference at Coral Gables, Florida, to announce "a significant increase in American's service at Miami and in the Caribbean." Baker refused to say that American was establishing a Miami hub, and he noted that the carrier was just going from nineteen to thirty-one flights a day. That was hardly enough to call Miami a hub. Still, company sources confirmed that if all went as management planned, a major hub was exactly what Miami would become. In short, the only reason Baker didn't add even more flights to Miami and immediately call it a hub was that, at that time, American was limited to just six gates spread out over two concourses at the Miami International Airport. But sources in the Dade County Department of Aviation said American officials were holding "intense" discussions with airport director Richard Judy to acquire a large number of gates in the airport's new Concourse D, which was scheduled to open that summer.

American's invasion of Miami, small though it was, obviously was intended to put more economic pressure on Eastern just when the faltering Texas Air Corp. subsidiary could least afford to fight a market share battle. Also, American wanted to start building its name identification in the Miami and Latin American markets, markets that it expected to be serving soon one way or another.

When Texas Air and Eastern officials began talking about Eastern's bankruptcy reorganization plan, they initially said they planned to raise $1.8 billion through the sale of assets. Everyone in the industry knew, however, that if Eastern really wanted to raise that much cash, it would have to sell its Latin division.

Obviously, American had both the desire and the available cash to buy it. And by mid-June, the two carriers were close to completing a $450 million deal transferring Eastern's Miami–to–Latin America route authorities, plus some rights to serve Latin America held by Eastern's sister carrier, Continental, to American.

But, as in most negotiations involving Lorenzo, elements of the deal began to change. At first, Eastern accepted American's decision not to buy the airline's Miami maintenance facilities. Then it said American had to take the hangers and other buildings or the whole deal was off. On another front, American has always wanted a side agreement to move Continental off six gates at Dallas/Fort Worth Airport's Terminal 2E and to four gates in Terminal 2W, which American owned but did not use. Those six Continental gates in Terminal 2E were the only things that prevented American from having total control of two full terminals at D/FW, 2E and 3E. At first, Lorenzo agreed to this. Then he changed his mind.

By early July, the pace of negotiations had slowed to a crawl as Lorenzo and his inner circle of advisors moved pieces in and out of the deal. They were trying to come up with solutions to several interrelated problems at once, and were having a devil of a time doing it. They wanted to get the maximum amount of cash for Eastern's assets, without making it impossible for the airline to make a successful come back. They wanted to appease Eastern's angry shareholders, whose cooperation would be necessary to get the airline out of bankruptcy. And they wanted to do everything possible to keep from hurting Continental and, if possible, to put Continental in position to benefit from the downsizing of Eastern that inevitably would result from a reorganization.

Finally, a frustrated Crandall called Lorenzo in early August to demand that they go through with the deal as originally negotiated, get serious about negotiating a different deal, or call the whole thing off. Their phone conversation didn't last very long. There was a short, angry, profanity-filled exchange in which Crandall accused Lorenzo of backing out of a deal, and Lorenzo warned Crandall against trying to bully Eastern or Texas Air out of business.

When they hung up, the deal was off.

For much of the next two months, Crandall was preoccupied with battening down American's hatches for the economic storm he saw building on the horizon and with preparing for the expected takeover battle.

Eastern, which by August was beginning to generate positive cash as it got more planes into the air during the peak summer travel season, focused on trying to sell old airplanes one or two at a time in hopes of raising the $1.8 billion in cash it needed to reorganize its debt.

But by mid-November, with Eastern's cash flow running negative once again, Eastern and Texas Air officials were under increasing pressure from their impatient creditors. Reluctantly they faced up to the fact that they needed a big asset sale in a hurry.

Delta already was sensitive to charges that it was responsible for Eastern's failure because Delta's massive Atlanta hub has smothered Eastern's hub there. So it wasn't interested in buying anything Eastern had to sell. United, in the meantime, still was in disarray following the failed employee-led buyout. Both the airline's unions and some of those UAL shareholders whose hopes for a huge payoff had been dashed were accusing Chairman Stephen Wolf and Vice Chairman Jack Pope, both ex-American senior executives, of having botched the deal. No other U.S. carriers could afford Eastern's asking price on the Latin American division. And foreign carriers were prohibited by law from buying international route rights issued by the U.S. government under international treaties.

So the call went out once again to American.

This time American officials were in no mood to be jerked around by Lorenzo and his people. They spelled out exactly what they wanted to buy, and exactly what they were willing to pay, and more or less told Eastern to take it or leave it.

By early December sources inside Eastern were reporting to the carrier's unions that a deal to sell the Latin American division and some other assets was all but done. The news media carried those and other stories about the pending American-Eastern deal for days.

Then, on December 18, American announced that it had reached an agreement to acquire international route authorities from another carrier. After literally years of off-and-on discussions, TWA finally had agreed to sell American its rights to fly from Chicago to London, plus its leasehold rights to some property at Chicago's O'Hare International Airport, for $195 million.

The announcement shocked the industry, and not only because it wasn't the deal with Eastern that everyone expected. The price tag on the Chicago–London route was huge, especially since American would not be getting TWA's rights to use London's vastly preferred Heathrow Airport and would have to shift the service to the less convenient Gatwick Airport. But the opportunity to land such a plum route for American's No. 2 hub at Chicago was just too great to pass up. American's plan to make Chicago its biggest international gateway got a huge boost. The airline obviously hoped that having the London route would help it to gain market share at Chicago—where the distracted United operated an even larger hub than American's— on other routes too.

"American has caught United flat-footed," Timothy Pettee, first vice president and airline analyst at Merrill Lynch Capital Markets in New York told a newspaper reporter after the deal was announced. "United has had to put its plans to expand into Europe for the first time on hold while it takes care of all this takeover business."

Then, on the very next day, December 19, American announced that it had finally reached an agreement to buy Eastern's Latin American route authorities, plus other Eastern and Continental assets, for $471 million. American got everything it had wanted from Eastern back in the summer: the Latin routes; the routes from Miami to

London, Madrid, and Toronto; valuable landing slots at Chicago, New York's LaGuardia, and John F. Kennedy airports and at Washington National Airport; hangar and support facilities at several airports, and the relocation of Continental's operations at Dallas/Fort Worth Airport from Terminal 2E to Terminal 2W. In addition, American won a promise from Continental that it would drop its participation in a long-running $1 billion civil antitrust suit filed by about a dozen airlines in the mid-1980s against American and SABRE in a Los Angeles federal court.

Julius Maldutis, airline analyst at Salomon Brothers, Inc., in New York, called American's two major route deals with TWA and Eastern "a big step in American's international route expansion strategy. And it's only the opening move in what I believe will be a much larger foreign presence that American can be expected to develop."

When he said that, Maldutis must have been looking at American's fleet plan, which at the time included 112 orders and options on MD-11s, Boeing 767-300ERs, and Airbus A300-600Rs, each of them long range airplanes designed for international service. Others who, like Maldutis, had taken the time to analyze what American's actions in 1989 were all about surely arrived at the same conclusion.

After conquering the U.S. domestic airline industry, Bob Crandall and American Airlines were going after even bigger game.

16

Chicago to Tokyo or Bust

SIX ROUTES to Japan?

It had to be a joke. The U.S. government had just negotiated a new agreement with Japan creating six new commercial air routes between the United States and Japan. The United States hadn't obtained that many new routes to Japan at once since shortly after General Douglas MacArthur gave up his throne as de facto emperor during the post–World War II rebuilding of Japan. The deal also allowed the United States to allocate one new all-cargo air route.

But it was true. In late 1989 the U.S. and Japanese governments signed an amendment to their bilateral commercial aviation treaty authorizing the United States to grant rights to up to six new routes to Japan. Preference was to be given to cities that did not already have service to Japan, though the routes could be awarded to any city. Only three of the routes could serve Tokyo. The others had to serve some secondary Japanese city. In its announcement that it was establishing a formal route allocation case, the Department of Transportation (DOT) said it would give preference to carriers that had few or no rights to serve Japan as a way of increasing competition in the U.S.–Japan air travel markets dominated by United and Northwest airlines on the U.S. side and by JAL on the Japanese side.

It was as if the new agreement between the United States and Japan had "American" written all over it, or so some in American's management seemed to think. And, in fact, the factors that the DOT said would carry the most weight in deciding which airline would get which route followed almost point-for-point arguments that Crandall and other American officials had been making in Washington for years. So, on January 18, 1990, American filed a petition with the DOT asking not for one, two, or even three of the six routes. American asked for all six.

Adhering to DOT rules, American listed its order of preference for new routes this way: Chicago–Tokyo, San Jose, California–Tokyo, L.A.–Tokyo, Chicago–Nagoya, Los Angeles–Nagoya, and San Jose–Nagoya. But American officials made it very clear that they wanted and expected to win all six routes.

In reality, American did have a distinct preference.

Chicago was the key. One of American's top corporate goals was to reach market parity with United at Chicago. Both carriers operated hubs at O'Hare International Airport, one of only four U.S. airports that still operates under "slot control" rules that strictly limit takeoffs and landings during any one-hour period. Thanks to the Chicago-based United's much longer tenure at O'Hare, it had about 45 percent of all slots—time-specific landing and takeoff rights. American, which had grown rapidly at Chicago in the mid- and late 1980s, had acquired about 30 percent of the slots there, mainly through deals with other carriers. But it was starting to run into a brick wall in trying to pull even with United in terms of both acquiring additional O'Hare slots and market share. Crandall and his senior people believed that American's perennial No. 2 carrier position at O'Hare meant that in a good year it didn't make as much money as it should there and that in a bad year its losses at Chicago would be worse than they otherwise should be.

Landing the Chicago–Tokyo route authority wouldn't mean instant parity in O'Hare slots, but American believed winning that route—and closing its acquisition of TWA's Chicago–London route authority—would shift the loyalty of many Chicago-area passengers away from United and to American, permanently. The only problem for American was that United, which already offered seventy-nine U.S.–Japan round trips each week, more than any other U.S. carrier, also filed a petition with the DOT seeking just one of the six new routes to be granted.

United went after the Chicago–Tokyo route as if its future depended on winning it. Given the potential impact getting that route could have on American's comparative strength in the Chicago market, it's no wonder. United's own numbers showed that it expected to earn $57 million in operating profits in the first twelve months of operating the Chicago–Tokyo route. If that revenue, and the attendant switch in market loyalties by travelers playing the frequent fliers' points game, went to American, American could reach relative parity at O'Hare with United. And if that ever happened, United officials feared that American's slightly lower operating costs and stronger domestic route network would make it very difficult for them to prevent an even more significant and costly erosion of United's market share in its own hometown.

The politically savvy Larry Nagin, United's senior vice president for corporate and external affairs and one of Chairman Steve Wolf's two closest advisors, was in charge of making sure his airline won the route. In less than five months Nagin lined up the political endorsements of Chicago Mayor Richard Daley, Illinois Governor James Thompson and the entire twenty-four member Illinois congressional delegation. Also in United's corner were the governors of Indiana, Kentucky, Nebraska, Virginia, and four other states, the Nebraska legislature, the twelve-member Virginia congressional delegation, and the mayor of Indianapolis.

Okay, so it was political overkill. After all, what in the world was the Nebraska legislature doing by getting involved in a route case that didn't even have an indirect impact on its state? At least Virginia's governor and congressional delegates could argue that their constituents would be affected because United's proposal called for same-plane service from Washington, D.C., to Chicago to Tokyo and back.

Still, United's political log-rolling caught American napping.

"We've never seen such a route case turned into such a political thing," said Don Carty, who by then had been promoted to executive vice president for finance and planning. "What's that tell you? It tells you they don't have much else to go on."

That, of course, was not true, and Carty knew it. For starters, United had a fleet of Boeing 747-400s, the newest and longest-range version of the 400-plus seat line of Boeing jumbo jets. That meant it would be able to offer more seats on each flight than American, which could offer only the 251-seat MD-11. Because the new route was going to a limited capacity route, meaning the carrier would be allowed to operate it only once a day, six days a week, having the biggest airplane made meant a lot.

Second, and most important, United had an ace up its sleeve—
one that everyone in the industry knew about but couldn't do anything to prevent United from playing. Samuel Skinner, a Chicagoan
who had run George Bush's 1988 winning campaign in Illinois was
Secretary of Transportation. Skinner also was a political protégé of
Illinois Governor Thompson and widely rumored to be interested in
running for governor himself some day. Also, though he was a Republican, Skinner had a good relationship with Daley and U.S. Representative Dan Rostenkowski, the state's two most powerful
Democrats.

American didn't like the way United was playing the game. And,
in fact, United wasn't playing by the sort of gentleman's rules that
previously had dictated the limits on how far up the political ladder
a carrier could take such a case. But, as they say, all's fair in love and
war, and United clearly understood the competition for new Chicago–
Tokyo route rights to be war.

AMERICAN DID something about United's first advantage. After
scouring the world for available 747-400s, which were not in abundant
supply because the model was only two years old, American announced a deal with Canadian Airlines International to pick up two
of the big airplanes for $330 million. Bob Crandall later admitted that
at $165 million apiece, American was paying far more for those two
747s—which troubled Canadian had ordered and was expected to
receive from Boeing in early 1991—than it would have paid had it
bought them directly from Boeing. But Boeing could not deliver
planes on such short notice, so American had to go to the secondary
market to find them.

Of course, that move highlighted what many of American's critics
over the years have called two of its biggest mistakes. First, American
had gotten rid of its small fleet of 747s back in 1983 because, as
Crandall said at the time, "American couldn't make money with
it. . . . When you've got an airline like ours, where demand patterns
change and flexibility is of tremendous importance, having fifty-five
DC-10s is a lot better than having thirty-five DC-10s and twenty
747s."

Despite the criticism, Crandall was right about that. The DC-10
was much more versatile in an economic sense than the 747. It could
be operated more cheaply than the 747 on about 85 percent of the

same routes. And in periods of low demand, the smaller DC-10 was much better than the 747. A 290-seat DC-10 that needed to fill 55 percent of its seats to break even on a flight could make money with only 160 passengers aboard. A 400-seat 747 with a 55 percent break-even load factor would need 220 passengers to make any money. But only the 747 could come close to meeting the demand for seats on very heavily traveled long-range routes. On the popular New York– L.A. route, American could offer five or six daily round trips on DC-10s to meet the demand. But because the Chicago–Tokyo route in question was to be a limited capacity route, American didn't have the option of adding a second daily round trip. Only the 747 could fill the bill, and American didn't have any. So, as is the case with most good decisions, American had to live with or adjust to its preference for the DC-10.

The second criticism related to American's lack of 747s stemmed from United's $750 million acquisition of Pan Am's Pacific division in 1985. Crandall, Carty, and even Tom Plaskett, who at the time was American's senior VP of marketing but later became Pan Am's chairman, argue that American never had a chance to buy the Pan Am Pacific division. "It was one of those dead-of-the-night deals we never had a chance on," Plaskett said. But American seriously had studied the possibility of acquiring Pan Am on at least three occasions prior to the 1985 sale of the Pacific division to United. And each time, American took a look at Pan Am's debts, high labor costs, and expensive-to-operate fleet of 747s and passed. Indeed, after United acquired the Pacific division, American officials ridiculed the deal as being abhorrently expensive, the kind of deal they'd never do.

Yet United had been able to bring its considerable financial resources to bear in improving the Pacific division's operations and in better utilizing route authorities Pan Am either had been underusing or not using at all. As a result, by 1990 United was raking in $500 million a year in profits from the Pacific division while American, which had only its D/FW–Tokyo run, looked on in envy. Had American been sharper and obtained Pan Am's Pacific division instead of United, it would have had to have a fleet of 747s and the tables might have been turned on United.

As for United's second major advantage over American in seeking the Chicago–Tokyo route—its political connections—American was utterly clueless about what to do to level the playing field.

John Ash, president of Global Aviation Associates, a Washington-based firm that consults airlines on international routes and other matters, predicted before the DOT hearings began that United would win the Chicago–Tokyo route based on the political considerations. But he also warned that American, which he said still had an outside chance of winning because the DOT's policy in establishing the route allocation case was "designed to break up the dominance of the two 900-pound gorillas in the Pacific [United and Northwest]," was about to blow its only chance.

"American hurts itself sometimes by the way it deals with these people [bureaucrats in the DOT]. They are so aggressive, and so self-assured that they sometimes offend people they're dealing with," Ash said.

It could be fairly said that while American thought it had reasonably good relationships with legislators in Washington, in many cases those relationships were not very good at all. And American's only relationships with many mid-level and even upper-level bureaucrats in the DOT were openly hostile.

American's principal lobbyist in Washington was William Burhop, who had been hired as vice president for federal affairs in 1989 to fill the vacancy left by senior VP Gene Overbeck's 1987 retirement. In contrast to the low-key Overbeck, Burhop quickly became known around the DOT and around congressional offices as "Little Bob Crandall" because he was perceived by many in Washington circles to be mimicking the angry-man approach for which his boss was so famous. The office staff of one congressman from Texas—American's home state, no less—was so offended by Burhop's tactics and attitude that they banned him from their office suite.

It had been Crandall's idea to bid for all six of the routes to be awarded and to make formal arguments claiming that the airline really wanted all of them. He and others at American had been arguing for years that the United States did not need to parcel out new routes to Japan piecemeal. Rather, they contended that the nation's best interests would be served by giving one strong airline—American, obviously—a large number of new route authorities to Japan. That, Crandall argued, would create the element of competition needed to break up the duopolistic control Northwest and United held over the marketplace, at least from the U.S. side, and to increase the U.S. side's overall market share. (By itself, JAL actually flew more than half of all U.S.–Japan passengers.)

Crandall made perfect sense from the business theory perspective.

But from a political perspective, the notion of giving a third U.S. carrier what amounted to a franchise to serve Japan was a nonstarter. No one familiar with Washington's handling of aviation issues believed American had a ghost of a chance of getting what it wanted. And many immediately noted that with its big application, American had just brought the rope to its own hanging. Ten other airlines, including the politically well-connected Delta, which like American had designs on becoming a significant player in the Pacific, petitioned the DOT seeking at least one of the six new routes to Japan. Amazingly, even the nearly bankrupt Pan Am, which had gotten out of the Pacific five years earlier, asked for one of the new routes. With so much at stake for so many parties, American had made itself every other airline's main target.

Perhaps he was enthralled by Crandall's logic for going after all six routes. Or perhaps he just was afraid to tell his boss no. But for whatever reason, Burhop either didn't tell Crandall that the idea of going for all six routes wouldn't fly in Washington or he failed to convince Crandall of that fact. Others in American's senior management, including Carty, supported the idea of going for all six, even though they knew it was a long shot. Several members of senior management later claimed that they thought asking for all six routes was dangerous. But apparently no one inside American's senior management tried to derail the plan; or if they did, they were unsuccessful.

In any case, by asking for all six routes, American gave the politically sensitive decision-makers at the DOT, some of whom hated American to begin with, all the ammunition they needed to shoot down Arrogant Airlines, as they sometimes called American. Bowing to political pressure from Skinner and to pressure created in Congress and at the state level by United, deputy assistant secretary Patrick Murphy, the senior career official assigned as the DOT's final decision-maker in the case, gave the industry's Big Three, American, United, and Delta, something they each could call a victory. United got the Chicago–Tokyo route. Delta got the Los Angeles–Tokyo route.

American got the booby prize: San Jose–Tokyo.

THE OLD adage—"Be careful what you pray for, you might get it"— applies here. American got some, but not all, of what it had prayed for to the DOT. But a good argument could be made that it might have been better off not to have gotten any new routes.

The San Jose–Tokyo route has been slow to develop for American. The airline has been unable to attract as many passengers away from San Francisco International Airport and United's flights there to Asia as it had expected. And it has been unable to market San Jose as a good jumping-off point for people traveling between the U.S. heartland and Japan. Even the runway at San Jose's airport has been a problem. It is too short for a fully loaded MD-11 to use for takeoffs, so the airline has had to severely limit cargo capacity on its San Jose–Tokyo flights. On particularly hot days when the thinner air makes it harder to generate lift, the airline even has had to limit seating on its MD-11s at San Jose. On a few occasions it has taken off from San Jose with a full load minus 100,000 pounds of fuel to save weight, then landed a few miles up the San Francisco Bay at Oakland Airport to have the fuel tanks topped off for the long flight to Tokyo.

After the decision was made final in November, a devastated American accused the DOT of playing politics. But that's like accusing the National Football League of sponsoring football games. Of course DOT played politics. It's in Washington. Its leader is a political appointee. And its senior officials, typically, are mid-career lawyers and political hacks trying either to hang on to their cushy jobs through ever-changing administrations or to land high-paying jobs as Washington lobbyists. So they do whatever they're told by their political masters. And American should have known that going in. Instead, the airline put itself in a position to be outmaneuvered, then cried "Foul!" when it happened.

Not surprisingly, six months after the Japanese route cases were decided, Crandall dismissed Burhop. It was one of the very few times in his career that Crandall had ever done the dirty deed himself. But in this case, Crandall had no one but himself to blame for Burhop's actions. He had hired Burhop precisely because he exhibited the same aggressive, tough, no-nonsense attitude that Crandall likes in all of his executives and of which he himself is the epitome. But while that approach works well in the real world of business, Washington is far from the real world. Logic and consistency matter in Washington only when doing the logical or consistent thing happens also to be in the best interests of those making the decision.

One thing American is noted for, however, is that even when it makes mistakes, it usually makes a good recovery. And, for a brief time, it looked as if American might come away from the 1990 Japanese route case a bigger winner by virtue of its loss. On August 7, 1990, five days after DOT administrative law judge John Mathias issued his recommendation to Murphy that United be awarded the Chicago–Tokyo route and that Delta be given the L.A.–Tokyo route, American immediately canceled its $330 million deal to acquire the two 747-400s from Canadian Airlines. When that deal had first been announced, Crandall had put a positive spin on American's uncharacteristic willingness to pay a premium price by saying "While we cannot actually buy the route, we are buying the airplanes because it was felt that we had to have those particular planes, and have them by next spring [1991] to win the route case. So, from our perspective, we are buying the route and planes [together] for a total of $330 million."

But, by canceling the deal for the two 747s, American suddenly had at its disposal the $330 million it had been willing to spend to acquire Chicago–Tokyo route. A call went out to Northwest, which had been serving the Chicago–Tokyo route without limitations since 1952. With United preparing to enter the market, Northwest soon would be competing against two hubbing carriers on that route: United, which has hubs at both Chicago and Tokyo, and JAL, which has a Tokyo hub.

In theory, Northwest's rights to fly between Chicago and Tokyo are more valuable than the rights to serve that route awarded in 1990 to United. Northwest's Chicago–Tokyo route was part of a package of virtually unlimited rights given to Northwest and Pan Am in the early 1950s when the United States and Japan concluded the basic treaty that governs international air service between the two nations. Northwest and Pan Am were allowed to fly not only to Tokyo from a number of U.S. cities, they also were given rights to fly on from Tokyo to other Asian nations, and to pick up local Japanese passenger traffic during their Tokyo stopovers. Then in 1985, cash-starved Pan Am exercised its rights under a long-standing U.S. Department of Transportation policy to sell international route rights it had been awarded by the government for free. It foolishly sold its U.S.–Japan routes to United in what proved ultimately to be a vain attempt to remain solvent.

However, the United States' lone route authority to fly between Chicago and Tokyo granted under the 1950s agreement with Japan belonged to Northwest, not Pan Am. So, when Chicago-based United bought Pan Am's Pacific Division in 1985, it did not get the one route that it wanted more than any other. Understandably, when U.S. and Japanese trade negotiators agreed in late 1989 to amend the commercial air services treaty between their two nations to open up six new routes to Japan for U.S. carriers, United saw that as the chance it had been waiting for to add the Chicago–Tokyo route to its portfolio of route rights in the Pacific.

It really didn't matter much to United that the new Chicago–Tokyo route it sought was subject to much more stringent Japanese-imposed limitations than were its other routes to Japan acquired from Pan Am. For example, United could fly its Chicago–Tokyo route only six days a week and could offer only one flight a day. Northwest, on the other hand, had almost unlimited rights to operate as many flights as it wanted each day on the Chicago–Tokyo route.

Crandall and Carty understood the importance of those technical differences between the Chicago–Tokyo rights held by Northwest and the Chicago–Tokyo rights granted to United in 1990. So, despite their extreme disappointment over not getting the Chicago–Tokyo route rights that went to United, the American duo began plotting a way to acquire Northwest's potentially more valuable Chicago–Tokyo route rights. With Northwest's rights, they figured American could offer two, maybe even three flights a day on the route during the peak summer travel period, using its new McDonnell Douglas MD-11s. Then, in the slow winter months, American could drop back to one flight a day. By using the MD-11, which it configures to seat 251 passengers compared with the 440-seat 747-400 United planned to use on its Chicago–Tokyo service, American would gain a cost advantage. The MD-11's three engines would not use as much fuel as the four power plants strapped to the 747. And, by adding extra sections—or flights—during the peak summer months, American would be able to overcome the single plane capacity advantage United would have held with its 747s. Then, in the slow winter months, American actually would hold the capacity advantage by flying one MD-11 daily versus United's one 747. If both airlines were able to attract an average of 150 passengers a day during the winter months, American's load factor—or percentage of filled seats— would be a slightly profitable 59.8 percent. But United's load factor would be an abysmal, money-losing 34.1 percent.

Of course, all that was based upon the assumption that American could induce Northwest to part with its Chicago–Tokyo rights. Carty thought he had that one figured out, too. He figured American could use the $330 million it previously had earmarked for the two 747-400s American planned to acquire from Canadian Airlines International as bait. After all, it was common knowledge around the industry that Northwest, heavily burdened by debt from its 1989 leveraged buyout, could use the cash. And it was obvious that once United, with its giant hub at Chicago providing lots of passenger feed to its international routes, started its Chicago–Tokyo service, Northwest's Chicago–Tokyo route would turn into a big money loser. Northwest had little or no ability to feed passengers from other midwestern cities to Chicago to fill up its Tokyo flights. And it had little reason to do that. Northwest also possessed rights to fly to Tokyo from both Detroit and Minneapolis/St. Paul and already was running its Tokyo-bound passengers from smaller cities through those two gateways, both of which happened to be major hubs on the Northwest system.

Carty's plan was to acquire Northwest's Chicago–Tokyo route, then fly it with American's new McDonnell Douglas MD-11s—which cost about $100 million each—rather than the 440-seat Boeing 747s, which at the time cost about $150 million each. In the peak summer travel season, American could offer two, or even three departures a day on MD-11s, while United, by law, would be stuck with just one daily departure on which it was committed to using a 747. Then, in the winter months, when demand for travel between the United States and Japan typically is slack, American could drop back to just one MD-11 flight a day on the Chicago–Tokyo route. Doing that—which essentially is matching aircraft capacity to changes in the level of passenger demand—would give American a better chance to make money even in the slow winter months, and an opportunity to carry the lion's share of the Chicago–Tokyo traffic in the peak summer travel season.

There was, however, one hitch in Carty's plan. Northwest didn't really want to sell its Chicago–Tokyo route. Or, more accurately, they couldn't.

Al Checchi and Gary Wilson, the financial wheeler-dealers who organized the 1989 leveraged buyout of Northwest, were in the midst of discovering the hard way that while airlines are glamorous, dynamic organizations that can generate huge amounts of cash, their historically low returns on investment and extreme sensitivity to downturns in the economy make them marginal investments in the best of times and bottomless money pits in bad times. Northwest had not made a profit since the takeover in mid-1989, and most of its free cash flow was going to reduce the buyout debt. But the consortium of banks led by Bankers Trust of New York that financed the takeover of Northwest wisely had included covenants in their agreements with Checchi, Wilson, and company that prevented the airline's new owners from lining their pockets with profits from the sale of Northwest's assets. Rather, because the banks considered such things as Northwest's international route rights to be their loan security, they had included provisions in the loan covenants requiring Northwest to use most or all of the money raised through the sale of such assets to pay down the debt incurred in the takeover. Because of that Wings Holding, Checchi's and Wilson's takeover vehicle and Northwest's ultimate corporate parent, had little incentive to sell assets like its Chicago–Tokyo route authority.

It didn't help American any that relations between the senior managers of both companies quickly soured. American's battalion of hotshot managers, most of whom were career airline industry people, had had little regard for Northwest's simple-minded management before the takeover. But their contempt for the Checchi-Wilson team of financiers, hoteliers, and political hacks was impossible to conceal. (By 1991 that contempt had turned to true hatred when Northwest hired several junior members of American's management team, all experts in yield management. American filed suit over the matter, only to see Northwest file what could be a landmark predatory pricing lawsuit against American in the summer of 1992 over American's introduction of a controversial new fare-pricing system.)

American's repeated attempts to buy the Chicago–Tokyo route from Northwest failed. American's only remaining option was to buy Northwest's entire Pacific Division. But because of its own losses, the price of such a transaction, the economic downturn in Asia (particularly in Japan) and concern about whether the U.S. government would try to block such a deal on anti-trust grounds, the idea of acquiring Northwest's entire Pacific Division was less than appealing to American's management. And the likelihood that Checchi and Wilson would sell Northwest's Pacific Division was pretty slim. For starters, most of the proceeds would have to go to the banks that financed the takeover back in 1989. Second, American wasn't about to pay as much for the Pacific Division as Checchi and Wilson thought it was worth. And third, selling the Pacific division would signal the beginning of the liquidation of Northwest. Traditionally, the Pacific

Division was the only regular source of profits for Northwest. Selling that division would mean that Northwest's weak, money-losing domestic division and its tiny Atlantic division would have to be sold or merged with another carrier.

American's top managers didn't like their predicament one bit, but they became resigned to the fact that for many years, the carrier was likely to remain only a niche player in the trans-Pacific markets with just two routes to Tokyo, from D/FW and San Jose.

In early December, a month after the final decision was issued giving United the Chicago–Tokyo route, American agreed to pay $140 million to cash-starved Continental Airlines for its Seattle–Tokyo route. But even that deal illustrated American's acceptance, at least for the time being, of its niche carrier status. Continental had hoped to sell almost all of its Pacific division—mostly rights to serve the South Pacific—and its South Pacific subsidiary, Air Micronesia, to Delta to raise the cash Continental needed to avoid bankruptcy. But Delta wouldn't bite on the full deal, so Continental shifted gears at the last moment and accepted American's standing offer to buy only the Seattle–Tokyo route. Hours after agreeing to sell Seattle–Tokyo to American, Continental filed a Chapter 11 bankruptcy petition, its second in eight years. American made a $140 million loan to the bankrupt carrier, secured by the Seattle–Tokyo route rights until American could get Transportation Department approval of the deal and take over service on the route in the fall of 1991.

In the late 1980s American had spent more than two years trying to win a smaller, but even more complicated international route authority to serve Japan. Before United acquired Pan Am's Pacific Division in 1985, it had Seattle–Tokyo rights. And for a couple of years after it acquired the Pan Am Pacific division, which included routes to Tokyo from both San Francisco and Los Angeles, United was permitted to keep the Seattle–Tokyo route as well.

But in response to the cries of other carriers who complained that United had the three most important gateways to Japan sewn up, the Department of Transportation set up a new route allocation contest. Initially, Continental won the case. But when the Transportation Department learned that the senior career official who made the decision had been negotiating with one of the parties in the case for a job upon his leaving government, his findings were thrown out and the case was relaunched. This time American and United fought hard, but American won. But the victory was short-lived. Continental, which had filed a federal suit when the first Seattle–Tokyo route case's decision was thrown out claiming that its rights of due process were violated by the Transportation Department, won its case and the Seattle–Tokyo route.

The upshot of American's two most fiercely fought international route cases was that American for a long time would be limited to being only a niche player in the vast and potentially lucrative trans-Pacific markets. Its San Jose–Tokyo and D/FW–Tokyo routes never would have the kind of profit potential of a Chicago–Tokyo route, or even of a Seattle–Tokyo route. American's position in the Pacific markets improved a bit in December 1990 when it got lucky—finally—and acquired from Continental the same Seattle–Tokyo route it had fought so hard to obtain a couple of years earlier when Continental was forced to sell it to raise cash it would need as it entered Chapter 11 bankruptcy.

EVEN WITH the Seattle–Tokyo route, American's presence in the Pacific is minuscule. And that is not likely to change at any time soon. The airline's priorities have shifted to building up its trans-Atlantic and Latin American service. And the tighter economic conditions of the early 1990s also have caused American to adopt a more conservative capital spending plan.

But that's not to say that if presented with the right opportunity, American would not shift gears once again and push hard to become a big player in the Pacific.

One such opportunity might be if Northwest were to have a change of heart. And that is not inconceivable. Northwest's financial problems worsened to the point that in late 1992 it was seeking another $300 million loan from its banks and part owner, KLM Royal Dutch Airlines, and $900 million in conversions from its labor unions. Thus it would not surprise anyone in or close to the airline industry to see American eventually acquire Northwest's Chicago–Tokyo route rights, or even Northwest's entire Pacific division.

Another opportunity to move into the Pacific could come through American's acquisition of an equity stake in Canadian Airlines International. By late November 1992, American was poised to rescue the nearly broke Canadian with a nearly $190 million investment that would give American 25 percent ownership of Canada's No. 2 carrier. As far as American is concerned, the deal would be paid for by also obtaining contracts from Canadian to provide it with a whole host of management information services, such as crew scheduling, yield management, and so on, and through greater Canadian support for the SABRE computer reservations system. But Canadian also has a number of rights to serve Japan. Just how American and Canadian could coordinate their schedules to allow American or its passengers access to Japan via Canadian route authorities is not clear. But if a way is found to make that idea work, American could get some of the Asian access it has sought for so long.

17

Riding the Storm Out

IT WAS as if the Reverend Billy Graham had said he no longer was sure the Bible was true. By the summer of 1990 Bob Crandall, the airline industry's high priest of rapid growth in the 1980s and the author of American's quasi-scriptural Growth Plan, was preaching heresy.

Speaking to a group of about 1,800 American managers gathered in Dallas in August for their annual management meetings, Crandall said: "Unless we can validate the assumption that we can consistently make money, we cannot keep investing in the airline business. And if we can't, the future of every American Airlines employee will be very different from what we all want it to be."

Was Crandall really threatening to abandon the Growth Plan? Or was he just trying to use fear as a motivational tool? Many of the American managers present that day, like a lot of other people around the industry who heard Crandall make similar statements in the late summer and early fall of 1990, thought he was just blowing smoke. Sure, it was starting to look as if the industry was going to go through a previously unexpected downturn. Fuel prices were rising rapidly in the wake of Iraq's invasion of Kuwait on August 2 and the international response against that action. Crandall had reinstituted the profit-improvement program concept that Don Carty had managed back in the early 1980s, and the company had been able to identify

fifty cost-cutting programs that were expected to improve its performance by $100 million.

Still, the conventional thinking among American's own managers
was that Crandall would never gut the Growth Plan, the brilliant
long-term strategic and operating plan that for nearly eight years he
and American had ridden all the way to the top of the industry.

One month after addressing his own managers in Dallas, Crandall
delivered a speech at the Wings Club in New York entitled "Storm
Clouds Ahead." Again he sounded like a very worried man. The
Persian Gulf Crisis, he said, was an important short-term concern
for U.S. airlines, especially since fuel prices were up 100 percent
following Iraq's invasion of Kuwait. But Crandall warned that "the
real bad news is not that the short term looks discouraging, but that
it's getting a great deal harder to be optimistic about the long term."

Despite its reputation for and intensified efforts at cost cutting,
American's costs, like those of the entire industry, were beginning
to spiral upward at an alarming rate. Demand for air travel was soft.
Financially weak carriers were pricing their product below actual
costs in hopes of generating needed cash, and the healthier carriers
were obliged to match those low fares or lose passengers and revenue.

But again, almost no one took Crandall seriously. After all, American had just agreed to pay $710 million to TWA for a variety of
assets, including four valuable routes to London, $140 million to
Continental for the Seattle-Tokyo route, and $471 million to Eastern
for its Latin division. Plus, it had more than 200 aircraft on firm order
and another 250 or so on option. And American officials, despite
their chairman's publicly expressed angst, insisted that the airline
still was committed to its growth plan and the $22 billion, five-year
capital spending plan that fueled it.

In short, regardless of what Crandall said, American hardly looked
or behaved like a company that was concerned about its long-term
profitability or survival.

Many people also thought Crandall was posturing for the benefit
of American's pilots, with whom management had been locked in
unusually contentious contract talks for more than a year. Crandall
desperately wanted to maintain American's significant cost advantage over United and Delta. But the numbers being sought by the
Allied Pilots Association threatened to wipe out much of that cost
advantage as well as, Crandall feared, American's chances of making
significant profits in the suddenly less rosy-looking early 1990s.

Indeed, the new decade certainly started off much tougher than anyone had expected. AMR Corp. reported a loss of $19.3 million in the first quarter of 1990, its first quarterly loss since the fourth quarter of fare war–plagued 1987. There was a modest rebound in the second quarter, in which AMR earned $129.2 million. But management was not fooled by that mild seasonal surge into thinking the picture was improving. In fact, that's when Crandall pulled the old profit-improvement program off the shelf and put it into effect.

And by the time Saddam Hussein gambled that the rest of the world wouldn't care if he attacked Kuwait, there were already significant signs of weakness in the airline's bookings for travel in the late summer and fall.

On top of all the U.S. airline industry's structural problems—too much capacity, rising costs, and below-cost pricing by weak or bankrupt competitors trying to generate badly needed cash—Crandall was beginning to see a major recession on the horizon.

Then when the Iraqis touched off the international crisis in the Persian Gulf, American was hammered by a near-tripling of fuel prices, from around 57 cents a gallon in July to around $1.45 a gallon by late September. To make matters worse, the threat of terrorist attacks against U.S. carriers rose sharply after President George Bush began sending thousands of U.S. troops to the Persian Gulf. People who otherwise would have traveled suddenly were too scared to fly.

Amazingly, AMR managed to scratch out a $65.6 million profit in the third quarter of 1990. But the bottom fell out in the fourth quarter, when the company reported a $215.1 million *loss*, easily the biggest quarterly loss in company history to that date. In fact, that quarterly loss was almost three times more than the largest previous *annual* loss.

However, by comparison with other carriers, American did pretty well in the fourth quarter of 1990, the worst single quarter in history for the entire worldwide airline industry. Continental filed its Chapter 11 bankruptcy petition in December. Eastern frittered away nearly all of its remaining cash in that quarter and finally ceased operations in early January 1991. In fact, of all the major U.S. airlines—those with revenues of at least $1 billion annually—only Southwest Airlines, the very nontraditional airline that eschews such industry conventions as hub-and-spoke operations and in-flight meals, made a profit in 1990.

Crandall couldn't resist an "I told you so."

"We have been saying for quite some time that 1990 was not going to be a good year," he said in January 1991 when he announced AMR's huge fourth quarter loss and its $39.6 million loss for all of 1990 (its first annual loss since 1982). "The dramatic rise in fuel prices, the loss of traffic due to a slowing economy, and a host of ill-advised industry pricing practices have had very adverse impacts on all carriers. American's situation was aggravated, particularly during the fourth quarter, by a number of pilot job actions which have made it difficult and expensive to provide the services our customers want."

The last factor he listed was a particularly galling one from his perspective.

About five hundred members of the Allied Pilots Association had called in sick over the weekend preceding Christmas in 1990. Management had understood the unusually long sick-call list—three times longer than normal—to mean that some union members were conducting a job action against the carrier at a time when it was extremely vulnerable to service disruptions: the Christmas–New Years holiday travel season.

Everyone in senior management was angry, but no one more so than Bob Baker, the airline's executive vice president for operations.

"I can understand guys wanting more money in their contract. That's part of life and I can deal with that. But to do something that disrupts a lot of our customers' holiday travel plans and makes them never want to fly on American again, that's not only unprofessional, it's dumb. How can we pay them what they want if by their actions they scare off our customers?" railed an exasperated Baker. The second-generation American executive added that he felt, in some ways, that those pilots who stayed away from work had betrayed not just management, but their fellow workers and all those thousands of people who for over sixty years had helped build American.

On the day after Christmas, American filed suit in federal court in Fort Worth seeking an injunction barring members of the Allied Pilots Association from participating in orchestrated efforts such as sickouts or work-to-rule actions. (Work-to-rule actions take their name from employees' decisions to perform their duties precisely as defined in the union's contract. When pilots work-to-rule they can have a devastating impact on the carrier's schedule because their contracts often retain arcane old language and concepts that, in effect, give them much more time than necessary to complete certain tasks. If they do that in large numbers, the airline's tight flight schedule can be devastated in a matter of hours.)

Officials at the pilots' union vehemently protested that no such orchestrated actions had taken place.

Still, American got its injunction from the court. But the sick call remained unusually long for the rest of the week. So, on December 27, Baker announced that American would reduce its daily flight schedule by about 4 percent because it no longer could afford to schedule 2,200 flights a day with so many pilots unavailable for duty. During each day of the sickout, he said, American had been forced to cancel a dozen or more flights because it was running out of pilots.

After the holidays, American took out very expensive full-page ads in major newspapers around the nation offering what it called an AApology to the thousands of passengers who were stranded, delayed, or otherwise inconvenienced by the Allied Pilots' disruption of American's operations during the holiday travel period.

Those ads touched off a firestorm among American's 8,700 pilots the vast majority of whom had heard only rumors or vague, quasi-coded messages on their extensive grapevine about a sickout, and who never would have participated in it had they had full knowledge of it. Most of those pilots expected and accepted a certain amount of bickering between the company and the union's leadership. That's a normal part of the contract negotiation process. And it was especially the case in the 1989–1991 contract talks, when the Allied Pilots' leaders often fought more fiercely among themselves than they did with management, which wound up being more of a convenient stalking horse for politically ambitious union leaders than a true negotiating adversary.

But American's AApology ads went far beyond most pilots' concept of fair negotiating tactics. As far as they were concerned, the ads were a blow below the belt. Management had gone too far this time.

In March 1991 American finally got a new pilots' contract, albeit one that allowed its pilots to greatly narrow the gap between the value of their pay and benefits and that of United's pilots, and one that Crandall bemoaned as "an uneconomic labor agreement." But merely signing the contract didn't heal the wounds or wipe away the profound lack of trust each side had in the other.

Just as many in American's management ranks believed that some pilots had betrayed the company by their actions, most pilots felt betrayed by a management that would spend so much money to blame them publicly for the actions of a relative few, and then fight them over what they viewed to be relatively small pay raises.

In the fall of 1991, Crandall quietly admitted in a letter to every pilot that management had made a mistake by running the AApology ads. He also offered his personal apologies to those pilots who had not participated in the sickout. Since Crandall issues formal written apologies for his actions about as often as Haley's Comet passes by the earth, most pilots understood his act to be a sign that he and management really were making a sincere effort to heal the wounds and patch up the relationship.

Still, while most pilots personally accepted the boss's apology, they could not forget that their company had turned on them. They quietly filed that memory away, just in case it would be needed during the next contract negotiations, which are scheduled to begin in the spring of 1994.

JACK POPE leaned back on the couch and chuckled when asked what he thought of United Airlines back in the early and mid-1980s, when he was American's senior VP of finance and chief financial officer.

"We assumed that United was asleep. We thought it was the God-given right of American and Delta to always be smarter, better, faster, quicker [and] more innovative than United," said Pope, who today is United's president.

And for nearly the entire decade of the 1980s, it seemed as if Pope's assessment was correct. United, one of the few carriers to support deregulation from the outset back in the mid-1970s, entered the de-regulated era with a sizable lead over the rest of the pack in terms of fleet size, destinations served, and passenger miles flown. But for a host of reasons—summed up under the broad term "bad man-agement"—United watched almost passively while archrival Amer-ican quickly transformed itself into a lean tiger and while Delta expanded methodically but relentlessly out of its niche in the South-east to become a huge national competitor. United, on the other hand, virtually stood still. Ultra-aggressive American blew past it to be-come the nation's biggest carrier. And the doggedly determined Delta closed the gap so much that at one point in the late 1980s in-dustry experts were openly predicting that it too would overtake United.

Things were so bad at United that twice, first in 1989 and then in 1990, the company narrowly escaped being taken over in leveraged buyouts organized by the carrier's own angry and estranged employees. Indeed, it seemed at times that United's workers were more concerned about the company's future than was management.

Pope jumped to United from American in 1987 when Stephen Wolf was brought in to replace Richard Ferris, the architect of United's failed 1980s diversification strategy. Ironically, Wolf had been the second choice of United's board. Bob Crandall was the first choice. He turned down a multimillion-dollar offer from United's board, but only after American's board trumped United's extremely generous financial offer by putting a long-term stock ownership incentive into Crandall's contract that promised to make him even wealthier if he stayed at American until he reached age sixty.

But by 1991, Pope could afford to laugh about how the whole situation had worked out. "Now, all of a sudden, something's happened here where the tables have been turned. And I think American and Delta are not too thrilled about that because United all of a sudden has awakened and we can go out and strike them back just as hard as they struck us all those years."

Indeed, beginning in October 1990, United started flexing its muscles in ways it hadn't for fifteen years. In just two weeks in October 1990 the carrier put together a string of triumphs that turned the rest of the industry on its ear.

First, United successfully turned back a $4.2 billion takeover attempt organized by its own pilots, who had hired Chrysler Corporation vice chairman Gerald Greenwald, the man many people thought would replace Lee Iacocca, to spearhead the attempt and to replace Wolf if they were successful.

Then the airline announced the largest single order in history for new airplanes! United ordered $22 billion worth of new widebody jets from Boeing. The order was for both more 747-400s and the first copies of Boeing's new 777, a twin-engine widebody designed for transcontinental and intercontinental service.

Perhaps the biggest, most startling move of all came on October 23, when United agreed to pay $400 million for most of Pan Am's lucrative rights to serve London's Heathrow Airport—along with other international routes and related facilities—in one of the most one-sided deals in industry history. Pan Am got the money. But not much else. And the way Pam Am was burning through cash in those days, the $400 million that it received from United wasn't likely to last a year. Sure enough, within fourteen months of that deal, Pan Am, despite subsequent major asset sales, was out of money and out of business forever.

Then in early November came the final word from the Department of Transportation giving United the coveted Chicago-Tokyo route.

All of that helped United's management convince its unions it really was serious about growing the airline and taking the industry crown back from American. Also, management's willingess to increase its contract offer to its pilots allowed both sides to put an end to their decade-old feud, which had been a major force behind both attempted takeovers. The new labor agreement between United and its pilots, signed in early 1991, was relatively generous, but it was not as expensive as either of the new pilot agreements signed in 1990 by Delta or by American in 1991.

CRANDALL AND company had been caught with their pants down. Not only was United's deal with Pan Am one of immense strategic importance to the entire U.S. airline industry, it was a major embarrassment for American.

Still, Crandall wasn't going to just give up without trying to get something for American. Two days after the United–Pan Am deal was announced, he faxed a letter to former protégé Tom Plaskett, who had become Pan Am's chairman in 1988. Crandall, who also released copies of his letter to the news media, wrote: "As I have told you many times in the past, most recently in our telephone conversation of Monday, October 22, we have for some time been interested in acquiring a number of Pan Am's international route authorities, including those to the United Kingdom. We would welcome an opportunity to make an offer to acquire the United Kingdom route authorities and believe, if given the opportunity thus far denied us, we would propose terms substantially better than those offered by United. Alternatively, we would welcome an opportunity to enter into an arrangement to acquire a package of assets that would provide Pan Am with superior economic benefits than that offered by United."

More ominously, Crandall implied that Plaskett had sold Pan Am's shareholders down the river and likely would be sued by some of them.

"We believe that the fiduciary duties owed by you and your fellow directors to maximize value for Pan Am's stockholders and creditors dictate that you afford us an opportunity to make a competing offer for these assets," Crandall wrote.

The next day Crandall sent Plaskett a second letter and again released it to the news media. This time he offered $500 million for just the route rights that Pan Am had agreed to sell United. That was a subtantially better price than United had agreed to pay, especially since United's offer also covered two of Pan Am's Boeing 747s plus a grab bag full of airport facilities around the nation.

Crandall's letters did no good. Pan Am and United had a tamper-proof deal. And to make sure Crandall and American understood that, United issued a news release with a thinly veiled threat to sue for tampering if American didn't knock it off.

The American chairman was furious. Problem was, he didn't know at whom his anger should be directed. Should he be mad at Wolf or Pope, both former members of his senior staff at American, for negotiating a great deal for their company? Should he be upset with his own staff for not anticipating such a deal and heading it off? Should he be angry with himself for not pursuing an assets deal more to Pan Am's liking before United entered the picture?

Or, should he be upset with Tom Plaskett, formerly his right-hand man at American, who had left the company in a professionally understated huff when Crandall made it clear he didn't think Plaskett had what it took to succeed him as president?

Ultimately, Crandall directed his general displeasure at all of those people, including—and perhaps most intensely at—himself. He was mad at none of them in particular and at everybody involved in general.

Yet, in all fairness, Crandall and American really had no one to blame but themselves. Maybe Wolf and Plaskett did purposely plant a sharp elbow in Crandall's ribs with their deal. But even so, American had had its chances to do a deal with Pan Am, and it passed. As Plaskett pointed out in a return of Crandall's first letter, "I had understood from our many conversations, including our most recent one, that American would be interested only in buying routes and did not wish to enter into a broad-scale agreement with Pan Am."

Throughout his four years at Pan Am, Plaskett had sought to form marketing alliances, operating partnerships, or even mergers that would keep the Pan Am franchise with its potentially valuable international routes and its highly recognizable name alive and most of the carrier's employees in their jobs. American, on the other hand, had not been interested in acquiring other carriers' labor problems, debts, or old beat-up airplanes. American wanted to do assets-only deals. It wanted only faltering carriers' international route rights, their landing and takeoff slots at restricted airports, and their terminal facilities at key airports.

Plaskett maintained that the key to Pan Am's deal with United was that United agreed to the creation of a joint marketing relationship. United promised to feed passengers to Pan Am's flights from Miami to Latin America, among other things. No one in the industry, with the possible exception of Plaskett and his aides at Pan Am, believed for one minute that United was going to do much, if anything, to help keep Pan Am alive. United had very little service to Miami, Pan Am's gateway to Latin America, and never took any serious steps to increase its service there to provide the promised passenger feed.

In reality, despite Plaskett's belief that the joint marketing agreement was an important piece of it, there was virtually no value added to Pan Am from the sale of its London routes to United beyond the $400 million cash payment. So when Plaskett maintained that what American was offering was of less long-term value than what United offered, he was being either coy or extremely naive.

In any case, the end result of the United–Pan Am deal was that American had been upstaged by its archenemy, United.

PLAYING CATCHUP is sometimes necessary. And nearly always expensive.

In mid-December, less than two months after United had announced its surprise deal with Pan Am, American demonstrated that. It also demonstrated once again its remarkable ability to move quickly when necessary. It agreed to buy all six of TWA's London routes, including its rights to serve Heathrow Airport, for $445 million. There also was a $70 million side deal moving some of TWA's slots at Chicago's O'Hare Airport and a handful of other facilities at several U.S. airports to American.

All of that spending, plus the $195 million American had agreed a year earlier to pay TWA for its Chicago-London route authority and related assets—a deal that the Transportation and Justice departments had delayed approving for a full year—meant AMR would have to issue stock at a price well below what company officials believed it was worth. At the time AMR stock was selling for about $48 a share even though Crandall said he believed it actually was worth more than $75 a share.

"But the fact is that when opportunity knocks, it is appropriate, we think, to pick that opportunity up. And if the price of doing so is to sell some numbers of shares at something approximating today's [low] market price, we think that's a price worth paying," he said.

American's and Crandall's critics—and there are many—had a field day with the American-TWA deal. Obviously, while the deal on the London routes was touted as costing $445 million, just $45 million more than United had paid Pan Am for its London routes, the real price of the American-TWA deal either was $515 million or $710 million, depending on whether you lumped the still uncompleted Chicago-London deal into the pot.

"Bob paid too much for the TWA assets. But Bob always pays too much," Plaskett snapped, perhaps as a payback for Crandall's earlier attempt to make it look as if he'd sold Pan Am's brithright for a bowl of porridge.

Thanks to a unique provision in the U.S.-U.K. air services treaty— known as Bermuda 2—neither American nor United could close their deals with TWA and Pan Am until the U.S. and British governments negotiated a change in the treaty. That's because under terms of Bermuda 2, neither of the acquiring carriers would be allowed to serve Heathrow Airport. Bermuda 2 specifically named Pan Am and TWA, or their corporate successors, as the only U.S. carriers allowed to serve Heathrow. Since both were to continue operating after the sale of their London routes, United and American did not qualify as their corporate successors. So the British government declared that United and American would have to move their flights acquired from Pan Am and TWA to the less-preferred Gatwick, which already was running out of terminal space and which business travelers avoid like the plague.

It took more than four months of intense and difficult negotiations to get the British to agree to alter the Bermuda 2 agreement to allow American and United in at Heathrow. And the only reason the British allowed even that change was that the United States finally agreed to give British Airways far more extensive rights to serve the United States than it had previously, more than it ever had given any foreign carrier.

Once that was done, the U.S. government approved both deals. But there was one hitch in the approval of American's deal. Citing American's already large presence in the trans-Atlantic market, the

Justice Department refused to allow American to acquire TWA's routes to London from St. Louis, Philadelphia, and Baltimore.

That was just fine with American, which had always viewed those as the three weakest of the six routes. But chairman Carl Icahn refused to cut the price of the deal just because three routes were lost. American, he said, had to pay the full $445 million for the New York-, Los Angeles-, and Boston-to-Heathrow routes, or it would not get any of them. After several weeks of public posturing, American gave in and met Icahn's demand.

Again American's critics hooted and howled. The supposed geniuses at American had been outfoxed again, this time by an industry rookie, Icahn, the corporate raider-turned-manager.

Even then, closing the TWA deal wasn't easy. Financier Kirk Kerkorian flirted publicly with making a takeover bid for TWA. Kerkorian's efforts were supported by Senator John Danforth, a powerful Missouri Republican with strong ties to the Bush administration, and by other Missouri politicians, all of whom were worried that Icahn would sell all of TWA's assets in piecemeal fashion and allow the carrier's St. Louis hub to wither and die, putting thousands of Missourians out of work. American, taking a page from United, publicly threatened to sue Kerkorian if he tried to tamper with its deal to buy TWA's London routes. Danforth and his supporters then tried to bluff American into backing off with a menacing letter, a suit filed in a federal court in St. Louis, and talk of special legislation. American, however, more or less ignored the threats and proceeded as planned. Kerkorian was not heard from again.

Ultimately, both American and United were able to launch service to Heathrow in the summer of 1991. Later that year Pan Am, unable to stop the flow of red ink, was forced to sell its remaining transatlantic routes and its Boston–New York–Washington shuttle operations to Delta. Then, in December, a second deal, which would have had Delta finance a drastically smaller Pan Am that served only its Latin American routes from Miami, fell through. Three days later, Plaskett ordered a final shutdown. Pan Am, probably the most storied airline in all the world, was dead.

Thus, the epic twelve-year battle for supremacy in the deregulated U.S. airline business had led to the creation of a clearly definable Big Three. And those three—American, United, and Delta—now were taking what had been only a domestic fight across the Atlantic, where a batch of high-cost national carriers, some still at least partly owned by their governments, nervously watched the invasion with growing concern. Would the U.S. titans, powered by their extremely efficient domestic hub-and-spoke networks serving the world's largest and most affluent aviation market (between 45 percent and 50 percent of the world's total aviation market), eventually run over the European carriers as they did the weaker U.S. airlines? Or would the Europeans find a way to stop the world's three largest airlines from conquering a second continent?

Actually, American had thrown the gauntlet down at the feet of Europe's top airlines back in April 1990. That's when Mike Gunn, American's senior vice president for marketing, introduced what American calls its International Flagship Service. Aimed specifically at first- and business-class passengers on international flights, American's new premium package of in-flight services was designed to neutralize the huge advantage European carriers previously had had over U.S. carriers because of their vastly superior passenger service. Europe's big international carriers, especially British Airways, SwissAir and Lufthansa German Airlines, had been feasting for two decades off the weak competition from Pan Am and TWA, whose shoddy in-flight service and shabby airplanes were legendary. Because their service was so bad, most of the high fare–paying business travelers crossing the Atlantic had deserted Pan Am and TWA years earlier and had switched allegiances to the Euro-carriers. As a result, Pan Am and TWA had been forced to survive by heavily discounting all of their trans-Atlantic seats. But the lower revenues generated by the heavy discounting left Pan Am and TWA unable to invest in passenger service improvements. As a result, the Euro-carriers had been picking the meat off Pan Am's and TWA's bones for years, so much so that they almost had come to believe it was their God-given right to carry 75 percent or more of all full-fare passengers traveling the Atlantic.

But with the introduction of its International Flagship Service, Gunn had said American was serving notice that the days were over when European carriers could run roughshod over their U.S. competitors in the trans-Atlantic markets.

"We intend to compete with the best airlines in the world," he said. "We feel there is a place in the market for a premier United States international airline, and our ambition is to be that, to become known as THE U.S. flag carrier."

Gunn, of course, was speaking only for American. But from the perspective of the European carriers, he might just as well have been speaking for United and Delta, too.

CRANDALL WASN'T kidding.

After watching his company lose another $195.6 million in the first quarter of 1991 and a total of $410.7 million in the six months ended March 31 of that year, he'd had enough.

"The formula no longer is working. And we're not sure that it ever will work," Crandall told a reporter after a luncheon speech in the summer of 1991. "We're going to have to change the formula, change the way we do business, or we may not be in business much longer."

Operation Desert Storm was over, most of the troops were on their way home, and the nation was celebrating its devastating defeat of Saddam Hussein's large but largely incompetent army in Kuwait and southern Iraq. But Crandall was on his soapbox once again, all but shouting that the U.S. airline industry was in serious trouble. The only difference was that this time, the senior managements of most other carriers were starting to see what he meant.

The airline industry was on its way to its worst year in history. And the war was not the only reason. All told, the major airlines lost about $6 billion in 1990 and 1991 combined. Four carriers, Continental, America West, Midway, and Pan Am filed Chapter 11 bankruptcy petitions between the time Iraq's invasion of Kuwait in August 1990 and the end of 1991. TWA followed with a Chapter 11 filing in early 1992. And three carriers—Eastern, Midway, and Pan Am— literally ran out of cash and were forced to cease operations and enter liquidation between August 1990 and the end of 1991.

The national economy did not rebound after the war ended the way some had hoped or expected it would. By late summer of 1991, despite President George Bush's politically ruinous denials, it was obvious that the U.S. economy was in recession. And by the end of the year, even Bush had to admit something was wrong.

Speaking again at the Wings Club of New York in September 1991, Crandall said: "When we last met, a year ago this month, the title of my talk was 'Storm Clouds Ahead.' With that as prologue, I think I might characterize my remarks today as 'Force 10 Blowing!'

"The industry's problem can be summed up in one word: profitability. We haven't achieved it recently, and we aren't going to achieve it soon—for a whole host of reasons," he said.

He then went over his list of reasons: the high price of new aircraft, increasing costs associated with protecting the environment, government's failure to build enough runways and airports to alleviate costly delays, higher taxes at every level of government, rising sales costs stemming from intense competition within the industry, and rapidly rising labor costs.

"Ladies and gentlemen, our industry is in big-time trouble!" he said. "The massive losses of late 1990 and early '91 have wiped out all the accumulated profits commercial airlines have ever earned. Today, U.S. carriers, believe it or not, have a retained net deficit of $1.4 billion. That means that from their founding through June of this year, U.S. airlines have lost $1.4 billion.

"What's most discouraging about all this is the probability that unless dramatic change occurs, the future looks decidedly bleak," Crandall said.

In deference to that bleak future, Crandall said American would drastically cut its five-year, $22 billion spending plan. Two months later American had worked out most of the details of those cuts. The airline canceled its options to buy more than 100 aircraft and shelved a host of other projects in order to cut $8 billion, or a little more than a third out of its capital spending plan.

But American wasn't throwing in the towel; just setting the stage for a remarkable shift in strategy every bit as bold and inspired as the Growth Plan had been back in 1983 and 1984.

Even as Crandall spoke to the Wings Club in September 1991, about 100 American executives, managers, and even front-line employees back in Fort Worth already were working on the development of a top secret plan that Crandall was betting would create the kind of dramatic, fundamental change that he believed was necessary if American, or any other airline, ever hoped to earn acceptable profit margins on a consistent basis.

Marketing chief Mike Gunn explained that the seeds of that top secret plan—called Project Radical Pricing—were planted during a casual meeting he had with Crandall and Don Carty in the spring of 1991, a month or so after the end of the war. In the course of their conversation Gunn expressed frustration over the "stacks and stacks of mail I was getting from customers who were saying 'we think your fares are too high, your fare system stinks and we're staying home because of it.' "

Carty added that he was just as frustrated by the airline's inability to significantly improve its yield.

"In the fall of 1990, during the build-up before the Persian Gulf War, we put in two huge price increases because of the big increase in the price of fuel. Our yields should have gone up but they didn't," Carty explained more than a year after that casual meeting with Gunn and Crandall.

"Then, in the spring [of 1991], when fuel prices went down, we didn't lower our prices. Again our yields did nothing. Every time we raised fares, a month later our yield was the same as it had been before. Every time we raised fares we just issued that many more discount tickets. It was a classic case of an industry that had priced its baseline service above the market's willingness to pay for that service. Something had to change. That's why when United tried [in March 1992] to raise prices 2 percent we didn't go along. We knew that was not the right answer to our problems," Carty said.

Together Gunn, Carty, and Crandall arrived at the same conclusion: "The formula no longer worked."

The trio took their thoughts to American's "planning committee," the airline's policy- and decision-making group that in addition to themselves includes executive vice president Bob Baker, the airline's eight other senior vice presidents and two staff vice presidents (who because of their functions—managing American's relationships in Washington and with organized labor respectively—report directly to Crandall). By late spring of 1991, the planning committee determined that the airline absolutely *had* to find some way to equalize what had become an intolerable, unequal, and unprofitable fare system. Doing that, they were convinced, was the best hope—maybe the only hope—they had of ever solving the airline's profitability problem.

Barbara Amster, a 25-year veteran of the airline who had been part of the original sales and training team when SABRE first was introduced to travel agents in the late 1970s, had risen through the ranks to become the airline's vice president of pricing and yield management. As such, she became the de facto project manager of Project Radical Pricing even though nearly all the members of the planning committee remained active participants in it.

Meeting on Saturdays during the summer, the initial project development team of about sixteen people—including some of Gunn's senior marketing staffers and several of Carty's top internal financial analysts—re-examined the many facets of airline ticket pricing. They rather quickly were able to uncover hard statistical facts that proved what Carty, Gunn, Crandall, and everyone else in management had come to understand through experience.

Through their buying behavior, business travelers—the airline's most preferred and best customers—had been telling management that unrestricted coach fares—the basic benchmark fares of the industry and the kind designed for business travelers—simply were too expensive. Across the spectrum of business travel there was unprecedented resistance to buying the high-priced, unrestricted coach fares then available.

For starters, big companies that generate hundreds of millions of miles of travel each year, were negotiating special unpublished discount fares for their employees traveling on business. While volume discount deals usually generate incremental revenue and profits for most companies, such deals only reduce the revenues airlines would have received otherwise. Unlike leisure travelers, who are likely to be enticed into buying a plane ticket they hadn't originally planned on buying if the fare sale prices are low enough, business travelers don't increase their travel just because they can get a great price.

Second, many business travelers had become sophisticated enough about their travel purchasing to learn all of the many tricks or "games" used to keep their travel costs down. Most of the "games" were nothing more than legal manipulations of the airlines' own bizarre and complicated fare system. But the airlines contended that some of the "games" used by travelers to subvert the fare system were, in fact, illegal acts of fraud or violations of published rules. But trying to enforce the rules—which they did sporadically—put the airlines in the position of having to suspect and play cop against their own customers. In addition, trying to track consumer fraud cost the airlines a small fortune, both in money and in employees' time eaten up by the low-return business.

Third, much to the surprise of virtually everyone in the travel industry, many businesspeople apparently learned something about themselves and their businesses as a result of the Persian Gulf crisis and the national economic downturn that began in 1990. When businesses drastically reduced their travel, and therefore their travel spending, as a result of the war or the economy, many of them discovered that their revenues and profits did not decline at the same rate. The lesson was obvious: They previously had been traveling more, and spending more on travel than was absolutely necessary. Prior to Saddam's invasion of Kuwait, a surprising number of businesses apparently had lost sight of the fact that it doesn't make sense to spend $1,000 on executive travel to close a $10,000 deal. That's why God created telephones, fax machines, and Federal Express.

In short, the war, the recession, and the purge of vast segments of the white-collar work force in a rapidly restructuring corporate America in the early 1990s took a huge and totally unexpected bite out of demand for business travel.

Thus, when the war ended in 1991, the expected bounce in travel, especially business travel, never occurred.

Amster and her Project Radical Pricing team were the first ones to fully document the changes in the buying behavior of business travelers. By the end of 1991, only 5.7 percent of all passengers on American were paying full coach fare prices. An even smaller percentage was paying the full rack rate on weaker carriers. Meanwhile, the average price of all discount fares sold by American at the end of 1991 was a staggering 63 percent off the published coach fare price.

With that detailed knowledge of their market, American's senior management was able to prove to their own satisfaction that simply coming up with a new kind of discount fare wouldn't solve the real problem. The entire fare structure had to be changed. And by September 1991, the basic rationale for that change—which ultimately became known as the Value Plan—was coming into focus.

At that point, Amster and other senior American executives began visiting with some of the most highly regarded professors at some of the top business schools around the nation, including those at Harvard, the University of Chicago, and the University of California at Los Angeles, in order to cross-check the conclusions at which they had arrived against the prevailing academic theories regarding pricing. All of the academics consulted were experts on the esoteric subject of "price elasticity."

Previously, the standard thinking in the airline industry was that business travel was inelastic, meaning that lowering the price of fares bought primarily by business travelers—i.e., coach fares—would not produce much, if any, increase in demand for business-type fares. But the ivory-tower residents confirmed that U.S. business travelers' growing aversion to high-priced coach fares and their willingness to fly roundabout routes or to break the rules to use leisure-type fares proved exactly what American's executives thought it did: that business travel is much, much more elastic than previously thought.

As a result, a substantial cut in coach fare prices coupled with a reduction in the complexity of buying an airline ticket should trigger a significant increase in demand. Coincidentally, the simplification of the fare structure also would save millions of dollars monthly in administration costs.

THE VALUE Plan was exactly the kind of radical change that Crandall had been talking about in his September 1991 speech to the Wings Club. Beginning with its announcement on April 9, 1992, American scrapped its old fare system that included sometimes as many as eighteen published fares—plus unpublished negotiated discounts—on a given route. In its place, American established four basic fares. There was first class, priced 50 percent below the previously existing first-class fares. Next there was coach—the "AAnytime Fare" in American's lexicon—priced at least 38 percent lower than the old coach fares. Then there were two levels of "Plan AAhead" advance purchase discount fares—twenty-one- and seven-days—that, unlike past advance purchase fares, could be reissued for use at a later date for only a $25 service fee. Ultimately, the fare simplication would reduce the carrier's more than 500,000 fare offerings in 13,000 markets to just 70,000 fare offerings in the same number of markets.

Crandall and company believed that if the Value Plan could be fully implemented, it eventually would increase American's revenues, and therefore its profits, as business travelers who had switched to low-ballers like TWA and Continental returned to American because of its superior service, schedule, and exceptional frequent flier program. Of course, as American's market share, and presumably that of both United and Delta, increased under the Value Plan, that meant weaker carriers' shares would go down. But American's management fervently insisted that even the weaker carriers would be better off in the long run despite a drop in market share. While the listed Value Plan fares would be lower than the listed fares in the old system, the absence of unpublished, negotiated discounts and other special category discount fares meant that yields (the average revenue per passenger mile flown) under the Value Plan would be higher than the incredibly low yields the weaker carriers had been recording.

The downside of introducing the Value Plan was that American could see as much as $100 million in advance ticket sales disappear in the first quarter the new fares were available. People who had already purchased their tickets would be allowed to exchange them for the new, lower-priced fares, meaning American would have to issue a lot of refunds.

But the potential rewards of making the drastic change in the way the airline sold its service simply were too great to pass up. The Value Plan team projected that once the new simplified fare system was fully in place, American could expect revenues of $300 million to $350 million more annually than if the existing fare system remained in place. And, because nearly all of that increased revenue would be incremental—meaning the airline's costs would not go up much because it already had the seating capacity in place to handle the higher demand—most of that added revenue would go directly to the bottom line.

THERE WAS never any doubt that American's principal competitors, United and Delta, would match the Value Plan. They had to. Not doing so would have meant allowing American to have a low price advantage. And besides, American's top management had faith that their respected counterparts at Delta and United were both disciplined enough to do a proper analytical review of the principles behind the Value Plan and smart enough to understand the results of such an analysis.

The only real concern was about what the industry's three bankrupt low-ballers—TWA, Continental, and America West—and the two wild cards in the deck—Northwest and USAir—would do.

Crandall and his planning committee determined that if any competitor tried to undercut the Value Plan prices, American would lower its entire four-tier fare system. If an airline tried to undercut American's twenty-one-day advance purchase fare price by $50, American would seek to retain the purity of its Value Plan pricing system by dropping that same fare by $50. The prices of its other three fares were cut by the same percentage that the first fare was cut. American also was prepared to loosen the restrictions on its two levels of advance purchase discount fares if the competition tried to undercut it that way.

After the Value Plan was introduced on April 9 at a New York news conference, Crandall, Carty, and other American executives took great pains to communicate publicly their determination not to allow the Value Plan prices to be undercut. They patiently explained to reporter after reporter their plan to match attempts to undercut the Value Plan prices by taking the entire four-tier price structure down on a percentage basis.

They all vehemently denied critics' charges that the Value Plan really was a cover for their "final solution," a devious plan to push some of the bankrupt or other weaker carriers over the edge. And, in fact, that was not their intent. Yet, they surely knew that some of the weaker carriers were so near the edge that a big change in the fare system might be enough of a shock to finish them off. In any case, by determining to move the entire fare structure up or down in order to meet competitor's attempts to undercut the Value Plan, and by broadcasting widely that determination, what American was offering its weaker competitors, was, in fact, a sucker's bet. If they tried to undercut the Value Plan, they would succeed only in reducing their own revenue because American, with its deeper pockets, was pledged to go as low as necessary to protect its new fare system.

As many within American's management had expected, TWA, under the leadership of corporate raider-turned-airline chairman Carl Icahn, was the first to try to undercut the Value Plan with lower fares and new levels of discount fares. Several other carriers also tested American's resolve to protect the sanctity of its new pricing system. All of them learned the hard way that Crandall and his team had not been bluffing. American matched them step-for-step down the price ladder, until mid-May, when the efforts to undercut the Value Plan seemed to subside.

For nearly a week all was quiet on the fares front. Then on May 26, Northwest rolled out the biggest challenge to the Value Plan to date. Northwest's "Grown-Ups Fly Free," a new twist on the "Kids Fly Free" ticket promotions in previous summers, had been in the works for months, and Northwest's senior managers—with whom American's senior management had developed a serious and highly personal feud—decided not to let American's pricing moves scuttle their own plans. The Northwest fare included many restrictions limiting its use to only passengers flying with relatives or guardians. Few business travelers could use it. Nor could two adults traveling together on vacation.

Naturally, everyone in the industry waited for American to respond. But no one expected the industry's most powerful giant to do what it did.

Citing its Value Plan dogma that no class of travelers should have special access to fares to which other travelers did not, American cut in half the price of what already were its most deeply discounted advance purchases fares. Adults didn't have to travel with children. Anyone willing to buy their tickets twenty-one days in advance could qualify for American's new fares. More astonishingly, American said the fares, which had to be bought by June 5, could be used on trips taken before September 13. American had broken—but only for a limited time—the 50-percent-off relationship between its lowest-priced Plan AAhead fares and its standard AAnytime fares. But by making the incredibly low prices it was offering available up-front to every traveler rather than to just adults traveling with their children, American officials felt they were protecting the Value Plan's integrity.

With that one decision, which ultimately was made by Crandall himself, the industry was plunged into the deepest, bloodiest fare war in history. Opportunistic leisure travelers swarmed travel agencies and tied up airlines' telephone reservations lines in the maddest dash to cash in on a bargain since the days of the Oklahoma land rush. As a result, U.S. airlines blew away virtually every record in the books for passengers carried, average load factors, passenger miles flown, and the like. Only, they lost a fortune doing it. American alone posted a previously unimaginable loss of $166 million in the second quarter and an $85 million loss in the third quarter. The second and third quarters normally are the industry's most profitable months.

GALVESTON, TEXAS, is hardly the center of the U.S. airline industry. In fact, the Texas Gulf island forty miles southeast of Houston doesn't even have scheduled airline service. But Galveston—or, more precisely, the U.S. Court House there—was the gravitational center of power in the industry for about five weeks in late July and August, 1992.

Most U.S. airlines put Galveston on their maps shortly after June 8, 1992. That night, at 9:58 P.M., CDT, an attorney representing Houston-based Continental dropped a package through the night delivery slot of the U.S. District Court's clerk's office there. The package contained a lawsuit in which Continental charged American with predatory pricing, which is defined as setting prices at below-cost levels in an effort to run a competitor out of business.

The next morning, attorneys hired by American filed a petition with the U.S. District Court in Chicago seeking a ruling that American's pricing actions were legal and not predatory. Neither the attorneys who filed the petition nor American's management was aware that Continental had beaten them to the punch the night before.

Northwest jumped on the Continental bandwagon a few days later when it filed an almost identically worded suit against American in the Galveston court. And bankrupt America West's creditors also asked the federal bankruptcy judge in Phoenix who was handling America West's Chapter 11 case for permission to go after American, too.

The coalition of carriers opposed to the Value Plan also went on a public relations offensive. Appearing before a Senate subcommittee in mid-June, Northwest senior vice president Barry Kotar said: "American Airlines set an entirely new pricing structure which the other airlines had no choice but to match. American came down like the elephant on the flea and said 'Either you're all going to play in my game, or you're outta here, fella.'

"Northwest pulled out the squirt gun and American responded with the water cannon. In my twenty-five years of being in this business, if that's not predatory pricing, I don't know what it is," he said.

Testifying at the same Senate hearing, America West's president, Michael Conway, was more blunt. "There is a predator on the loose, and that predator is American Airlines. This industry has been turned into a game of pure staying power. The last one with any money left will certainly win."

Crandall, who also testified in Washington that day, told the Senators his antagonists were just chronic complainers who could not compete with American in a deregulated market. He admitted that the 50-percent-off fare sale would cost the industry hundreds of millions of dollars that summer. But, he said, it was the result of unfettered competition, the kind of pro-consumer competition the Senate had said it wanted when it led the way in deregulating the industry in 1978.

"It was a foolish sale which will cost the airline industry dearly," he said, "but it was the natural result of competition . . . . Consumers are extraordinarily price sensitive. They will move toward the lowest fare. Thus, the industry also moves toward the lowest fare."

Because predatory pricing is so difficult to prove, few suits of that nature ever reach the trial stage. But in this case, the chances of the case reaching trial are remarkably high. Both Continental and Northwest are in extreme financial difficulty. And their creditors view their predatory pricing lawsuits against American as potential assets. Unless American makes a substantial cash settlement offer—which is highly unlikely—then Continental, Northwest, and their creditors have little to lose by pursuing the case all the way to trial. While American appears to be in a strong defensive position, nothing is a certainty in a jury trial.

It is remotely possible that one of the two main plaintiffs, Continental and Northwest, could drop out as the result of some financial transaction with American, though American officials say they won't knuckle under to what amounts to corporate extortion via the courts.

Indeed, Northwest officials approached American in the late summer of 1992 with an offer to sell a variety of assets. Included in the offer was the chance for American to buy Northwest's Chicago-Tokyo route rights and more than sixty landing and takeoff slots at Chicago's O'Hare Airport. Northwest, American, and Federal Express also discussed a three-way deal in which American would give FedEx its entire fleet of McDonnell Douglas MD-11s and Northwest would turn its fleet of 20 Airbus A-340 long-range aircraft over to American; Northwest, meanwhile, would get out from under its obligations to buy $2 billion worth of the A-340s.

American dearly wanted both the Tokyo rights and the Chicago slots. And both its huge disappointment with the MD-11 and its favorable view of the A-340 were well known. But in each case, the amounts Northwest sought were way beyond American's willingness to pay, especially in the midst of the worst downturn in industry history. Because the promise to drop the predatory pricing suit went along with the offers, American officials recognized that the premium prices sought by Northwest for the assets it knew American coveted actually represented a way to settle the predatory pricing litigation via a back door.

Crandall reluctantly declined Northwest's offers, though he might have been much less reluctant had the national economy not been in the tank at the time.

"I DON'T know what to think about this," said Don Carty, his mischievous grin spreading across his long face.

"On the one hand, the government says it's going to sue us for fixing prices too high. On the other hand, our competitors have ganged up to sue us because we set our prices too low. Now what am I supposed to make of this? Go figure! Is this a crazy business or what?"

It was December 15, 1992, and Carty had just delivered a luncheon speech to the Petroleum Club of Fort Worth. Actually, he had stood in for Crandall, who had to beg off from his agreement to speak to the Cowtown high rollers so he could attend President-elect Bill Clinton's two-day economic conference in Little Rock. Earlier that week there had been stories in the Fort Worth and Dallas newspapers saying that after nearly three years of looking into allegations that airlines used their computer reservations systems and public statements to signal each other regarding pricing, the U.S. Department of Justice was preparing to file a civil antitrust price fixing suit against most of the nation's major carriers. In effect, the Justice Department was trying to scare the airlines into entering into a consent decree in which they would promise not to do certain things when raising fares, such as announce fare hikes days in advance of the effective dates of those price changes. American, and several other major carriers, insisted that there was nothing either illegal or unethical about their pricing methods and refused to sign a consent decree. A week later, the Justice Department filed its suit.

In any case, the answer to Carty's question is clear.

The airline business is, in fact, a crazy business. And it is getting crazier all the time.

While a few vestiges of the Value Plan remain in place, as a practical matter the Value Plan died sometime in the fall of 1992. Crandall himself said as much in October when he said that because competitors insisted on pricing their services in old, unprofitable ways American reluctantly would "match whatever cockamamie fare anyone puts out there."

Accordingly, throughout the fall the industry pushed the price of coach fares—American quit referring to them as AAnytime Fares—back up beyond the original Value Plan fare levels. In fact, though a series of starts, stops, and delays created tons of confusion along the way, by mid-December fares on most routes had risen to within a few dollars of their pre–Value Plan price levels.

Given that, Carty was asked after his December speech in Fort Worth: "Doesn't this mean that if benchmark coach fares were too high before the Value Plan was introduced they're too high now?"

"Of course they're too high," he replied. "So we're all just going back to negotiating under-the-table (corporate discount) deals. It doesn't make sense. We lose money doing it. But that's what the market says it wants, so we'll give it to 'em.

"But I still believe we were right, that the Value Plan would have worked had our competitors given it a chance. Our only mistake was that we underestimated the stupidity of some of our competitors. I don't know why they didn't do a thorough analysis, but they obviously didn't. If they had, they would have joined us in supporting the Value Plan. But my best guess is they just emoted. Instead of responding to our move rationally and doing a thorough study, they just responded emotionally and determined they weren't going to let us at American tell them how they should price fares," Carty said.

NINETEEN NINETY-TWO was an ugly year for all airlines (except Southwest). And that goes double for the Big Three: American, United, and Delta. All three had to cut way back on their aircraft orders, sharply reduce their other capital spending plans, and drastically curtail their growth plans because their huge losses simply no longer would support such expansion plans. Delta and United, arguably, are damaged more by the need to cut back than American, which because it got the jump on the growth cycle back in the early 1980s was already past its peak in growth when the cuts had to be made. But while American cut its fleet growth and acquisitions plan once after the middle of 1991, Delta and United both went to that well twice during the same time frame. Delta also instituted its first layoffs in forty years when in the fall of 1992 it trimmed about five thousand part-time and temporary workers. The nation's third-largest carrier also announced just before Christmas plans for a five percent across-the-board pay cut to take effect February 1, 1993.

But American's workers did not escape 1992 unscathed. In December, more than 650 middle managers and technical specialists either were laid off or left the company voluntarily (mostly through early retirement). The cuts were made in response to Crandall's decision to trim the 1993 budget line item for salaried employees by 10 percent.

What a contrast those cuts make in comparison with the situation a few years ago, when it seemed as if American's team of senior managers had the carrier's future all mapped out through the year 2000 and beyond. Nothing, it seemed, could stop American from achieving its goals.

Now nothing about American's future appears certain. It's not even certain that there will be an American Airlines in the future.

Crandall basically said so in a September 1992 speech to about fifty airline analysts from Wall Street gathered for breakfast at the Harvard Club in New York. After running down a long list of major, expensive problems facing all airlines, Crandall asked the rhetorical question: "How do we fix the problem?"

Then he answered it.

"I don't know," he said, "particularly since the industry has not even been able to establish a sensible basic rate structure. But unless we find a way, the industry cannot hope to be profitable."

There was a stunned silence in the room. The analysts all had heard Crandall issue dire warnings about the industry's future before. But none of them could recall ever having heard him say he didn't have a clue about how to solve the problems. Nor had they ever seen from him anything like his display that morning of his own great personal angst over American's new predicament.

RoseAnn Tortora, airline analyst at County Nat West in New York—and a former American financial staffer in the 1970s—said: "The man raised more questions than he had answers for. I'm not sure he has the answers at all. It seemed like there was a certain sense of frustration coming through his remarks, or even a sense of a lack of control."

Maybe it was a coincidence. Then again, maybe it wasn't.

Either way, within a month of American's admission in October 1992 that the Value Plan, indeed, was dead, a British trade journal ran a story quoting Crandall on the subject of his retirement.

"I will be gone from American Airlines sometime soon. I've been here a long time, and I'm going to retire sometime soon, in three or four years," Crandall said.

The magazine story certainly caught everyone back at American's headquarters by surprise. Nearly two years earlier, in some of his annual President's Conference meetings with employees, Crandall had referred to American's "thousand-plane fleet in the year 2000, when I retire." Even Ted Tedesco, American's vice president of corporate affairs and Crandall's old fraternity brother in the late 1950s at the University of Rhode Island, was shocked.

"This is news to everybody here. I've never heard Crandall say anything about leaving. We around here don't expect him to leave any time soon. He should be here a long time," Tedesco said of his old friend.

But when the news of what Crandall had said began to circulate through American's headquarters and reached the local press, he issued a statement saying: "I meant every word of what I said."

American's new director of corporate communications, Tim Doke, said his boss "does not recall ever saying that he was going to hang on 'til he was 65." Furthermore, Doke said, Crandall was looking ahead "three or four years" as "a good time for him do go do something else."

Crandall, who turned fifty-seven in December 1992, makes $600,000 a year in base salary, and in 1991 earned $275,000 more based on the performance of AMR's stock, already is set financially. But, if he waits to retire until after January 1, 1996 (he'll turn sixty in the preceding month), he can walk away with 355,000 shares of AMR stock worth nearly $23 million, based on the stock's New York Stock Exchange price in late 1992. That's the result of a 1987 attempt by the board of directors at United's parent company, UAL, to steal Crandall away from American. To counter UAL's lucrative offer, and to ensure that he would not be spirited away by some other company offering big bucks, AMR's board came up with that long-term employment incentive agreement.

So why the apparent change of heart? Is Crandall finally approaching burnout? Is he starting to feel the fatigue brought on by an entire career of pressure-packed sixteen-hour days? Was the ultimate failure of the Value Plan a psychologically devastating blow?

Tom Plaskett recalled: "Bob and I used to have talks about retiring at fifty-five. It's a real rat race. I don't think people understand the real intensity that executives in the airline industry have to work in, and the stressful environment they've worked in since deregulation fourteen years ago.

"By the same token, Bob loves his job. So I wouldn't make too much of those comments. My personal view is that they'll have to carry Bob out of there feet first," Plaskett said.

Shearson Lehman Brothers Inc. senior advisory director Robert Joedicke, who has been an airline analyst on Wall Street since shortly after World War II, probably knows Crandall better than anyone in the financial world. And he doesn't think Crandall is quite ready to pull the ripcord.

"Bob has never walked away from a challenge. He might walk away someday, but he won't do it until American has turned the corner and started a financial comeback. If I know Bob, he won't leave until he feels like American's future is secure and it's in good hands. He won't leave the job undone," Joedicke said.

MARKETING CHIEF Mike Gunn was sitting at his desk on the afternoon of April 10, 1992, the day after American introduced the Value

Plan, literally watching the planes fly by his window. He was still on an emotional high left over from the day before. Like everyone else at American, Gunn felt certain that the Value Plan would revolutionize the airline industry and return both American and its competitors to profitability.

"You know, I'm just sitting here doing some media interviews on the phone and sort of watching the planes take off over at the airport (D/FW)," Gunn said. "I've never been prouder of my company than I was yesterday. It's sort of like the locker room after the Super Bowl around here today. We all feel like popping open some champagne and celebrating.

"At least for another hour or so. That's when Bob's plane is due in from New York, and when we all get to work. That's the thing about Bob that makes him different from the rest of us. We're all sitting around enjoying the afterglow from yesterday," Gunn said. "But I guarantee you he's already thinking of what we need to do next. When he gets back in the office later on this afternoon it'll be back to work for all of us. We're all scheduled to meet with him once he gets back in the office. But that's Bob. There's always another dragon to slay somewhere."

Yes, that is Bob Crandall—quintessential Bob Crandall. Yesterday's accomplishments may have been grand. But achieving today's goals and tomorrow's dreams are infinitely more important.

That perpetual pursuit of a better way to do things, of a smarter way to achieve the same or better results, has become the hallmark of American Airlines under Bob Crandall. It was the single most important factor in American's fifteen-year climb to the top of the industry. And it continues to be the key to American's ceaseless—though, so far frustrating—search for solutions to the problems that slowly are killing the U.S. airline industry.

Even if he weren't a financial expert, a data processing visionary, a great communicator, or one of the most talented people managers around, Crandall still might go down as the most important figure in American's corporate history, which is saying a lot given the huge impact that C. R. Smith had on American in his more than forty years as chairman. But Crandall did bring all of his considerable business skills with him to American. And it is the combination of those skills and his incredible, relentless drive to be best that have made Bob Crandall the biggest figure not only in American's history, but in the history of the entire commercial airline industry.

INDEX